An introduction to systems for the educational administrator

GLENN L. IMMEGART
University of Rochester

FRANCIS J. PILECKI
Labouré Junior College

An introduction to systems for the educational administrator

ADDISON-WESLEY PUBLISHING COMPANY

Reading, Massachusetts
Menlo Park, California · London · Don Mills, Ontario

to
Mary Lou and Julie

Preface

The application of system theory to educational administration seems most appropriate in these times of crisis. For, on the one hand, there is a strong need to reduce organizational ineffectiveness. The weakened buying potential of the dollar is complicated by the diminishing quantity of tax dollars. The Federal government urges "accountability" in education. Citizens demand to know just *what* it is they are supporting in the schools. Teacher organizations also voice increasing concern regarding the operation of the schools.

On the other hand, in a society which is becoming more aware of the abuse of individuals in organizations, there is a grave administrative responsibility to develop an organizational efficiency, in the broader sense of Barnard's terms. That is, it behooves the administrator to become concerned with the meshing of organizational goals with individual needs both at staff and student level.

The authors believe that in the systems movement can be found an operating methodology which confronts squarely and satisfactorily the issues of organizational effectiveness and efficiency. This work is designed as an initial reading for those concerned with the use of systems methods; it presents the common properties of systems along with numerous schemata for application and analysis.

The manuscript was prepared following the authors' involvement in several related research projects, and takes into account in no small way their personal experiences in the practice of educational administration, as well as contacts with a number of forward-looking educational administrators.

Numerous colleagues and students have contributed greatly to the development of the ideas herein presented. We acknowledge with gratitude their contributions. We are especially eager to note the valuable criticisms of Dean Stephen P. Hencley, of Hugh Fraser, John Burroughs, and Charles Case, then students at The University of Rochester, and David Marion of Boston University. For their testing of the analysis schemes presented herein, we wish to acknowledge the research work of Carl Thompson and Arthur Benvenuto of The University of Rochester, as well as Jerry Johnson, Gerry Dowd, Ernest Schuttenberg, Carolyn Mikan, and Richard Ellis of Boston University.

To all the unnamed forces who drove us to this writing or helped us in its development, we shall always be indebted.

Rochester, N.Y.   G.L.I.
Boston, Mass.   F.J.P.
May 1972

Contents

Part I / A generalized introduction to the systems movement

Chapter 1 / The development and potential of the systems movement

Administering the educational organization today is indeed a formidable task. Increasing student enrollments, the expanding role-functions of education, larger staffs, and a snowballing educational technology all contribute to this challenge. Likewise, shifts in the financial bases of education, modifications in the decision-making structures for education, and such vital current concerns as negotiating with teachers groups, seeking the equality of educational opportunity for all, and changing state and federal roles for education all add their share to the magnitude of the task of administering education.

Administrative science has helped educational administrators to meet these challenges through the study of administration and organization, and the refinement of more useful procedures and techniques. Administrative science has also shaped the goals and content of improved training programs in educational administration. However, many are raising the question: With the challenges and complexity of education today, have administrative science and improved training programs prepared administrators to (1) grapple with the important dynamics of their jobs, (2) entertain creative solutions to pervasive problems, or (3) practice "preventive" administration? What is needed is a systematic relational perspective capable of dealing with complex unfolding problems. Unfortunately, too many educational administrators presently seem able only to "keep up with the brushfires," putting them out one at a time.

Maybe this is just administrative life—maybe there is no other way. Possibly, however, this need not be so. *The systems movement, for example, offers real promise for aiding and improving the practice of educational administration.* In particular, the systems movement offers a perspective for the administrator that, in and of itself, can facilitate his job. The systems movement has also produced numerous administrative support systems whose techniques and procedures can greatly simplify and systematize many of the burdensome aspects of administering. There are ways available in the systems movement to free the educational administrator to cope with some of the more important matters that face him.

The authors' bias should be stated at the outset. We hold that the systems movement has great potential for improving and facilitating the practice of educational administration. It is our hope to demonstrate that potential in this document. Specifically, we will seek in the first section of the book to indicate the relevance of the systems movement for the practicing educational administrator. In the second section we will discuss the theoretical perspective of systems thought. In the third section we will examine the concept of administrative support from the point of view of systems science and also illustrate the application of selected systems approaches to the milieu of the educational administrator.

This book is not intended as an exhaustive or comprehensive treatment of the topic. Rather it is our intent to provide the reader with some basic feeling for systems thought, to illustrate its relevance for a field of practice, and to demonstrate in explicit terms how systems approaches can aid the practicing school administrator. Our approach will be suggestive and indicative, and focused toward opening up for the reader an emerging movement and its approaches. We hope the interested educational administrator will view this as a springboard for a more intensive examination of systems relative to his professional charge.

Accordingly we will begin in this chapter with a generalized look at the systems movement. We will seek (1) to set forth briefly the essence of the systems movement, (2) to identify the various forms or approaches systems thinking has taken, (3) to indicate in broad strokes the potential of the systems movement for educational administration, (4) to identify a number of specific systems administrative support devices that have relevance for educational administration, and (5) to note some of the major problems of drawing on the systems movement (that is, applying systems thinking and approaches to educational administration).

THE ESSENCE OF THE SYSTEMS MOVEMENT

Systems terminology and concepts are sufficiently in vogue that they are fast becoming universals in a number of scientific areas and applied fields, as well as in the society at large. This is neither by accident, nor totally by design. The systems notion was initally developed as a general construct, but its very generality has led to such widespread acceptance that the popular usage of its terms and concepts is somewhat vague and imprecise. It seems important, therefore, that at the outset we try to get at the heart of the "systems" concept or movement and endeavor to make sense out of it. To do this we will attempt to glean from the systems movement the gist of systems thinking. As Ackoff has already cogently pointed out, definitions and terminology in this area should not be taken too seriously.[1] In fact, just as the definition of the term system itself depends on the user, so do definitions of many systems concepts and approaches. To grasp meaning (or to understand) we can, rather, explore the essential characteristics of systems thinking and, possibly more precisely, the perspective of the systems scientist.

What is the "essence" of the systems movement? First of all it should be made clear that it is not a theory—that is, not a systems theory or General Systems Theory or what-have-you in the pure sense of the word theory. Actually there is no such thing as systems theory in the sense of "theory" as used by Allport or Fiegl.[2] Although there are theoretical aspects of systems thinking—and there is much that approaches theory in the systems movement—there is, in fact, no single, all-inclusive, universally accepted, and well-enunciated body of knowledge that can be accurately called systems theory—even though the theory label is often attached to systems thought and concepts.

Rather, and more importantly, what the systems movement has produced is a *mode of thought*. This mode of thought can be characterized as cross-disciplinary, or interdisciplinary, in nature; it is thus a mode of thought that is both conceptually rich and ultimately practical. Systems thinking provides a viable approach to asking and answering questions. In the cogent terms of Hitch, it offers a "perspective on uncertainty."[3]

Systems thought is both holistic and contextual. Not only does it focus on wholes (totality) and relevant (component) parts, it is also concerned with environmental context. By definition, (open) systems exist and flourish in a dynamic exchange relationship with other (open) systems and with their environments.

Most simply and most pointedly, *systems thought is systematic, relational thought*. That is, it is *thought*—the conscious process of reflection. Secondly, it is *systematic*—methodical, coherent, designed, and analytic in nature. Finally, it is *relational*—it accounts for referents, connections, interconnections, and direction.

To illustrate, we might look briefly at the application of systems thought to a typical administrative problem, one of an administrator's replacing a teacher in mid-Februaray as a result of her husband's employment transfer on short notice to another state. There are several standard or "stock" solutions to this problem: (1) Hire a new full-time teacher (e.g., a January graduate from State U., someone new to the area, or whatever). (2) Hire a substitute to finish out the school year. (3) Use several substitutes as available to finish out the year. Most administrators would most likely take a typical or experientially tested solution and implement it. They would, in all probability, react in a reflexive or preconditioned way.

The principal using the systems approach would proceed somewhat differently. First, he would set forth the criteria to be employed in selecting a replacement – such as, for example, the following:

1. Availability
2. Salary
3. Experience
4. Job (subject or grade level) preference of candidate
5. Knowledge of school
6. Recommendations
7. Training
8. Interview impression
9. Certification

10. Prior experience
11. Etc.

He would then consider all possible reasonable alternative solutions to the problem situation (Table 1.1). Further, he would consider certain important relationships such as those of (1) the outgoing teacher to the replacement, (2) this emergency staffing problem to next year's staffing needs, and (3) the incoming teacher to the pupils in the room. Aware of the relatively low probability of an "ideal" solution, he would proceed to assess the relative time, cost, and benefit aspects of the situation (Table 1.2). A temporary substitute might be employed, or even a candidate might be "tested" as the "systems administrator" worked toward his solution.

The administrator using the systems perspective would, through analysis of subjective probability including time-cost-benefit considerations and other relevant criteria, select the most desirable solution (optimization) to his problem. Rather than a conditioned response, hurried action, or ill-considered alternative, the systems approach would yield a decision resulting from *systematic, relational* thought.

Systems thought has a number of advantages as an analytic framework. First, it has provided an approach to functional or behavioral analysis in terms of *antecedent conditions* and *developmental trends.* Phenomena in the systems perspective are viewed not as isolated events but instead are assessed in totality, in context, and in a chronological sense. Put another way, the systems perspective places import on the evolutional aspects of all events and problems, and is concerned with the totality of behavior or function in an unfolding time sequence. It is concerned with *linkages* and *patterns* in *time-space.*

Systems thought has also provided an approach to structural analysis in terms of *relationships* and *connections.* Structures in this perspective are not, therefore, abstracted or invented but are analyzed through empirical referents, real proximity, relevant factors and parameters,[4] and pertinent connections or interfaces of their component parts.

The systems movement also offers an approach that is both *practical* and *operational.* A system problem is not mechanical, psychological, or sociological, for these are ways of looking at a problem.[5] In this sense problems are simply nonfunctional or dysfunctional aspects of systems. To solve them one must look at the system and the forces affecting it, and then ask and answer the right questions (the ones that make a difference!).

The systems perspective is, further, *futuristic*—that is, one that projects events, situations, and processes developmentally. Whether improving an existing system or creating a new one, use of the systems approach focuses on *what will be.* For example, tradition and the past are important only as antecedent conditions because time, relative to open systems, is nonreversible—*optimizing what will be* is the task.

Systems thought as well provides a *realistic departure* for working in a complex context. The systems analyst is aware of the scarcity of materials and energy, and, while seeking system maximization through optimization

Table 1.1 A systems comparison of five candidates for a teaching position

Candidate	Experience	Prefers this grade level	Knows our school	Availability for next year	Recommendations	Training	Interview impression	Certification	Has taught these children
A	None	Yes	No	Maybe	Good	BS	Satis-factory	Yes	No
B	Sub.	Yes	Yes	Yes	Very good	112 hrs.	Good	No	Some
C	12 yrs.	No	No	Yes	Good	MA	Poor	Yes	No
D	20 yrs.	No	Yes	No	High	BS+	Satis-factory	Yes	No
E	Sub.	Yes	Yes	Yes	Low	BA	Barely satis.	Yes	Yes

Table 1.2 Availability, cost, and benefit comparison of five candidates for a teaching position

Candidates	Availability	Cost	Effectiveness (rated)
A	Now	$5900	Good student teaching
B	In two weeks	5400	Excellent
C	Now	7800	Good
D	In one week	8150	Excellent
E	Now	6100	Marginal

or suboptimization, he explores rigorously the relative costs and benefits of alternatives. End results are not viewed through "rose-colored glasses" but are assessed in terms of relevant conditions and actual payoffs. Additionally, such matters are viewed in relation to all other categories of cost and gain impinging at a given time or in the foreseeable future.

Finally, the systems movement has provided a *unifying force* for practice, development, and science. Systems thinking spans a number of disciplines and has brought together the efforts of scholars and practitioners from a number of fields. Together these scholars and practitioners have explored common concerns and have established a useful way of thinking in order to attack problems.

In sum, the systems movement has resulted in a mode of thought that has yielded a useful perspective on reality. This mode of thought—systematic, relational thinking—offers a unique approach to practice, development, and science. It provides a helpful perspective for dealing with complex, unfolding problems.

With this somewhat generalized attempt to set forth the essence of the systems approach, we can now turn to a brief consideration of the various forms systems thought has taken.

THE FORMS SYSTEMS THINKING HAS TAKEN

At best it is difficult to label the "father" of systems thinking or to state precisely when systems thought as such emerged. Clearly identifying all of the relevant antecedents of the systems approach is likewise difficult. To some the father is von Bertalanffy,[6] to others Lotka or Ampere.[7] To some the antecedents are relatively recent (e.g., a natural outgrowth of the development of the sciences or a disenchantment in this century with the limitations imposed by the boundaries of the traditional sciences). To others the antecedents can be traced back to the writings of Plato.[8] Such arguments have little relevance except for the scholar or historian. What is important, however, is that the systems movement—at least in its present form—began about 40 years ago and has had its greatest period of development in just the past 20 or so years.[9]

It is also important to observe that regardless of who started it, or when, several approaches or emphases have been pursued. These branches or approaches are to some extent distinct but at the same time overlap a great deal. Some lines have emerged quite independently while others merge or intertwine to such an extent that separating them is at best an academic exercise. The major strands are, however, identifiable and the differences, no matter how subtle, can be delineated. To be noted is the fact that overlaps occur not only in terms of the theoretical or conceptual aspects of the systems movement but also with respect to scholars, literature, research, and applications. It follows then that some inherent conceptual confusion, some variation in what is important, and some disagreement regarding boundaries can be expected in pursuing the systems literature.[10]

The major approaches to systems thinking are the following:

1. General System Theory
2. Cybernetics
3. Holism
4. Operations Research
5. Systems Design
6. Information Theory
7. Systems Analysis
8. Systems Engineering
9. Output Analysis
10. Mathematical Programming
11. Computer Science

General System Theory, or system theory, is the label given *"to describe a level of theoretical model-building which lies somewhere between the highly generalized constructions of pure mathematics and the specific theories of the specialized disciplines."* [11] As first set forth by von Bertalanffy it forms "the skeleton of a science,"[12] and seeks to integrate all of the sciences within a common conceptual framework using uniform and systematically derived terminology. Of interest to General Systems scholars are the nature of systems, the universality of systems properties and states, and the generalization of scientific findings from one kind of system to another. The perspective and methlodogy of this emphasis ranges from the purely descriptive to the most rigorous of mathematical formulations. The dynamics, functions, development, and composition of systems are studied to generate further research as well as a universal scientific theory.

Cybernetics represents the movement within the general body of systems thought that holds that *humans and society can be best understood through study of their messages and communication facilities.*[13] It is the thesis of cybernetics that any system can be effectively analyzed through the communication and control activities of the system. Cyberneticians have sought to develop a language and techniques to attack and deal precisely with the problems of control and communication. Their efforts are directed toward classification and development of those processes which function so as to combat (move in a direction opposite to) nature's tendency toward disorder and degeneration. The model of cybernetics affords a vehicle for assessing feedback and its effect on system state, the monitoring of system activity, and the adaptation of the system in the light of information (knowledge).

Holism is the branch of the systems movement centered in continental Europe. This approach is quite similar to the General Systems movement in terms of its interdisciplinary emphasis and truly generic focus (as contrasted to the precise focus of cybernetics). It is different from General System Theory in that it tends to incorporate to a greater extent the concerns of philosophy, theology, and the humanities (along with the social, behavioral, and physical sciences). Both Eastern and Western thought are of interest in

Holism. A metaphysical approach is taken toward the analysis of systems, structures, and wholes; implications for society, broadly conceived, are projected. The holistic approach per se is of import, as well as its application to the sciences and humanities. Most recently this movement has been applied particularly to concerns normally falling into the traditional realms of philosophy and religion.[14]

Operations Research (O.R.) represents the first attempt in the general systems movement to move directly to applied practice. OR (as it is popularly known) *"is concerned with increasing the effectiveness of operations of man—machine systems."*[15] According to Churchman its objective is to provide managers of an organization with a scientific basis for solving problems involving the interaction of components of the organization in the best interests of the organization as a whole.[16] It is the application of interdisciplinary science to organizational decision-making and the use of optimization and suboptimization (situations such as those in which goals and activities of an organization or its components are involved) in making organizational choices. The process includes research on problems of organized systems to provide solutions which best serve the organization as a whole (or a major part of it as a whole) by interdisciplinary teams through the use of the scientific method.[17] Its general model $[E=f\ (xi, yi)\ ]$ views effectiveness as a function of controllable and noncontrollable variables.[18] Solutions in Operations Research may be either analytical (mathematical deduction) or numerical (trial and error iteration).[19] OR is a product of both General Systems Theory (the interdisciplinary approach) and Cybernetics (the scientific control of organizational activity).

Systems Design represents an outgrowth of the General Systems Theory emphasis and the Operations Research movement. It is interdisciplinary and based in the generalizability of systems findings, but in contrast to OR is less concerned with what is . Rather, it *is concerned with the creative development and structuring of new, different, and unique systems.* It can be applied to man, machine, or man-machine systems of either simple or complex nature. Systems Design likewise can be achieved through rigorous-mathematical procedures or logical-subjective techniques.

Information Theory is direct outgrowth of Cybernetics and the first purely quantitative branch of the systems movement. According to Miller, Information Theory itself is now about 15 years old. Originally developed for problems in communications engineering, it has more recently been applied to telephone communications and radar,[20] as well as, less sophisticatedly, to a variety of information systems in machines and organizations. *It has been observed that the possibility of defining information quantitatively improves one's chances of making the right guess.*[21] This is the end toward which information theorists work and have become increasingly successful. Central to the information theorist is the energy potential (in a quantitative sense) of messages, such as for the administrator a message's potential for aiding in decision-making.

Systems Analysis represents a refined "systems" process for business and industrial problem-solving.[22] Churchman observed that OR and systems analysis are often equated or confused.[23] He points out that OR is oriented primarily to human systems (organizations) while systems analysis is concerned with mechanical and man-machine systems. Like OR, systems analysis is an interdisciplinary scientific attack on problems; in contrast to OR, systems analysis breaks wholes into parts and reassembles these into some kind of whole (weather the same whole, a new whole, or a somewhat different one). OR, on the other hand, always works in terms of the organization as a given. *Systems analysis involves (1) systems decomposition (analysis) or the dissection of a system, and (2) the resulting systems synthesis (often, systems design) into another whole system.* Of import are components, functions, activities, and relationships and the restructuring of these based on interdisciplinary scientific analysis and projection.

Systems Engineering is a product of Operations Research, the somewhat more subjective Systems Design approach, and the general development of engineering science. As such it has a true disciplinary flavor (further attested to by its label) and increasingly represents a growing body of knowledge and professional pursuit in and of itself. Unlike OR, which is concerned with existing systems, Systems Engineering directs itself toward the planning and design of new systems (as well as to the improved performance of existing operations).[24] Like Systems Design (which actually is probably a less rigorous or sophisticated form of Systems Engineering) *Systems Engineering is primarily focused on the creative development of better "systems," be they man, man-machine, or mechanical.* In Hall's words, Systems Engineering is "a creative process in a time series of actions or events which leads to a novel system that satisfies the objectives of a group at some point in time."[25] Systems Engineering, however, more than OR, Systems Design, or Systems Analysis, tends to be a discipline in the traditional sense and thereby has tended to create its own specialists, procedures, and body of knowledge.

Output Analysis, though a highly specialized branch of Systems Analysis, bears some mentioning since this form of systems activity has been clearly developed and effectively applied in the past few years.[26] *This form of analysis holds that a system (organization) can best be studied in terms of the results of its actions (activity).* The focus is, therefore, on (1) outcomes or output, (2) the evaluation of output in terms of system goals, and (3) subsequent feedback to the system as to how its operations and processes can be altered or restructured to better achieve system goals. Implicitly, Output Analysis is premised on the notion that feedback is the controlling force of system activity—and since feedback is derived from outputs, the way a system operates can most satisfactorily be assessed in terms of its output.

Mathematical Programming is one of the most widely known and successfully applied quantitative techniques in management decision-making.[27] It has been applied to a variety of problems from transportation management to investment portfolios. With obvious antecedents in the science of

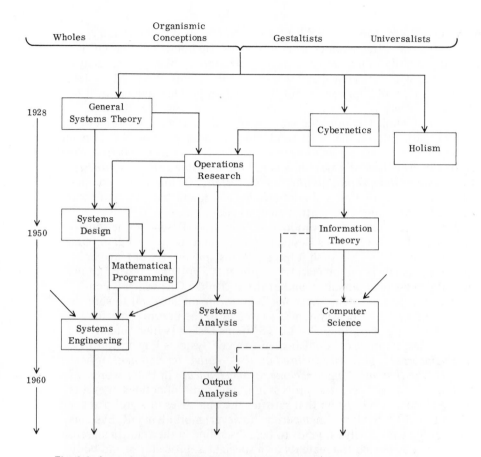

Fig. 1.1 An evolutionary view of systems approaches and emphases.

mathematics, the use of Mathematical Programming in the systems movement resulted from a need for increasing quantification and more accurate
prediction wherever possible in OR, System Design, and Systems Engineering. It has proved to be an effective method of finding optimum allocation
schemes for a number of classes of problems. *Mathematical Programming
involves the use of mathematical formulae, such as the linear equation, to
solve complex organizational problems,* such as those of production sched-
ules and worker deployment.

Lastly, *Computer Science* represents a highly technical and applied aspect of the systems movement. Little elaboration is needed here since of
all the outcomes of the systems movement and systems related activity, the
computer and computer science are probably best known. It should be
pointed out, nevertheless, that while the educational administrator has seen
and used the computer's scheduling and/or accounting potential, little has

been done in this field to explore the computer's possibilities for other administrative assistance, such as in assisting in the process of organizational decision-making.[28]

The evolution and relationships of the emphases or approaches in the systems movement described above can be pictorily represented in time-space to illustrate the similarity, differences, and linkages already discussed (Fig. 1.1). This chart distinguishes and relates the major threads of the systems movement in a chronological perspective.

THE POTENTIAL OF "SYSTEMS" FOR EDUCATIONAL ADMINISTRATION

The movement outlined above has great relevance for educational administration. It is relevant as a general orientation and as a source of specific administrative practices as well. We can, therefore, look first at the potential of the systems movement for research, theory development, practice, and training (preparation) in educational administration, and then identify specific models, procedures, or techniques that have emerged from the systems movement that can facilitate the task of administering an educational organization.

In regard to *research* in educational administration, the systems movement has much to offer. The systems literature is rich in what Miller terms "cross-level" hypotheses[29] and already has attracted interest by researchers in this field. Using "systems theory," Griffiths has generated a number of propositions that are pertinent for educational administration and merit testing through empirical study.[30] More recently Swanson, drawing on the work of Thomas, has explored the potential of research into the cost-quality relationship in education using systems concepts and models.[31] Other systems concepts such as the stress reaction syndrome identified by Miller (that stress leads to overcompensation, undercompensation, and ultimately total collapse)[32] also suggest avenues and even specific hypotheses for studies related to educational administration and organization.

In addition, the systems notion regarding the similarities of all forms of systems has meaning for research activity in educational administration. To the extent that this is true, findings can be brought together from a number of areas of inquiry and related in such a way as to extend the knowledge in this field far beyond its present boundaries.

The systems movement is also contributing greatly to research methodology. Particularly relevant here is the adaptation of methodology from one field to another, the refinement of methodologies, the development of more rigorous and sophisticated mathematical and quantitative procedures, and the advancement of models, model building, gaming, and simulations.

Finally, we might note, relative to the research potential, that systems thought as a body of concepts, (partial) theory, and perspective is peculiarly applicable to the entire basic or action research processes—the identification and formulation of a problem, the design of investigation, the methodology of scientific study, the analysis of data, the organization of findings, and the translation of findings into operations and action programs in real systems. In fact, no other body of knowledge has as extensive utility for all phases of research, both basic and applied, as does systems thought. The advantages of one conceptual framework guiding this entire process should be obvious.

The systems movement as well has a potential for *theory development* in educational administration. Here it has certain advantages over field theory (restriction to a single medium) and Gestalt psychology with its emphasis on supersummation (the whole is greater than the sum of its parts). Systems notions, therefore, can be used to theorize within, across, and through systems. Also, such theorizing can account for the fact that although in system activity input roughly approximates output, it usually involves a loss (i.e., is less than, not supersummated). Theory development drawing on systems thinking is ultimately empirical, operational, and focused on the real dynamics and totality of systems as well as the forces that affect them. The already demonstrated universality of certain systems properties and laws have obvious value for theorizing as attested by the literature in this field. Also, the utility of systems ideas, apparatus, and approaches along with the relational power inherent in the systems perspective is helpful in theoretical activity. Implied above in the work of Griffiths and Swanson is the potential of systems thought for generating relevant theory to guide research in educational administration.

The systems movement can also contribute greatly to the *practice of educational administration.* Some of the specific contributions will be discussed in the next section of this chapter but here we can look at the more general implications for administrative practice. Most relevant for the "practitioner" is simply the systems perspective itself. To the extent that any practitioner can understand the systems mode of thought and apply it in his work his task will be facilitated. Systems thinking will force him to look at situations or problems in their totality, to take a long-range view regarding his organization, to analyze consciously antecedent conditions and possible future effects, to be cognizant of relations and connections in the life space of the organization, to utilize cost-utility approaches to making choices, and to optimize (maximize) for the total organization. Hopefully, the administrator's predictive power should be enhanced through a more skillful approach and an improved ability to deal with uncertainty. Lastly, the many heuristic vehicles, procedures, and tools created by the systems movement contribute each in its own way to the facilitation of administrative practice. (Some of these devices will be identified and described in the next part of this chapter.).

The systems movement also has meaning for the *preparation* of *administrators* because of the systems potential for research, theory building, and the practice of administration. But this relevance extends beyond useful content (viz., concepts of the integrating or sensitizing variety, theory, and processes) and a high level of explanatory power to even the provision of a unifying thread for preparation programs. Systems concepts facilitate the logical collation of knowledge and stimulate knowledge synthesis. They are also optimally interdisciplinary, and the relating of concepts and theory is assisted when systems constructs and approaches are used. As well, a program of administrator preparation can be conceived and structured as a system in and of itself. The value of certain systems concepts such as "feedback" (evaluation) or "output" (results) as focal concerns in developing programs of preparation should be obvious. Maybe in this way traditional approaches toward the preparation of educational administrators can be supplemented by better and more useful training sequences.

In sum, the systems movement is profoundly relevant to research, theory building, and the practice of educational administration, and to the preparation of administrators. Likewise, many of the methods developed by the movement can aid the practicing school administrator.

SOME SPECIFIC CONTRIBUTIONS OF THE SYSTEMS MOVEMENT

The "systems" movement has prompted a number of specific models, procedures, and techniques that are relevant for administrative practice in education. Because educational administrators have yet to capitalize to any great extent on these, we will seek only to identify and discuss briefly some of the more popular and well developed systems devices.

Selected *models* with relevance for the practice of administration in educational organizations are:

1. *The "Black Box" Model.* Ashby's classic input-output process model provides an analytic framework which graphically focuses attention on outcomes of system activity as the results of system inputs and system processes and, further, shows that feedback is the evaluative or monitoring process through which a system modifies and/or improves subsequent outputs.[33] (See Fig. 1.2.)

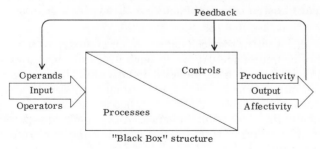

Fig. 1.2 The classic "Black Box" model (after Ashby).

2. *Output Analysis.* From his work in business and industrial problem solving, Optner has derived a comprehensive and detailed scheme (model)

for attacking management problems through the application of systems analysis techniques to the control functions in organization decision-making.[34]

3. *An Outcome Analysis Scheme.* Related to Optner's approach, but somewhat more subjective, is a scheme developed in a recent research project that assesses a variety of the outcomes of organizational activity. This model can be used to assess the extent to which productivity, organizational integration, organizational health, and feedback (evaluation) are present in organizational outcomes.[35] (See Table 1.3)

Table 1.3 T.O.B.E. scheme for organizational outcome analysis

Dimension	Measure	Scale
		0 1 2 3
1. Productivity	a) Product utility	┼───┼───┼───┼
	b) Service(s) utility	┼───┼───┼───┼
2. Integration	a) Self-actualization	┼───┼───┼───┼
	b) Group decision-making	┼───┼───┼───┼
	c) Individuals' flexibility to change	┼───┼───┼───┼
3. Organizational Health	a) Capacity to test reality	┼───┼───┼───┼
	b) Identity sense	┼───┼───┼───┼
	c) Adaptability	┼───┼───┼───┼
4. Evaluation (Feedback)	a) Desirability of	┼───┼───┼───┼
	b) Penetration of	┼───┼───┼───┼

4. *Mathematical Models.* The mathematical programming movement has resulted in a number of linear, integer, stochastic, and dynamic programming techniques that may be applied to organizational problems. The usefulness of mathematical equations to solve problems if resource allocation, personnel deployment, and a host of other problems has already been demonstrated.[36]

5. *Simulations.* Management science (using systems approaches) has developed a number of computer simulations through which organizations or organizational components have been modeled and decision alternatives are tested to assess their outcome and effect on the system and its goals. Through these procedures, variables can be controlled and alternated and effects assessed in a rapid time reduction sequence. Also, simulations permit the manipulation of vast arrays of variables that would be too numerous and complex for human solution.[37]

6. *Political Decision Model.* Easton's work in political science using systems concepts and principles has resulted in a systems model of group decision-making. The model has relevance and implications for group decisions in any context and can be used to better understand group decision-making

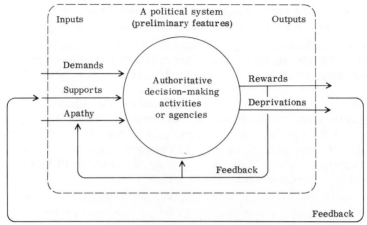

Fig. 1.3 A systems model of the political system.

in the organizational setting as well as in the larger societal arena for which it was intended.[38]   (See Fig. 1.3.)

7. *A Communications Model.* Churchman has explicated a communications model for use in analyzing activities in business organizations. The model accounts for (1) organizational communication network(s), (2) knowledge of the goal-direction processes of organizational control, and (3) knowledge of goal-changing processes.[39] The model and its components have been operationalized and could be applied in the study of educational organizations. (See Fig. 1.4.)

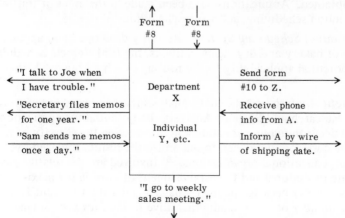

Fig. 1.4 Communication model.

Some of the *procedures* growing out of the systems movement that can facilitate the practice of educational administration are the following:

1. *The Critical Path Method.* The critical path method (CPM), or PERT, as it has been more recently labeled, is a "powerful but basically simple technique for analyzing, planning, and scheduling large, complex projects."[40] This procedure involves breaking a project into its component parts or activities, determining which of these are "critical," and then scheduling the project in terms of its parts or subactivities in order to meet a target time at minimum cost. CPM can be applied to many things, from the construction or a building or the production of a play, to a research study or a plan for improving instruction. (See Chapter 8 for a detailed discussion of PERT and its application to a typical administrative problem.)

2. *The Planning, Programming, Budgeting System. (PPBS).* An outgrowth of military planning and decision-making, PPBS has had wide application in government projects and more recently in university planning. PPBS involves budgeting by programs, rather than by the traditional objects of expenditure, and the extension of programs "far enough in the future to show to the extent practical and necessary the full resource requirements and financial implications of the programmed outputs."[41]

3. *Computer Programming.* Some educational organizations already use computers in scheduling and, to a lesser extent, in information storage and retrieval. The utilization of computers has not, however, been extended fully to such matters as organizational information systems, personnel deployment, personnel records, organizational research, or similar fields where applications could well be made.[42]

4. *Linear Programming.* Through the use of linear equations (linear programming), solutions to problems involving two quantifiable interacting variables can be obtained. Applications have been made in the areas of traffic control, production scheduling, and work scheduling.[43]

5. *Transportation Scheduling System.* Recently developed and applied to the routing of bakery and dry cleaners trucks, the IBM Vehicle Scheduling Program has potential applicability to the routing of school buses.[44] (See Fig. 1.5.)

6. *Cost-Benefit Analysis.* Cost-benefit analysis has been used extensively in Operations Research and Systems Analysis. Its potential for applications in educational decision-making are abundant considering the scarcity of resources and the corresponding need to maximize the results achieved by, or the products of, educational organizations.[45] Involved are the relative payoffs of alternate procedures and the establishment of criteria for maximizing choices. (Refer back to the list on page 5 and Tables 1.1 and 1.2.)

Finally, a number of specific administrative *techniques* have emanated from the systems movement and, more precisely, the models and proce-

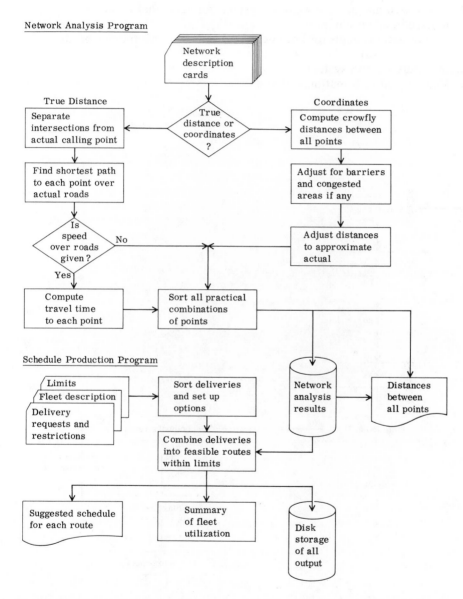

Fig. 1.5 Systems chart of the IBM vehicular scheduling program. (By permission from *H20-0464-IBM Vehicular Scheduling Program.* © by International Business Machines Corporation.)

dures discussed above. A few of these are:

1. The flow chart. (See Fig. 1.6.)
2. Automated manpower inventory systems for personnel selection, deployment, and evaluation.
3. Instructional systems for both delimited and extensive training needs.
4. Information storage and retrieval systems.
5. Inventory control systems.
6. Management information systems.

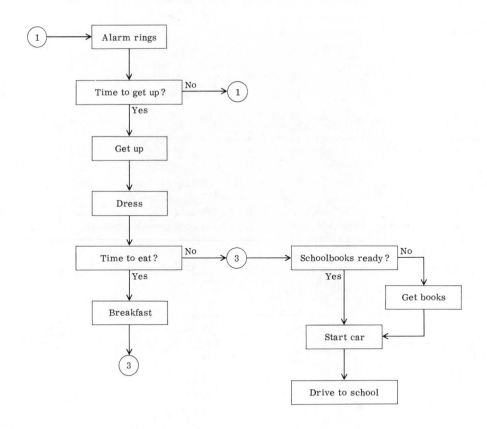

Fig. 1.6 A flow chart. (From Enoch Haga (ed.) *Automated Educational Systems,* Elmhurst, Illinois: The Business Press, 1967, p. 27. By permission.)

SOME PROBLEMS

All-in-all, the systems movement is rich in potential for educational administration. It provides a heuristic mode of thought, viable concepts, and a
number of management tools that can be of benefit to the field of educational administration. However, before we look to the systems movement
as a source of solutions to all of our problems, or blindly begin to adopt its
approaches, methodology, or tools, we ought to recognize some of the problems that bear on the use of "systems" in educational administration or any
other applied field.

There is grave danger in viewing the systems movement as a panacea, or
cure-all. Rather, the products of the systems movement might be viewed
more as facilitators or "freers" for educational administrators. In a sense,
the systems movement enables us to ask better questions and seek better answers. Also, it provides us with a number of tested procedures and tools for
solving some of our problems. To the extent that educational administrators
utilize administrative support devices they will be free to explore the more
knotty and emerging problems of our times. But by no stretch of the imagination do systems approaches yield all the answers. There are many categories of management problems not amenable to sytems techniques or for
which the techniques lack sufficient refinement. "Systems" as a movement
is itself young and emerging.

A second problem in borrowing from the systems movement relates to
the appropriateness of systems models and procedures for the dynamics and
variables with which the administrator deals. Administrators must be critical and they will need to assess carefully the potential of each procedure or
device they seek to use. They will need to be cautious not to borrow without adequate clarification by the "systems expert" as well. To the extent
that systems models and procedures need adaptation, the administrator must
be aware of the possible loss inherent in the changeover process. It is imperative that applications not be forced and that administrators be aware of what
the models, procedures, and techniques they borrow can do and cannot do.
Systems vehicles, as all others, have their limits, a relative or restricted scope
of applicability, and inherent limitations.

Another potential problem in capitalizing on the systems movement
can be an over-zealous preoccupation with the mathematical aspects of the
systems movement. "Over-sophistication" and the desire to utilize more
quantitative approaches can well get in the way of applied practice. If the
situations and problems of the world of practice are conducive to the mathematical procedures used in some of the more rigorous systems approaches,
this drawback is not a matter of concern. But of course the science of mathematics does not yet have the capacity to provide models or solutions for
everything. Thus the administrator needs to realize that the quantified systems approaches cannot solve all problems and, equally important, *that the
systems movement has numerous approaches that can facilitate prediction
and dealing with uncertainty that are less quantifiable, more subjective, but
nonetheless systematic and rigorous in a logical or empirical sense.*

In looking to the systems movement, one must further avoid a preoccupation with models, procedures, techniques, and terminology per se. More important are the principles and processes (methodology) of systems scholars and the "mind set" or mode of thought these scholars employ in scientific and applied activity. Administrators need to guard against long intellectual reflections or discussions and need to push toward the practical implementation of systems approaches in educational administration.

The traditionalists in the ranks of educational administrators pose another problem in drawing on systems knowledge. Although one gets the strong feeling that the systems approach is ultimately a common-sense approach, it can be anticipated that widespread acceptance of systems ideas and devices will not be immediately forthcoming. Although this may be due to a natural resistance to "different" ways of thinking, implementing even the most obviously useful systems models and procedures will be no less difficult than promulgating a new school curriculum, passing a bond issue for a new school building, or modifying teacher certification requirements.

Lastly, there is the problem of just plain getting started. There has been a lot of talk recently about the relevance of systems for educational administration. It remains now for those practicing administrators who see relevance in the systems movement for their field of practice to do something about it.

In this chapter we have sought to explore the "essence" of the systems movement—in a capsule, *systematic, relational thought*; to identify the major lines of development in the systems movement; to indicate the relevance of the systems movement for research, theory building, practice, and preparation in administration; to suggest a number of systems models, procedures, and techniques that can facilitate the practice of administration; and, finally, to focus on a few of the problems of using systems ideas and approaches in educational administration. We can now turn to a discussion of the theoretical aspects of systems and to illustrating their relevance for the world of educational administration.

NOTES

1. R. L. Ackoff, "The Development and Nature of Operations Research and Its Relevance of Educational Media Research," Paper for the Conference: New Dimensions for Research in Educational Media, Center for Instructional Communications, Syracuse University, 1964, p. 7.

2. See F. H. Allport, *Theories of Perception and the Concept of Structure.* New York: John Wiley & Sons, 1955, pp. 8-12, and H. Feigl, "Principles and Problems of Theory Construction in Psychology," in Wayne Dennis et al., *Current Trends in Psychological Theory.* Pittsburgh: University of Pittsburgh Press, 1951, p. 182.

3. C. J. Hitch, "Uncertainties in Operations Research," *Ops. Res. 8,* No. 4 (July-August 1960), pp. 437-445.

4. Variables within a system can be referred to as *factors,* and variables external to a system can be termed *parameters.*

5. After Ackoff, *op. cit.,* p. 9.

6. See F. J. Pilecki, "An Investigation of the Predictive Value of Intermittent Feedback and Relay Feedback in Task Accomplishment," Unpublished doctoral dissertation: The University of Rochester, 1966, p. 31.

7. *Ibid.,* p. 31; See also L. von Bertalanffy, "General System Theory," in *Gen. Syst., 1,* (1956), pp. 1-10.

8. *Ibid.,* p. 31.

9. There is little question that the systems movement as we now know it is directly linked to L. von Bertalanffy's early papers dating back to the late 1920's. However, the greatest development of the movement has occurred since 1950. Significant in this regard is Wiener's work in Cybernetics; the work of von Bertalanffy, Ackoff, Ashby, and Rapoport; the well-known Chicago Conference reported by Grinker; and activity in the Society for General Systems Research.

10. There is no need to dwell on these matters here. This should be apparent to anyone who has perused the systems literature; and for those who have not, a little reading in the area will make the point obvious.

11. K. Boulding, "General Systems Theory—The Skeleton of a Science," *Gen. Syst. 1,* (1956), p. 11.

12. *Ibid.,* p. 11.

13. N. Wiener, "Cybernetics," in S. Ulmer, *Introductory Readings in Political Science.* Chicago: Rand McNally, 1961, pp. 298-306. See also N. Wiener, *The Human Use of Human Beings.* Boston: Houghton Mifflin, 1950.

14. This section is based on documents of the International Society for the Comparative Study of Civilizations (S.I.E.C.C.), Salzburg, Austria, Residenz.

15. R. L. Ackoff, "Systems, Organizations and Interdisciplinary Research," *Gen. Syst., 5,* (1960), p. 1.

16. C. W. Churchman, R. L. Ackoff, and E. L. Arnoff, *Introduction to Operations Research.* New York: John Wiley & Sons, 1957, p. 6.

17. Ackoff, "The Development and Nature of Operations Research. . . ," *op. cit.,* p. 7.

18. Churchman, Ackoff, and Arnoff, *op. cit.,* p. 13.

19. *Ibid.,* p. 14.

20. M. Alexis and C. Z. Wilson, *Organizational Decision Making.* Englewood Cliffs, N.J.: Prentice Hall, 1967, p. 313.

21. A. Rapoport, "What is Information?" in Ulmer, *op. cit.,* p. 307.

22. S. L. Optner, *Systems Analysis for Business and Industrial Problem Solving.* Englewood Cliffs, N.J.: Prentice Hall, 1965.

23. Churchman, Ackoff, and Arnoff, *op. cit.*, p. 7.

24. A. D. Hall, *A Methodology for Systems Engineering.* New York: Nostrand, 1962.

25. *Ibid.*, p. 81.

26. See Optner, *op. cit.*

27. Alexis and Wilson, *op. cit.*, p. 224.

28. See J. W. Loughary, *Man-Machine Systems in Education.* New York: Harper and Row, 1966; P. Allen, *Exploring the Computer,* Reading, Mass.: Addison-Wesley, 1967; J. I. Goodland, J. F. O'Toole, Jr., and L. L. Tyler, *Computers and Information Systems in Education.* New York: Harcourt, Brace and World, 1966.

29. James G. Miller, "Toward a General Theory for the Behavioral Sciences," *Am. Psychol., 10,* (1955), pp. 513-531.

30. D. E. Griffiths, "The Nature and Meaning of Theory," in *Behavioral Science and Educational Administration,* Sixty-Third Yearbook of the National Society for the Study of Education. Chicago: University of Chicago Press, 1964, Chapter V.

31. A. D. Swanson, "The Cost-Quality Relationship," in *The Challenge of Change in School Finance.* Committee on Educational Finance, NEA, Washington, D.C., 1967, pp. 151-164.

32. Miller, *op. cit.*

33. W. R. Ashby, *An Introduction to Cybernetics.* New York: John Wiley & Sons, 1956, Chapter VI.

34. Optner, *op. cit.*

35. G. L. Immegart, "Systems Theory and Taxonomic Inquiry into Organizational Behavior in Education," in D. E. Griffiths (ed.), *Developing Taxonomies of Organizational Behavior in Educational Administration.* Chicago: Rand McNally, 1969.

36. Alexis and Wilson, *op. cit.*, pp. 222-240.

37. See, for example, J. Kagdis and M. R. Lackner, "Introduction to Management Control Systems Research," Technical Memorandum 708/100/00, System Development Corporation, October 15, 1962.

38. D. Easton, "An Approach to the Analysis of Political Systems," *Wld. Politics, 9,* (1956-57), pp. 383-400.

39. Churchman, Ackoff and Arnoff, *op. cit.*, Chapter IV.

40. F. K. Levy, G. L. Thompson, and J. D. Wiest, "The ABC's of the Critical Path Method," *Har. Bus. Rev., 4,* No. 5 (September-October 1963), pp. 98-108; D. L. Cook, *PERT: Applications in Education.* Cooperative Research Monograph No. 17, OE-12024, 1966, U. S. Government Printing Office, F55.212.12024.

41. C. J. Hitch, "Program Budgeting," *Datamation. 13,* No. 9 (September 1967), pp. 37-40.

42. Although such applications have been suggested and discussed at length in recent years, there is little evidence that educational organizations have attempted more than superficial uses of computer technology, particularly in regard to management applications.

43. Alexis and Wilson, *op. cit.,* pp. 226ff.

44. "System 1360 Vehicle Scheduling Program Application Description," IBM Technical Publications Department, H20-0464-0, White Plains, New York, 1967.

45. Swanson, *op. cit.,* and J. A. Thomas, "Efficiency Criteria in Urban School Systems." Paper read at the AERA Annual Meeting, 1967, New York City.

**Part II / The theoretical premises of
systems and systems thought**

Chapter 2 / The concept system

In order to understand and apply the products of the system movement, a basic understanding of the concept system and its theoretical premises is essential. As we have already noted, systems notions are: (1) relatively recent in origin, (2) derived from many varied sources, and (3) subject to mounting confusion due to their "vogueness." And although the goal of systems scientists, and of the movement itself, is the unification of findings from the existing discrete sciences and bodies of knowledge into a single, all-inclusive theoretical perspective to facilitate science and practice, no comprehensive, single systems theory, as such, presently exists.

There are, however, a number of closely related, more or less complete, rigorous, and empirically verifiable theories or sets of concepts emanating largely from von Bertalanffy's conception of general systems theory,[1] the science of cybernetics,[2] and the operations research movement.[3] The diverse sources of systems ideas should in no way be disconcerting, since the similarities and consistencies of resultant theories or conceptual frameworks give evidence of their potential for eventual incorporation into a unified, general theory which should ". . . contain universal principles applicable to all systems."[4]

The pioneering efforts of systems scholars have resulted in this exciting movement which has, in fact, *begun to link disciplines and fields of practice together in both a communicative and productive dialogue.* The potential of systems thought has been cogently summarized by Hearn:

> In each locality, scientists from diverse fields are working together for a twofold purpose. By examining what has been learned in other fields they hope to discover paths to new knowledge in their own spheres; and and they hope through their collaborative efforts to contribute to a growing body of unified theory.[5]

At this point it may be appropriate to reinforce our caution regarding the systems movement so that it is not construed as an attempt to develop some sort of "super-science." According to Guilbraud:

> Its only function is to devise new and fundamental techniques of research and analysis, which each specialist can then apply in more specific forms to his own field . . . It simply borrows problems from . . . other fields, hoping that the solution it discovers may have some useful applications, but not taking even this for granted.[6]

Systems theory further does not purport to be a discipline per se. Rather, as we have observed, it is a methodology, an approach, a mode of thought, if you will, for dealing with problems or situations based on the conviction that

> . . . it is possible to represent all forms of animate and inanimate matter as systems. . . (The systems scientists) are impressed by the number of times the same principles have been independently 'discovered' . . . in different fields . . . They believe that the unification of theory in the physical and nonphysical worlds is desirable and ultimately attainable, at least to some degree. Accordingly, they contend that there are properties which are common to systems of every order . . . and that there are universal laws which describe the structure of systems and their manner of functioning.[7]

Rapoport, stating it in another way, has noted that the systems movement

> . . . subsumes an outlook or a methodology rather than a theory in the sense ascribed to this term in science. The salient feature of this outlook is, as its name implies, an emphasis on those aspects of objects or events which derive from general properties of systems rather than from the specific content.[8]

The potential of systems concepts or theories as constructs of value to the practicing educational administrator needs to be made explicit. In this chapter we will begin to do this by first discussing the basic notion of system. Next, the relevance of the universal properties of systems will be described. Finally, we will identify the major approaches to conceptualizing open systems and the characteristic states and properties of open systems. Also, the pertinence of open systems concepts to educational administration will be treated.

THE NOTION OF SYSTEM

A system can be defined quite simply as "a set of objects together with relationships between the objects and between their attributes."[9] *A system is, in other words, an entity composed of (1) a number of parts, (2) the relationships of these parts, and (3) the attributes of both the parts and the relationships.* Or, in another vein, a system can be conceived as "some form in structure or operation, concepts or function, composed of united and integrated parts."[10]

The term "system" can, therefore, be used to refer to a vast array of things from the smallest "whole" to the total universe. An atom, a cell, a plant, a man, a bird, a committee, a city, a nation, the world, and the universe are all examples of systems. Or, automobiles, typewriters, heating plants, computers, buildings, and the nation's highways are systems. Or, in addition to "living" or "physical" systems, there are conceptual systems such as number systems, game strategy systems, and theoretical systems.

And there are practical systems such as traffic control systems, food service systems, refuse collection systems, code systems, and even betting systems. All of these examples share the above description of system in that they are composed of related and functionally interconnected parts that possess qualitative factors all of which stem from inclusion in the particular system.

Systems all have a *uniqueness of character* which enables them to be distinguished from other systems, even quite similar ones, and from their environment.

Obviously school districts, school buildings, school staffs, teachers' associations, supervisory staffs, classrooms, programs of studies, and even teaching units or lessons are systems, and, further, can be profitably analyzed as such. But, before moving in this direction, we need to explore more deeply the notion of system.

There are two basic types of systems—"open" and "closed." Open systems are those which exchange matter and energy with their environment. Closed systems are self-contained, and are unaffected by other systems or their environment. All closed systems (best exemplified by certain chemical reactions or people in advanced stages of psychic disorder) move toward entropy, a "death-state" of inertia. Open systems, since they interact with and use their environment, combat entropy and thus exist in a dynamic "life state," typified by increasing order, differentiation, variation, and complexity. Schools, or most any of the systems the educational administrator must work with, tend to be "open" systems in the true sense of the word. Certainly the school exists in an exchange relationship with society. For example, the school takes its clients from society's young population, extracts other needed resources, and "processes" the clients into more educated beings, ultimately a contribution to society.

The matter of system "openness" and "closedness" is not, however, a simple either/or proposition. Certain properties, as we shall see, pertain to all systems, both the "open" and the "closed." For example, all systems ultimately tend toward entropy or death regardless of whether they are open or closed. The unique quality of the open system is its ability to counteract the entropic tendency. But an open system can reduce entropy only through work, which requires tapping other sources of energy. The tendency toward entropy is constant, and requires continual attention in order to maintain and improve the system's qualitative life state. At any point in time an open system may be more open or more closed than it was before, or might be in the future. Thus we can say that systems can exist on an open-to-closed continuum, some systems being more open while others are more closed. Further, all systems have subsystems which are definable entities or systems in and of themselves, and any of these subsystems can be relatively open or closed at any given time.

The point here is precisely that just because a system, such as a school, is characterized as "open," this does not mean the system is or will remain maximally functional, dynamic, or contributing. To be maximally open implies a conscious effort on the part of the system to maximize both its existence and its relationship to its environment. Just as people with physical or psychic disorders are isolated from—rather than open to—their environment or the real world, so can all systems or subsystems become disordered, unresponsive, or inert. Therefore, a school that fails to combat the entropic tendency, or a department in a school that fails to strive for openness, is subject to increasing isolation from the real world (environment) around it. Persons such as educational administrators can also succumb to the universal entropic press. Witness in this regard the superintendent who does not keep up-to-date and who attempts to run his district of 20,000 pupils today as he did his 1,000 pupil district of two decades ago. His decreasing relevance and increasing isolation from reality eventually will render him relatively useless, and when such "closedness" reaches a dysfunctional point for the system or the larger environment the administrator finds himself replaced. This is not, of course, complete entropy but is rather an illustration of *functional* entropy. It might be added that increasing or cumulative functional entropy (whether in people or with the Studebaker Motor Company) does accelerate the system's movement toward total entropy. There is a point at which less open, or more closed, systems just can no longer combat the tendency toward entropy.

We are led then to the key property of the open system, and the challenge confronting all open systems that wish to magnify their existence—that of growth and development in order to overcome the systemic tendency toward death. The key to the existence of all open systems is *growth and development of the system from a primitive or embryonic initial state to a state of mature functionality, of increasing order, differentiation, variation, and complexity.* As the open system evolves and draws on resources, itself, and its environment, the system's dynamic existence and contribution to itself and the environment are increased. Such an evolution, through system activity, ensures openness.

Also characteristic of all system activity is energy transformation through the system's processes and structure into output or a terminal state. For the closed system, activity progresses unimpeded until all energy is dispelled and a final stage of inaction or entropy is reached. In terms of open systems, input in the form of energy from the system or its environment is transformed by system structures and processes into output or contributions to the system and/or its environment. Thus, system activity is rational and purposive as opposed to random or accidental. It seeks, in the open system, to maximize the system itself and the system's function in the larger environment of which it is a part. Important to the system and its activity are rationality (purpose), the dynamic exchange relationship existing between the system and its environment (the steady or life state of the system), and the evaluation or assessment of system activity (feedback). Only as the system engages in energy transformation or activity which is purposive, dynamic, and feedback-governed does it counteract entropy and move to a more open and dynamic state typified by functional variation, order, differentiation, and complexity.[11]

There are in the basic notion of the open system several immediate implications for the educational administrator and his work. First and foremost is the idea that any system is more than simply its definable parts. Also integral to any system are (a) the relationships between its parts and (b) the attributes of its parts and their relationships. Systems are, therefore, complex entities with both quantitative and qualitative dimensions. *In order to understand or work with any system one must know not only the system's components but also how these components are functionally related and the qualitative aspects of the components and their interdependence.* For example, if the newly appointed administrator really wants to get to know his school or school district, this implies more than getting to know just the staff, the pupils, the facilities, and the existing educational materials. Equally important are the relationships of teachers and pupils, of teachers and materials, of teachers and facilities, and so forth. And even more important, the qualitative effects of all elements and relationships are also essential to understanding a school as a system. Systems, especially large social systems, are inherently complex, and if one wishes to cope effectively with them, since the effect of any system is a "total system effect," one must attempt to comprehend the entire system in its full complexity. This process involves more than the obvious surface characteristics that are immediately apparent. At this point the notion of system alerts the reader to such complexity; in probing more deeply it will be apparent that systems concepts can contribute to the detailed understanding of systems.

A second implication from the discussion so far is that *systems, in order to continue to function or to increase their effectiveness, must constantly and consciously combat the natural systemic tendency of increasing entropy or, ultimately, death.* Public schools have, by virtue of their support and legitimation in our society, a captive and ensured existence quite unlike other organizations such as many business firms. However, if schools (or for that matter, any open systems) are to maximize their effects, attention must be given to system relevance and contribution. Since the administrator as the executive head or director of the school enterprise is primarily responsible for the maintenance, growth, and development of the school organization as a system, he must directly assume responsibility for keeping his school "open." That is, he must attend to open system needs in terms of providing for increasing order, differentiation, variation, and complexity of the total organization and for all of its subunits. Anyone in a focal position like that of the educational administrator must deal with a wide variety of both independent and interdependent "systems." The educational administrator copes with staff systems, student systems, transportation systems, facility systems, instructional systems, and even systems of educational thought. *Not only must the administrator understand and mesh the activities of such systems in his work, he must also maximize the effect of all of these systems on the learner so that the school may fulfill its function.*

Finally, the administrator must also view himself personally as an open system. Possibly more important than whether a leader or executive is "autocratic" or "democratic," more or less able, well-trained or not well-trained, is whether he or she is vital, relevant, and functionally contributing. *Self-awareness and personal growth and development are crucial if the administrator wishes personally to combat entropic tendencies and to maximize his job performance.*

Before probing more deeply into the characteristics of open systems and the various theoretical approaches available for analyzing open systems, we should examine the universal properties of all systems and the relevance of these properties for conceptualizing, analyzing, and ultimately understanding systems.

UNIVERSAL SYSTEM PROPERTIES

From the perspective of the systems scientist, all systems—whether open or closed, or more or less open or closed—exhibit certain properties, usually labeled *universal system properties.*[1][2] Such characteristics or properties can be used to contribute to the conceptualization of a system and ultimately to the understanding of that system.

1. *Tendency toward entropy.* We have already noted one of the universal properties of systems, that of *the tendency toward entropy.* All systems, regardless of nature, size, or type, tend toward a state of randomness, disorder, inertia, or ultimate death. By definition, "system" implies existence and activity. But all systems, whether living, mechanical, or conceptual, are subject to use, wear and tear, and malfunction. Only the most vital and open systems survive over prolonged periods of time. To the degree that a system can capitalize on its resources and its environment and can continue activity, growth, and development, its existence is enhanced. To the degree that functional entropy or certain of its important subsystems degenerate to entropic or nonfunctional states, the system's life state is threatened. All systems to some extent can suffer from partial entropy, such as the loss of a limb to a living system or the loss of a circuit in an electrical system. However, through adaptation or regeneration these systems can restore a normal state of existence. On the other hand, if the partial entropy strikes key subsystems of a larger system, or if by sheer weight or magnitude this partial entropy exceeds the system's tolerance level, the system is in danger. The important implication here for the administrator is that "dynamic existence" can not be taken for granted; rather this is a system state that must be *sought.* All open systems must strive through evolution, adaptation, and development to maximize their existence.

2. *Existence in time-space.* The second universal property of systems is that *all systems exist in time-space.* All systems involve the transformation of energy (activity), and while certain closed systems (such as certain chemical reactions which can be reversed) have a reversible time sequence, most closed systems and *all* open ones exist in a *nonreversible* time sequence. Systems are, therefore, evolutionary and either grow or degen-

erate over a period of time. It follows that to understand any system one must look at its life history, but to do anything with the system one must project into the *future*. Most relevant here for the parcticing educational administrator is the fact that although the present state of his organization and the organization's history are important factors as he plans ahead, these are, at best, only data on which to build for future system activity. Past and present successes and failures are events that through evaluation may give the directions for future activity but which, as time moves on, mean little beyond their effects in the past. Those working with systems need, then, to monitor and assess system action, but the focus of their concerns should be with adapting the system for the future.

3. *Boundaries.* The third universal systems property is that *all systems have boundaries* which are more or less arbitrary demarcations of that which is included within the system and that which is excluded from it. The boundary for a system can also be viewed as that point, or those points, beyond which the unique aspects of the system are no longer distinguishable. In any event, system boundaries in most cases are quite arbitrary and for analytic purposes are determined by the pragmatic considerations of utility, feasibility, and sensibility. Boundaries of some systems such as an automobile or a typewriter are somewhat finite, while boundaries for other systems such as a school, a society, or Parsonian sociological theory are quite imprecise. Or, even in the case of the typewriter, if it is an electric one and is plugged in, precise boundary demarcation becomes difficult and is ultimately arbitrary. Illustrating equally well the arbitrary boundaries of systems is the current state of the practice of medicine. To the general practitioner, a patient is a total being subject to a wide variety of stimuli and pathologies but to the heart specialist, the allergist, or the psychiatrist, the patient is a more delimited system because of both practical and professional reasons.

For anyone dealing with large and complex systems such as schools, implications regarding system boundaries are numerous. First of all, with any system that lacks finite boundaries, mere definition and comprehension are difficult. One can easily grasp and, with study, "understand" a simple watch or clock as a system. But defining a school and understanding it is another matter. To the degree that all those working with a system with fuzzy boundaries define and conceive of the system differently, concerted action will indeed be difficult. On the other hand, since system boundaries are at best arbitrary, to the degree that definitional and conceptual aspects of a system can be made explicit and agreed on, understanding in this regard will be facilitated. Also, to the degree that useful or feasible boundaries of a system can be established, system activity can be enhanced. For example, for purposes of revising the school cirriculum, the school may be defined to embrace the faculty; for purposes of selling a bond issue for a new school building, it may embrace the faculty and all employees and friends; and for purposes of working with a problem student it may be only those staff with special diagnostic and guidance skills. In each case, system activity will be facilitated by the boundaries drawn. Although system boundaries need some precision for functional activity the fact that they can be modified or arbitrarily drawn is beneficial.

From another perspective, since system boundaries reveal system inclusions and exclusions, system growth and development (functionality) can often be enhanced by extending or restricting system boundaries as needed. In the case of a crisis, a single member of a system can take action for the total system, while in other situations other talents and resources can be brought into the system to foster system action.

Finally, there is some relevance in the fact that it is easier to move within or without a "boundary" than across it. It is, therefore, easier for a teacher or any member of a system such as a school to adjust within the system than to enter it or leave it. Unfortunately, some feel that expulsion from or attraction to a system is a solution to problems. Often this is not the case, since adaptation and modification within the system offer more feasible alternatives.

4. *Environment.* The fourth universal systems property is that *all systems have an environment.* A system's environment is everything which is outside of the system's boundary. Environment, then, is contingent on the definition of the system and may vary as the system's boundary varies. Further, system environment is of two kinds: *proximal,* or that of which the system is aware; and *distal,* or that of which the system is unaware. Environment is important to all system activity since it has the potential to affect both the system and its functioning. However, for open systems—which by their nature exist in a dynamic exchange relationship with their environment—the environment is crucial to the system. Since the environment evaluates and, in effect, controls the system and its action, and since it contains many other systems, often competing or even conflicting ones, it is imperative for open systems to extend their awareness of environment—as well as of forces and dynamics from the environment—which can affect the systems and their activity.

Consequently, systems need comprehensive knowledge about all related aspects of their environment. They need to enlarge their proximal environment and reduce their distal environment. Also, systems need intensive knowledge about those aspects of the proximal environment which are most critical to system activity. For example, as school administrators today seek additional funds for schools, they need to be aware of all population elements and their dispositions toward increased spending for education, not just the "patrons" or "friends" of the schools. Further, school administrators need intensive understanding of antitaxation groups and other governmental agencies that might also be seeking added fiscal support. For a system to be maximally functional and its activity to be relevant, extensive and intensive knowledge of its environment is crucial.

Another implication concerns the system-environment relationship. In this respect the ultimate evaluation and control of system activity rests with the environment. Thus, while systems such as schools, clubs, or individual human beings act for their own good and benefit, they are ultimately judged by their service to the larger environment. To the extent that systems contribute to and enhance their environment, the environment will reward and enhance the system. However, when the system becomes malfunctional or nonfunctional, its existence will be threatened or thwarted.

5. *Variables and parameters.* The fifth universal systems property is that *all systems have factors that affect the structure and function of the system.* Factors within the system are *variables*; factors in the system's environment are *parameters.* By definition, closed systems are, of course, affected only by factors within the system or by system variables. Open systems are affected by factors—events, situations, energy dynamics, forces, malfunctions, and so forth—from both within and without the system. In other words the relevance of this system property is obvious: all systems are vulnerable and open systems are vulnerable to both internal and external occurrences. Considering also the notion of *proximal* and *distal* environment, one may see that open systems are vulnerable not only to internal and external factors of which they are aware, but also to external factors (from the *distal* environment) of which they are *not* aware. Although such factors do not always affect the system adversely (they may have a positive or facilitating affect), system activity in time-space is constantly subject to impingements from both the system itself and from its environment. The dynamic state of a system and the system's structures and functions are "open" to effects from a variety of sources.

The implication is twofold. First, one needs to be aware of the potential and probability of such impingements in planning and implementing system action. Second, the open system, in order to maximize its existence, needs to consciously tap and utilize those factors with a positive or facilitating potentiality. Open systems, in fact, do not exist in isolation, and all systems are vulnerable to impingements. System action of any kind is not self-contained; rather, it is related at all stages to all other system activity at that time, to the total system (its components, relationships, and attributes), and, with open systems, to the environment.

6. *Subsystems.* The sixth universal systems property is that *all systems have subsystems*—or a bit more accurately, all but the smallest systems have subsystems. (Actually, few deal with the smallest molecular or micro-entities, so for practical purposes, *all* systems have subsystems.) Like a system, a subsystem is a bounded unit composed of parts, relationships, and attributes. Likewise, subsystems themselves have subsystems. Thus the same definition used for systems can be used for subsystems, and any subsystem is a system in and of itself. It functions or is classified as it is in relation to a suprasystem. The subsystem concept is quite valuable in analyzing any system, particularly those that are large or complex. In fact, it is very often difficult to deal with total systems per se, and in such cases breaking a system down into its subsystems is important.

For example, if one is having trouble starting his car, in all probability he would not leave it at a service station and say simply, "Fix it." Rather, one would try to describe symptoms before the mechanic would begin his work. Or, if one had transmission problems, the car may go directly to a transmission shop where the mechanics concern themselves only with the transmission subsystem of the car.

Subsystems, like all other systems, have more-or-less arbitrary boundaries which are, further, more-or-less precise. In larger systems, an extremely large number of definable, distinct, and overlapping subsystems can be identified. The importance of this concept lies primarily in the facts that (a) *system action is the result of the functional interplay of subsystems* and (b) *subsystems represent a fundamental and basic unit for system analysis.* They are, further, a feasible and useful point of focus for attending to system malfunctions and problems.

As the administrator looks at his organization, he sees that school (system) action is the result of the functional interplay of many subsystems. School operations result from activity by administrative subsystems, teacher subsystems, supervisory subsystems, classified staff subsystems, and student subsystems. A particular student's learning results from teaching subsystems, guidance subsystems, learning materials subsystems, curricular subsystems, and often disciplinary or control subsystems. School policy results from the school board subsystem, administrative subsystems, citizen's committee subsystems, parental subsystems, state department of education subsystems, and so forth. Thus functional subsystems and their interplay are vital elements in system action and provide a useful basis for analyzing system actions. In any system like the school there are an infinite number of distinct and overlapping subsystems which can be used in understanding and working with the school as a total system.

The relevance of these ideas for the administrator—or anyone involved in meshing or linking subsystems into the context of larger system activity— is that system action is simply the result of *the functional interplay of subsystems.* Subsystems, therefore, must be related to each other and to the total system, in real and productive ways. Subsystem isolation or inactivity inevitably affects and is costly to system activity and the system itself. System effort, in sum, is the orchestration of many diverse but functionally related components, processes, and structures.

7. *Suprasystems.* The seventh and last universal property of systems is that *all systems* (except the largest and some few closed systems) *have suprasystems.* Thus, just as all systems can analytically and practically be broken down into subsystems, all systems are, in fact, subsystems to larger and more complex systems. For example, the school as a public agency is a subsystem in the state governmental system just as are state police systems, judicial systems, legislative systems, and taxation systems. It can now be seen that system boundaries are arbitrary and are ultimately dictated by utility or feasibility. Further, the *environment* of a system is magnified in importance in that in this environment are more embracing systems—suprasystems of which the system is a part. There are, therefore, systems which along with

the system under consideration must relate functionally as subsystems of even larger or suprasystems.

To illustrate this point we may look at the city school district which is fiscally dependent on a large municipality. The large city school district, of course, has subsystems. Its effect depends on the functional interplay of its subsystems. Likewise, the municipality as a larger, more encompassing system has subsystems such as the police (sub)system, the sanitary engineering (sub)system, the judicial (sub)system, the parks (sub)system, and the city school (sub)system as well, to name but a few. The effect of the larger municipal system similarly depends on the functional interplay of its subsystems, including the school subsystem.

All systems are in this sense analytic units of larger systems. Their importance is ultimately in terms of the larger context. Schools are not organizations in and of themselves, independent and isolated from other aspects of community or social life. Rather they are, and need to be, functionally related and relevant to other subsystems of the community, nation, and state. To yield maximal results, schools need to contribute as subsystems to each of their suprasystems.

THE PROPERTIES OF OPEN SYSTEMS: UNIQUE CHARACTERISTICS

Just as the systems movement has resulted in the identification and description of *universal* properties for all systems, so the movement has yielded a number of characteristics which are *unique* to open systems. As a wide variety of phenomena have been subjected to observation and analysis by systems scholars, the recurrence of the same properties—states, processes, and tendencies—in open systems has resulted in the identification and formulation of the characteristic properties of open systems. Since these are unique and peculiar to the open system, the power of such concepts for analyzing and understanding the open system is enhanced. Thus the basic notion of system provides a viewpoint from which to examine a system in terms of its components, relationships, attributes, and complexity. The universal properties of all systems enable one to look at systems with greater precision, and analyze them in more detail. Open system properties, however, permit one to move to an even greater level of specificity in examining the open system—to precisely the properties which are unique to, or typically characteristic of, all open systems.

1. *Inputs and outputs.* The first unique property of the open system, and one already referred to in defining the open system, is that *open systems maintain themselves by exchanging energy and information with their environment.* That is, open systems have *inputs* and *outputs.* The action of the open system involves the transmission of inputs, or action stimuli, into outputs—terminal results or outcomes. Open systems have, therefore, a *dual* role: to maintain themselves and to serve their environment.

The relevance of this property rests in the fact that all system action is prompted by stimulus conditions and results in outcomes. System action is not automatic nor necessarily reflexive (although, in the latter case, it may be) but usually it is the conscious application of system structures and processes to conditions, situations, and events which confront the system. In order for a system to maximize its dual role of system survival and environmental service, the system must purposively and rationally handle input stimuli and transform such energy or information into desirable results. In other words, it is the open system's task to make order out of the randomness, uncertainty, or chaos that faces it.

In a recent research project which sought to use systems theory as a basis for developing a taxonomy of organizational behavior in educational administration,[13] it was found that the method of processing inputs by educational organizational systems was, in fact, important to the outcomes realized. Regardless of whether inputs were rational (purposive) or irrational (expressive), if formal, legitimized (consciously planned) structures and processes were used to deal with the input, then output or outcomes were rational. However, when irrational or expressive inputs were processed by informal or *ad hoc* arrangements, output was also irrational. The implication here is clear for the open system: the conscious, planned transformation of action stimuli into output is imperative to effective system functioning and ultimately system survival and environmental service.

Further relevance of this idea is found in the degree to which a system uses input stimuli in the form of energy and information to enhance the system's growth and development and to maximize its environmental contribution. For example, if schools consciously use action stimuli, whether human, fiscal, or material resources or information, to develop into more dynamic and viable organizations, their life state or level of existence is augmented. If, on the other hand, they fail to capitalize on or use available resources for systems facilitation, maintenance of the system is threatened and degeneration or entropic tendencies will inevitably increase. Similarly, if the school capitalizes on resources or information from its environment, it will foster its existence in terms of productivity and the availability of energy and information for future system usage.

In both of the above instances, as we consider the school as an open system, the importance of the role of the administrator is apparent. Since the administrator is largely responsible for both the planning and the direction of school system activities, it is he who must ensure that input or action stimuli are consciously and properly handled, and that the school as a system maximizes its use of the energy and information received from its environment for the dual purposes of the system—survival and contribution.

2. *Steady state.* The second characteristic of open systems is that *the open system tends to maintain itself in a steady state.* This means that open systems maintain themselves at a high level of integration as typified by a *dynamic ratio* of system components and properties. Dynamic ratio here refers to a life or evolutionary state—an existence that seeks increasing order, differentiation, variation and complexity rather than tendencies toward

the randomness and chaos that surround it. Systems do this through controlled, adaptive, and synergistic activity. Dynamic ratio also implies an imbalance in the forces of, and the forces affecting, the system as opposed to the balance of forces that characterizes a state of equilibrium or inaction. In order to move to increasing order and complexity, action as a result of imbalanced forces is necessary. This is the "life" or evolutionary state which implies an active coping with forces to maintain or foster system existence.

Also, relevant here is the fact that *open systems maintain themselves.* That is, the open system may ultimately affect its own destiny. This is, of course, not the case with closed systems. (For example, in the advanced stages of psychic disorder, the patient has little control over his destiny. Even other systems, such as physicians, no matter how competent and viable, have very little control over the destiny of that patient.) Thus, open systems can choose and control their evolutional patterns. A school district or an administrator, for example, may choose (a) whether they want to be minimally, adequately, or maximally effective, (b) whether they will become increasingly or decreasingly so, and (c) at what rate of speed they wish to do so. Although other forces both internal and external impinge on the open system and affect its destiny, the open system can, to a large degree, through action and adaptation, control its life state. For example, the Latin teacher, when Latin is removed from the curriculum, can suffer from the loss of the job or can seek retraining as a teacher of another subject, a position as a professional association official, and so forth. Similarly, schools with outdated or inappropriate curricula can suffer the fate of irrelevance, or they can move toward more relevant and contributing programs of study.

Open systems are alive and dynamic, and are therefore self-determining. They succumb to "fate" only as a result of excessive wear and tear, or when they choose to succumb or are no longer functional. When the open system no longer exists or chooses to exist in an exchange relationship with its environment, it becomes in effect a closed system and the tendency toward entropy and death is increased.

3. *Self-regulation.* Thirdly, *open systems are characteristically self-regulating.* That is, the open system itself orders and controls the forces that affect it. The human body or the thermostat on a furnace are classic examples of this property. When the human body is subjected to increasingly hot temperatures, sweat begins to cool its surface in order to maintain the body temperature within a tolerable range. When the body is cooled, sweating stops, as this control is no longer needed. In the case of the thermostat, when room temperature falls below a certain point, the closing of an electrical circuit starts the furnace. When the room temperature reaches the tolerable range, the thermostat triggers a break in the circuit to stop the heating process.

By virtue of their ability to be self-regulating, open systems are able to realize and maintain a dynamic life-state even in the face of adverse forces. And by consciously developing or institutionalizing or mechanizing self-regulating procedures and mechanisms, systems are automatically able to control such forces, thus freeing the system for more important kinds of work. If one's home has both heating and air-conditioning systems, there is a choice between independent and integrated controls. With the former, one thermostat works the heating system, but another works the air-conditioning. When temperatures fluctuate in the spring and fall much family system activity is expended turning one temperature control system on and the other off. However, with an integrated control, the control device itself can shift from circuiting hot or cool air depending on whether the temperature rises or drops out of the tolerable range.

Schools, like all other open systems, have self-regulating devices. Budget elections, boards of education, administrators, negotiation procedures, and review committees are all types of self-regulating or control devices. One of the challenges to the administrator, by virtue of his controlling position, is to create various self-regulating (or homeostatic) devices so those dysfunctional imbalances caused by predictable and regular forces are handled automatically, and order, rather than disorder or disarray, is ensured.

4. *Equifinality.* The fourth property of the open system is that *it exhibits equifinality.* This means that open systems have the capacity to achieve identical results from different conditions or by the employment of different processes. Quite simply, "there are many ways to skin a cat," or "there are many roads that lead to Rome!" This does not mean that a system can do just anything and reach a particular end, but it does mean that given different initial conditions or using different system processes, identical results can be realized as long as system action is rationally, purposively, and causally directed to that goal—provided, of course, the goal is feasible.

Implications here are both obvious and numerous. Both rural and urban, small or large, schools can be equally effective. Children can learn to read by phonics, look-say, ITA, or a variety or combination of teaching methods. Further, students can learn by experience or by consciously planned training, individually, or in groups. *The greatest implication of this property of the open system is that it opens the horizons regarding alternatives, and it underscores the need for goals and the rational progression from an initial state using appropriate procedures to the goal.* Initial states or procedures, in and of themselves, do not condition or determine goal realization. More precisely, goal realization results from appropriate, planned system activity directed toward real and feasible goals.

5. *Dynamic interaction.* The fifth property of the open system is that *the open system maintains itself through the dynamic interaction of functional subsystems.* The subsystem concept is of ultimal importance in considering the open system, since system effects are the result of system activity. We have already discussed the relevance of the subsystem concept as a property of all systems in terms of the functional interplay of the subsystems and their direct relationship to total system results. In the case of the open system the activity, linkage, and adaptability of subsystems is crucial to the system's life state. For, if subsystems are not functioning, if they are malfunctioning, if they are pursuing inappropriate or irrelevant goals, if they are

conflicting, if they are not working in concert, or if they are not open or adaptive, the system is in trouble. The net effect of the open system depends on the functional, relevant, and coordinated activity of all of its subsystems.

Just as the human being with a broken leg, the radio with a malfunctioning circuit, or the animal with a ruptured lung cannot function properly in some, or all, ways so the social system such as a school with inept administrative leadership, a conflict between the "old" and "new" faculty members, or teachers who physically or mentally browbeat children is functionally hampered. The implication here is precise: the educational administrator must attend to all of the subsystems in his school. He must link and coordinate their activities effectively, and he must constantly adapt these subsystems and their linkages as needs dictate if the best school or system is to be realized. No matter how many resources a system has, unless its subsystems are functionally integrated and their activities relevant, its effect will be minimal.

6. *Feedback.* The sixth characteristic of the open system is that *open systems, in part, maintain their steady states through feedback processes.* Feedback is the evaluative or monitoring process whereby open systems assess their outputs and their processes. Steady-state maintenance is realized as the system receives information about its past actions and uses this information to assess and, when necessary, modify or adapt system structures and processes for future action.

We will deal more explicitly and in greater detail with feedback in a subsequent chapter. However, it should be obvious that conscious and continual evaluation of system activity is essential to ensuring system relevance and contribution, as well as to ascertaining the life state of the system. Since open systems exist in nonreversible time-space and are subject to both evolutional and entropic forces, constant monitoring of the system is needed in order to maintain a viable existence.

It is interesting that some administrators who periodically attend to personal medical or dental health checkups, or to fire prevention or audit checkups in their schools, fail to systematically seek and use feedback about their school organization as a system. The best example of the value and potential for maximizing and utilizing feedback is found in the exploration of outer space. Success here is contingent on comprehensive feedback and a highly integrated system of subsystems with optimal and precise information exchange. This may well be contrasted to schools or other systems where often "the left hand does not know what the right hand is doing."

7. *Progressive segregation.* The seventh property of open systems is that *all open systems display progressive segregation.* This is the process of a division into a functional and hierarchical ordering of subsystems. Inherent in an open system's evolutional development and movement from randomness and chaos to order and complexity is the system's own ordering of its components (subsystems) and their functional relationships. This system process ensures internal system effectiveness and integration, and contributes to the system's ability to cope with the forces affecting it. At a basic level

this is the tendency of open systems to determine what subsystems it will formally create, what subsystems it will use to process work, the nature and order of subsystem activity, and the priority of subsystem duties and obligations within the overall system perspective.

Schools offer excellent examples of this systemic tendency. As they get larger they define new and different subsystems such as remedial learning subsystems, guidance subsystems, instructional resource subsystems, transportation subsystems, research subsystems, and so forth. Schools also define precisely the work of their subsystems, such as discipline to the administrative subsystem, instruction to teaching subsystems, counseling to guidance subsystems, and student accounting to clerical subsystems. Further, an ordering of subsystem activity occurs as minor disciplinary actions are handled by teacher subsystems, more problematic disciplinary cases by administrative subsystems, and acute discipline problems by subsystems of specialists such as attendance personnel or psychologists. Finally, priorities are established regarding certain of a school's subsystems. For example, instructional subsystems have priority over food service subsystems; when budget cuts are made, academic instructional subsystems most often have priority over extracurricular activities subsystems.

The relevance of this property is that the open system can organize, order, and, if needed, adapt its functional subsystem structure to best accomplish system work.

8. *Progressive mechanization.* The eighth property common to open systems is that of *progressive mechanization.* This means that in all open systems there is an ordering of certain procedures or processes into fixed arrangements. In other words, open systems take care of the "regularity" of action stimuli in themselves and in their environment through this process. Self, or homeostatic, regulation is a form of progressive mechanization, but the latter concept is more extensive. Homeostatic regulation applies primarily to deviations in the system state, while mechanization applies to all regulation, whether normal or crisis, preventive or custodial.

The open system, therefore, is able to adopt and use procedural and regulatory practices to facilitate its processing of work. Schools "mechanize" to report pupil progress, to handle incoming phone calls, to regulate visits to classrooms, to excuse student absences, to distribute instructional supplies and in many more ways. The establishment of policy or rules and regulations are other appropriate examples. The result of this process for the open system is maximal control for adaptation of its structure and processes within the system's environment.

9. *Negentropy.* In our discussion of the concept system, we have already discussed entropy and the ability of the open system to combat it. At that point the relevance of negentropy (the opposite of entropy) was implied and implications for administrative practice discussed. We might well stress here the fact that while the entropic tendency is universal, *the tendency toward negentropy is something only an open system has.* As noted before, the open system has great control over its existence and destiny; it can choose

whether or not to fight entropy or to maximize its existence. All living or open systems exist for a finite period in time-space. Few, indeed, have infinite lives. *However, the duration and quality of life for the open system is, in large measure, in its own hands.*

MAJOR APPROACHES TO OPEN SYSTEMS THEORY

Systems may be examined and analyzed in a number of ways. They can be looked at as total entities per se, or as total entities in an environment. They can be examined in terms of their structure or function. Also, they can be analyzed in terms of subsystem (microscopic) or outcome (macroscopic) analysis. Further, they can be scrutinized in terms of components, type of organization, kinds of activity, or processes. Such ways of looking at systems illustrate the various perspectives used in the formulation of theories of open systems. Resultant theories are neither mutually exclusive nor all-inclusive. This suggests, at least at the present time, that to understand a system to the fullest extent, a multiperspective approach is most advantageous. Before looking at the advantages of a multitheoretical perspective in analyzing a system, we should first identify briefly the major forms open system theories have taken.

A review of the systems literature reveals basically five distinct theoretical approaches toward conceptualizing systems:

1. *Comprehensive systems theories, or "theories of the whole."* These theories focus generally and often subjectively on total or "whole" systems and their obvious components, together with the components' attributes.[14] Systems, by definition, are units or wholes. An obvious advantage of this concept of a system is its inherent concern for totality as opposed to isolated aspects, idiosyncratic characteristics, or selected parts of wholes. In these theories, systems, as entities, take their unique meaning from the components, attributes, and relationships of which they are composed.

Such theory has somewhat limited utility, since it tends not to reduce ambiguity, does not minimize subjectivity, and due to the complexity of most meaningful systems, is unable to cope with certain important aspects of detail. However, these kinds of theories are excellent points for beginning the examination or analysis of a system.

2. *"Process" or subsystem theories.* Theories of this type are concerned with microscopic analysis and focus on the processing of inputs through system (system-subsystem) activity into system output.[15] The fundamental aspect of the open system is the energy-information transformation process that occurs as the system exchanges energy and matter with its environment in time-space. Through the processing of action stimuli in the open system's dual role of survival and service, the *raison d'etre* of a system's existence is revealed. Thus, process systems theories provide analytic frameworks that deal with action stimuli (inputs), the subsystems (structures and processes) which act on input, and the output or resultants of system action. Since the potential forms of input and output for a system are relatively in-

finite, and a finite but extensive variety of functional, processing subsystems exist in any system, this kind of approach for analyzing a system or its activity is most detailed and extensive.

Through this theoretical perspective not only can an extensive number of aspects or attributes of a aystem be examined, but also their linkage and relationships as revealed in system activity, can be scrutinized. Process theories of open systems provide both a comprehensive and detailed means for understanding systems. The approach is, further, descriptive and evolutional.

3. *"Feedback" theories or theories of open system control.* Feedback theories, emanating from the science of cybernetics, are premised on the thesis that all systems can best be understood through their communication and control activities.[16] These theories posit that system activity, life state, and adaptation are all monitored and evaluated by information about the system and its effects, all of which may be generated either internally or externally. Through feedback, or "evaluative information," the system is able to plan and project future action more wisely as a result of the review and analysis of past effects. Theories of this kind are concerned with the quantitative and qualitative aspects of information, information flow, and its value and affect on the system and system functioning.

The perspective of feedback theory for analyzing a system is helpful in determining the control dynamics of the system and the regulation and development of processes used by the system to maintain its relevance. Such analytic frameworks can be used for surveillance of both the monitoring and evaluative processes of a system as used for survival and service. The focus of feedback theory is on the system's future on the basis of a rigorous assessment of the system's past.

4. *Theories of system properties.* These theories represent macroscopic analysis and derive from the recurring properties and states evinced in the life-space of a wide variety of systems.[17] One of the striking outcomes of the systems movement and the application of systems notions to a wide variety of phenomena has been the consistent observation of a number of properties, or characteristic states, tendencies, and processes, in the systems studied.[18] This recurrence has given rise to theories of systems properties which consist of characteristics of open systems as discussed in the last section of this chapter. Systems can thus be examined, analyzed, and/or compared in terms of the presence or absence of properties and in terms of their evolutional stage related to these properties. This process permits an assessment of the system's open or life state at a given point in time-space.

The advantages of analysis of the open system using these theories are those of a macroscopic view of the system in terms of unique systems properties and the assessment of a system's viability relative to a particular point in the system's evolution. In plotting such observations over time, evolutional analysis of a system can be achieved.

5. *Output theories or output analysis.* Theories of this type focus on the outcomes or products of system action relative to their impact on the sys-

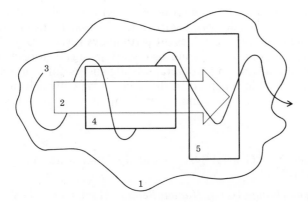

Fig. 2.1 Basic theoretical approaches to systems. (1) Comprehensive systems theories. (2) Process theories. (3) Feedback theories. (4) Universal properties theories. (5) Output theories.

tem or its environment.[19] These theories, which derive largely from the operations research movement, are primarily concerned with the overriding results of system activity. It is held that although such approaches are often "subjective," the best way to understand a system is to look at its effects, or the results of its activity. Outcome (or output) is multidimensional, in that there are internal and external, tangible and intangible, and productive or affective results from the actions of a system. Together, all categories or dimensions of outcome provide a framework for the analysis of the system.

As analytic vehicles, outcome theories provide perspectives that permit both objective and subjective assessment of the system. Also output analysis is ultimately based on real data regarding what happened to, or as a result of, the system. This kind of system examination is most appropriate for the analysis of large, complex social organizations like schools.

The five above approaches to open-systems theorizing can be graphically represented as in Fig. 2.1 in order to pictorially show their relationships and differing emphases.

The value of these different theoretical perspectives for analyzing and understanding goes beyond those values already noted in discussing each theoretical approach. Certainly, as we have implied, the multiperspective analysis of a system facilitates understanding in and of itself. But also as one moves from more generic or macroscopic analyses of a system to more specific or microscopic examinations, and from more subjective to more objective ones, the process of analysis is aided and understanding is magnified. In this sense, moving from analyses using comprehensive or properties schemes to analyses of system processes, and finally to analyses of system output and feedback, is most helpful in understanding a system. *Thus, one of the greatest values of systems thought is the potential for the evaluation of any system.*

It has been indicated in this chapter how the general analysis of a system might be begun. The reader wishing to undertake systematic and detailed analysis along the theoretical lines set forth above is referred to the writers' previous research on systems and taxonomy in organizational behavior in educational administration for several specific and useful analytic schemes.[20] In the remaining chapters of this section, we will probe more deeply into more specific systems concepts and approaches that will facilitate analysis.

NOTES

1. L. von Bertalanffy, "General Systems Theory," *Main Curr. Mod. Thought, 2,* (1955), p. 77.

2. N. Wiener, *The Human Use of Human Beings.* Garden City, N.Y.: Doubleday Anchor Books, 1956; and W. R. Ashby, *An Introduction to Cybernetics.* New York: John Wiley & Sons, 1956.

3. C. W. Churchman, and others, *Introduction to Operations Research.* New York: John Wiley & Sons, 1957.

4. Adapted from von Bertalanffy, *op. cit.,* p. 1.

5. G. Hearn, *Theory Building in Social Work.* Toronto: University of Toronto Press, 1958, p. 39. By permission.

6. G. T. Guilbraud, *What is Cybernetics?* New York: Criterion Books, 1969, p. 2. By permission of S. G. Phillips, Inc. English translation by Valerie Mackay, © William Heinemann, Ltd., 1959.

7. Hearn, *op. cit.,* p. 38.

8. A. Rapoport, "Mathematical Aspects of General Systems Analysis," *Gen. Syst., 11* (1966), p. 3.

9. A. D. Hall and R. E. Fagen, "Definition of System," *Gen. Syst., 1* (1956), p. 18.

10. R. R. Grinker, *Toward a Unified Theory of Human Behavior.* New York: Basic Books, 1956, p. 370.

11. See F. K. Berrien, *General and Social Systems.* New Brunswick, N.J.: Rutgers University Press, 1968.

12. See, for example, Hearn, *op. cit.,* pp. 44-50; and D. E. Griffiths, "Use of Models in Research" in J. Culbertson and D. Hencley (eds.), *Educational Research: New Perspectives.* Danville, Illinois: Interstate Printers, 1963, pp. 116-117.

13. D. E. Griffiths (ed.), *Developing Taxonomies of Organizational Behavior in Educational Administration,* Chicago: Rand McNally, 1969, Chapter 6.

14. See, for example, Hall and Fagen, *op. cit.,* pp. 18-28.

15. See, for example, Ashby, *op. cit.,* Optner, *op. cit.,* pp. 36-51 (in particular); and J. G. Miller, "Living Systems: Structure and Process." *Behavioral Science, 10,* No. 4 (October 1965), pp. 337-379.

16. See, for example, F. H. George, *Automation, Cybernetics and Society.* New York: Philosophical Library, 1959; and J. O. Wisdom, "The Hypothesis of Cybernetics," *Gen. Syst., 1* (1956), pp. 111-122.

17. See, for example, Hearn, *op. cit.,* pp. 43-51, Griffiths, "Use of Models in Research," *op. cit.,* pp. 116-118; and G. S. Maccia, "An Educational Theory Model: General Systems Theory," Ohio State University Center for the Construction of Theory in Education, Occasional Paper 62-126, 1962.

18. L. von Bertalanffy, "General Systems Theory — A Critical Review," *Gen. Syst., 7* (1962), pp. 1-19; and J. G. Miller, Living Systems: Structure and Process," *op. cit.*

19. See, for example, Optner, *op. cit.;* and E. H. Schein, *Organizational Psychology.* Englewood Cliffs: Prentice-Hall, 1965, pp. 96-106.

20. In Griffiths, *Developing Taxonomies of Organizational Behavior in Educational Administration, op. cit.*

Chapter 3 / Some particular systems concepts with relevance for educational administration

Since the basic key to systems thought lies in the concepts that have been developed to describe, explain, and predict systemic behavior,[1] it is important for the potential user of the products of the systems movement to be aware of, and to understand, those systems concepts that are most relevant for his field. Young,[2] in his comprehensive survey of systems thought, has identified four general categories of systems concepts. They are:

1. Systemic and descriptive factors
2. Regulation and maintenance
3. Dynamics and change
4. Decline and breakdown

The first category of concepts, *systemic and descriptive factors,* contains those concepts which can be used (a) to make important distinctions between systems, (b) to organize and analyze large quantities of data about systems in relevant ways, and (c) to conceptualize the fundamental nature of various (and various types of) systems. These are the kinds of concepts explored in the last chapter as the authors developed the notion of *system* and set forth the universal properties of all systems—along with the unique characteristics of open systems—by drawing on available "theories" or theoretical elements. Such concepts represent an essential first step in understanding and analyzing systems—their organization, their function, and their relationships to other systems.

The other three categories of systems concepts are also relevant both to the understanding of systems, and ultimately, to the application of systems approaches in educational administration. Although the discussion of the concept of a system has already touched on a number of these ideas, there are some concepts under each of the other categories that should be further explicated and their relevance clarified. Particularly meriting such treatment are the concepts of steady state, homeostasis, information, and feedback under the *regulation and maintenance* category; the concepts of adaptation, growth, and change under the *dynamics and change* category; and the concepts of stress, disturbance, and overload under the *decline and breakdown* category.

In the *regulation and maintenance* category of systems concepts are those notions which deal with the regulation, control, maintenance, and stabilization of systems. The concept category of *dynamics and change* includes ideas regarding the adaptive, learning, growth, dynamistic, and internally generated change processes of systems. In the *decline and breakdown* category of systems concepts are those concepts which deal with the systemic problems of stress, disruption, dissolution, disturbance, and breakdown.

The concepts embraced by each of these three general categories are too extensive for detailed treatment here. Accordingly, this discussion will focus generally on those concepts noted above for each category and in more or less detail regarding each of these. The interested reader is referred to Young's survey of the systems movement[3] and the sources identified by Young[4] to facilitate further understanding of basic systems concepts. Here, for each of the three concept category areas, we will focus primarily on one concept, the one held to be most relevant for the administrator. The other related ideas will be used as necessary to introduce or amplify the discussion.

It should be noted that not all of the categories or concepts from systems thought receive, or have received, the same emphasis in the systems movement. For example, in the early days of the movement, the category *systemic and descriptive factors* was the primary area for scholarly concentration. More recently the concept *regulation and maintenance* has been emphasized, possibly in part because as systems notions have been applied in various fields of practice the control and stabilization of systems were of utmost, or at least primary, importance. Most recently there has been a tendency to focus on the concept category *dynamics and change* or on the dynamic and adaptive "life" processes of systems, a popular concern of many at the present time. And, finally, as Young has observed, concepts from the category *decline and breakdown* have been relatively disregarded.[5] This poses a problem in the systems movement itself and for those in fields of practice which hope to capitalize on the systems movement. For example, notions regarding system breakdown (and the concept, stress) are relevant to anyone connected with administrative life, whether it be in education or some other field.

The order of treatment of the systems movement will continue as begun in the last chapter. In this chapter we will examine first the regulation and maintenance concepts, move then to notions of system dynamics and change, and finally, conclude with stress and the idea of system decline and breakdown.

SYSTEM REGULATION AND MAINTENANCE

All open systems such as schools, human beings, or plant life exist in a *steady state. The steady state existence is characterized by a dynamic or "living" ratio among and between all system components and properties.* This is, further, a state of disequilibrium where all system forces are active and activating, as opposed to a state of true or stable equilibrium which is a state of rest caused by the balancing (or cancellation) of system forces or

activities. This is a state of unstable equilibriumwhere the system is receptive and responsive to forces and energy from both within and without the
system which perpetuate a constant imbalance in the system's life state and
which in turn cause system action or activity in order to restore appropriate,
although not perfect, system balance.

For example, on an extremely cold day when a person goes out of
doors, the environmental force of a $-10°$ temperature threatens the life
state of the human system. Hence, he puts on additional clothing to pro-
tect his "life state." However, if it is also a sunny and windy day, then a
comfortable state is difficult to maintain, depending on whether he is in
direct sunlight or shade, exposed to the wind or shielded from it, active or
inactive, or moving from one of these conditions to another. So the person,
as a system, attempts to maintain a life state *within* a tolerable range by
guarding against over- and under-exposure and too much or too little
warmth. For example, as one adjusts to activity or sunlight by unloosening
the protective clothing, the forces of wind and cold prompt further adjustments so that an appropriate balance of elements is maintained. Relative
departures in the direction of system "warmness" or "coldness" trigger
constant system activity to maintain a "healthful" or comfortable life state.

Similarly, when a school system's steady state (which is seeking a
higher level of relevant activity by adding an instructional materials annex
onto the secondary school complex) meets with a negative bond issue vote
and finds that citizens actually want a better facility than that projected,
the system can capitalize on such a force, through its response, to enhance
its life state. Possibly by involving citizens in the planning of the new facility the school system will realize more than it had initially expected,
(e.g., greater citizen understanding of school goals as well as a favorable
vote) and will arrive at a still higher level of existence. The imbalance of
the "negative" vote can be used, if the situation is right, to provoke regula-
tive system activity to maximize the open system's life state. The open or
"living" system is active and responsive to forces affecting it, and by regulating or maintaining such forces perpetuates its dynamic existence. On
the other hand, the system that accepts the negative vote and does nothing,
even if the voters want more for the system than it wants for itself, is not
maintaining its highest level of life state through its activity. Rather, the
forces in such an instance result in balance or inactivity, or in a state of
system rest. In any event, the steady state of an open system is an active,
dynamic life state wherein the system reacts to forces and imbalances by
regulating and maintaining a dynamic ratio among and between all of its
parts.

Schools as systems maintain their "steady states" through self regulation and life state maintenance prompted by a wide variety of external
forces—such as criticism of the·instructional program, negative votes at the
polls, or demands by powerful elements in the citizenry—and a variety of
internal forces—such as teacher demands for new and improved instructional materials, an expanding educational technology, and student requests

for more relevant programs of studies. The threats or forces that bear on all open systems such as schools cause these systems to behave in such a way as to restore a tolerable balance in their life space; this activity, or the manifestation of system action, is the dynamic (living) state of such systems. It is achieved through the regulation of forces and the maintenance of system viability itself.

System life state maintenance and regulation is realized through processes of *homeostatic* control. Homeostasis is the process by which a system stabilizes itself and its contents within a tolerable and even variable[6] range of limits. It is a conscious, or consciously devised, process that seeks through system activity the dynamic relationship of system components necessary for system life as a result of extreme or significant forces in, or on, the system. As observed in the last chapter, the temperature control thermostat is a classic and simple example of homeostatic control.

Other illustrations of this process or control activity—not often thought of in these terms, but nonetheless helpful in realizing the importance of the concept—can be briefly identified. The programmed text or computerized instructional package, for example, contain certain homeosatic devices. When the student using a programmed text gives an incorrect response he is often admonished "Go back to page so-and-so and reread a section of text," since he has not yet mastered that material sufficiently to move on. Another example of "homeostatic control" is the individual's desire to seek medical help when ill, a desire triggered by certain body reactions such as a runny nose, a temperature, and/or a headache. Likewise, a principal's asking his secretary to "Hold all phone calls until I get this report done," a recuperating teacher's request to be relieved of all extra duties until fully well again, or the submission to arbitration of differences over next year's salary plan for teachers all represent instances of the employment of homeostatic procedures or controls.

Whenever a system needs regulation, or the maintenance of its steady state requires attention, it consciously devises a procedure or homeostatic process (or utilizes one that is consciously devised) to bring its life state back into a tolerable range of limits (imbalance), or into a dynamic, workable relationship (ratio) among its components. Homeostatic controls, whether in mechanical systems such as a motor cooling system, in living systems such as a person's thought processes regarding his personal health, or in social systems such as grievance procedures for adjudicating teacher dissatisfactions in a school district, are all processes for open system life state maintenance.

Central to the concept of homeostasis and steady state are the related concepts of *information* and *communication*. Information in this sense is simply knowledge—facts or data about events, situations, or conditions affecting the system. Communication is the process or sequence of activities that is used to transfer information from one place to another or to create system "awareness." The fact that one's temperature is rising is information. This is important in and of itself, but unless the individual's neurological structure (the internal human organism's communication system) transmits characteristic reactions about such information to the brain for processing—that is, creates system awareness of the condition—system action will not be forthcoming. But even if this information is transmitted, unless the person has other information which will enable him to recognize that such characteristic reactions are danger signals, the system cannot take appropriate action. *However, it is through information, its transmission (communication), and processing that system threats or imbalances (beyond tolerance limits) are acted on.*

With the thermostat it is not enough that the room temperature drop below 70 degrees. In order to initiate appropriate action from the heating system, this information must first be obtained, then communicated to the processing sector of the thermostat which is programmed on the basis of other information—specifically, that this temperature level is beyond the tolerable range, that the heating unit switch must be activated when such a temperature is reached, and that the room temperature requires continued surveillance to make sure that the temperature does not increase too much.

In the case of the school system seeking to increase its operating funds through an added tax levy, the "information" or facts about opposition from senior citizens, private school patrons, and the taxpayers' league must be obtained, communicated to those responsible for working on public opinion, and linked to other information (e.g., the fact that the opposition of any two of these groups could defeat the levy). Then intelligent system activity can be undertaken to regulate and maintain appropriately the community-school system's steady state.

FEEDBACK

Of central concern in the regulation and maintenance of a system steady state is a particular kind of information and communication process called *feedback.* Feedback is *evaluative* information *about* system action or the results of system action. It is after the fact; that is, feedback is the assessment of some portion of a system's past. Sources of feedback may be from within or without the system, but regardless of the source, feedback is the literal feeding back into the system, into its structure and processes, of evaluative information about the system, its activities, and its effects.

The relevance of the feedback concept lies in the facts that (1) feedback is basic in homeostatic processes, and (2) it is ultimately a *valuing* of system viability and contribution. For example—and again in the case of the thermostat and heating system operations—proper system functioning is based on the constant feeding back of information about the temperature state in the area being heated. Or, in the case of the teacher giving remedial assistance to a student with a reading problem, system functionality is based on the feeding back of information about the student's reading behavior to the teacher and the feeding back of evaluative information about the student's progress (or lack of progress) to the student by the teacher.

Secondly, feedback is a special case in information communication. Feedback is not random or disorderly; rather it is purposive and evaluative *about* the system or something the system did. In this sense, even though it is after the fact (or an outcome), it is also something the system can use or capitalize on (that is, input for future system action or adjustment) in order to increase the system's function and contributing potential. Thus, if the school counselor receives feedback that his "directive" approach to students is driving them away from his office, such feedback can be used by the counselor to modify his behavior toward less directive styles in order to better serve his clients. Or, if the school finds its graduates are not prepared for college-level work and this, in turn, causes parents to fail to support the schools, this feedback can be used to improve the school program in order to enhance the school's products, and ultimately, in order to raise the level of school support.

Numerous studies of organizations, including some from the educational setting, reveal the relevance of feedback for the open system and particularly for social systems like human groups or school organizations. Although it is neither feasible nor necessary to document these studies in detail, it is germane to our consideration of systems concepts to focus in more depth on the feedback concept by exploring further the nature of feedback, its utilization potential, and some of the implications of the concept for the practicing educational administrator.

The Nature of Feedback

Feedback is communicated information which is basically judgmental in nature. With it a system is able to adjust future action and behavior by reviewing its past performances in terms of goals or objectives, or in terms of system functionality or contribution. In other words, by reviewing its output (activities, achievements, and outcomes) as perceived both internally and externally, a system is in a position to decide whether or not its processing of future inputs needs adjustment or modification. This is system evaluation. For example, the computer system—or the thermostat—utilizes a controlling mechanism within the system in order to process feedback. This is essential to the operation of these systems. But, in contrast to this provision in electronic or mechanical systems, social systems do not always provide for such a function or attend to the evaluative function necessary for system relevancy and growth or development. And all too often the willingness of those in social systems to utilize or to act on feedback can be seriously doubted.

Information flow, or the transmission and utilization of evaluative information (feedback) is not, however, without cost to a system. For every bit of information transmitted and handled, there is a dissipation of energy and a consequent movement, or tendency of movement, toward entropy.[7] And there is a significant problem for any system in determining that amount of feedback which is either too little (thus harming the system through lack of information) or too great (that which hampers the system by sheer load or excessive costs).[8] *It is, therefore, essential that social systems not only devise efficient means for receiving, handling, and using evaluative information but also that constant attention be given to the need for feedback and the kinds of evaluative information that are most helpful or beneficial to the system.*

Typically, when feedback occurs through fixed arrangements or consciously devised channels, it is termed *formal.* When evaluative information does not conform to fixed or prescribed arrangements, it is *informal* feedback. The importance of the need for and development of formal feedback channels is seen in the fact that, for open systems, feedback is imperative to system survival,[9] because only in this way can a system maximally ensure that the evaluative information that is taken in by the system is the type that can be utilized appropriately by the system.

Feedback also may be either *positive* or *negative;* that is, it either reinforces or opposes the system's action or direction.[10] Much of the vitality and functioning of the open system is contingent on its receptivity to, and utilization of, both of these general types of feedback. Positive feedback serves to point to system "strengths" and areas where maximal functionality and relevance has been achieved. This contributes directly to system efficiency. However, positive feedback has a built-in risk toward blindly reinforcing the sytem and its activity or toward restricting change or adaptation, which ultimately may be at the expense of the system. In other words, positive feedback can contribute to the "mutual admiration society" syndrome. On the other hand, negative feedback, in opposing system action or direction, stimulates or justifies system modifications, adaptations, and change. It is, in effect, "critical" of the system. The importance of negative feedback is stressed by Miller: "When a system's negative feedback discontinues, its steady state vanishes, and at the same time, its boundary disappears and the system terminates."[11] Negative, critical feedback is obviously most necessary for open system survival and functional relevancy.

In a study of the flow of feedback between a school and its community, Rusche found that not only does negative feedback to the school system occur more frequently than positive feedback, but also it tends to be specific, pointed, and critical. The same investigator has, however, reported that "negative feedback was viewed (by school personnel) as noncritical, chronic complaints about which little could be done."[12] It can be conjectured that the minimal or unwilling receptivity to negative feedback can be costly to a school's vitality as a system, and to a school's functional relevancy to its environment. For example, if a school gets precise feedback that the practice of reporting pupil progress on report cards does not provide adequate communication to either parents or students about the students' progress in school, the school would do well to explore other alternatives of reporting pupil progress so that communications would be improved and goals or objectives could be better realized.

Carlson and others offer yet another classification of feedback into four distinct categories. As reported by Hearn this categorization further contributes to an understanding of feedback:[1][3]

1. *Continuous feedback.* In this type of feedback a controlled quantity of evaluative information is continously monitored. More appropriate in electronic or mechanical systems as opposed to social systems, this type of feedback requires a mechanism designed to receive and review constantly all incoming information. An assumption is made in such a case that the desirability of feedback has been established; also it is assumed that the relative energy dissipation involved in handling data (feedback) has been taken into account.

2. *Intermittent feedback.* In this type, evaluative information is channeled at certain times which are usually, though not necessarily, defined. The weekly administrative or teachers staff meeting is an example of formal intermittent feedback. This type of feedback may also be thought of in terms of *when* the monitoring occurs. For example, the principal's door may be "open" at specified hours of the day, or the principal may visit classrooms on Wednesdays and Fridays to supervise teachers.

3. *Proportional feedback.* In this type of feedback, the quantity of evaluative information is controlled proportionate to system needs. In other words, an adjusting mechanism compensates for the desirability and utility of the feedback in terms of the actual needs of the system at a given time. Evaluative information may thus be combined, summarized, or meted out in the quantity needed for specific purposes. For example, in a crucial bond-issue campaign, feedback on "voter feelings" or needed issue clarifications would receive preference over other evaluative information such as possible student reactions to a new extracurricular activities schedule.

4. *Relay feedback.* Here evaluative information is either solicited or not. The system channel and processing is either "on" or "off." For example, until the principal asks for feedback, and indeed, unless he asks, no feedback is desired or processed. Or the superintendent might reject criticism of the school program unless he is in session with the curriculum committee, a time when such feedback is actively sought.

Two of these types of feedback (intermittent and relay feedback) were investigated in a study as predictors of success of failure in task accomplishment.[14] When intermittent feedback was required of a person engaged in the task used in this study, there was less success in accomplishment than when only initial or pre-task relay feedback was utilized. Until more studies are conducted in this area, it appears that continuous feeback, which on the surface has a great monitoring capacity (but potentially high energy cost), has a less favorable affect on successful task accomplishment because of its interruption potential and effort consuming nature. In fact, both continuous and intermittent feedback have a high cost factor and a real hindering potential. Relay feedback, in contrast, has a greater risk factor in terms of what it misses or fails to tap. *On this basis, proportional feedback would appear to be the most usually satisfactory type of feedback for social systems.* For, in a word, this type of feedback yields information when it is

desired and to the extent desired, but no information is transmitted when
such would be undesired or unnecessary. This is, however, a difficult type
of feedback to implement in a social system and is particularly so in one in
which a changing, evolving time perspective rules out certain system evaluations until conditions may reach a critical nature. The ideal for systems like
schools may well be a combination of relay and proportional types of feedback when viewed in terms of ultimate costs and value; continuous and intermittent feedback might necessarily be restricted to crisis or emergency
situations when information is needed regardless of cost.

Numerous other studies have been conducted to test empirically the
optimal uses of feedback mechanisms both with individuals and with social
groups, including formal organizations. To further underscore the relevance
of feedback for the school administrator, several selected studies germane to
our discussion should be noted.

Since the late 1930's it has been shown, for example, that a student's
learning will be significantly greater when he is aware of his progress—the
correctness or wrongness of his attempts to learn. Prominent among such
studies is the work of Hull, in which the notion and function of reinforcement are stressed.[15] Subsequent studies have distinguished other roles of
feedback in the learning process in terms of the "information" and "motivation" dimensions in addition to reinforcement.[16] More recently various
studies have shown that feedback is an asset to learning in group instructional situations. Such feedback may range from the flashing of a colored light
on the student's desk when a correct response is given, to written teacher
comments on a test being returned.[17] (We should observe explicitly that
these are all cases in which feedback comes to the subsystem from a monitor, just as in the case of a thermostat.)

Just as feedback of various types and during defined time durations facilitates and fosters individual system processes, so also will evaluative information in the group setting stimulate and increase the movement of the
group per se towards its goals. In working with discussion groups, for example, Jenkins found that without constant awareness of group progress and
knowledge of current relationships to their goals, groups may lose themselves through intermember aggressiveness or overall apathy. Jenkins has
suggested the need for an observer to give feedback in order to provide information on progress, participation, and other factors of general importance to
the work of the group.[18] Somewhat similarly, Leavitt and Mueller have
concluded that when sufficient freedom to afford feedback exists, the degree of interpersonal confidence is proportionate to the extent of freedom
for feedback. Conversely, low feedback in the group context results in sus-
picion and hostility among group members.[19] Further, when work groups
receive feedback regarding task accomplishment, these groups were found
by Pryer and Bass to develop higher motivation and to utilize group resources
more in solving the new work problems that confronted them.[20]

It is apparent that task accomplishment or system goal achievement,
whether by individuals or groups, is enhanced when the individuals or groups
are informed of their performances in the light of certain kinds of evaluative

criteria. The question that may now be raised concerns the qualitative and quantitative aspects of this information. That is, in systems terminology, does positive or negative feedback have greater value? And is there a discernible affect based on the frequency of such feedback?

It would appear that in learning situations, maximizing positive feedback—as opposed to negative—is most important. Even more significantly, the findings from various studies indicate that complete feedback based on accuracy or inaccuracy of performance is more desirable than reduced feedback.[21] That is, when the task is completed, whether the item is learned or not learned, feedback is beneficial to the learner in terms of his future actions, or behavior, directed toward learning.

But in all of these types of feedback, the direction is from the observer (a monitor) to the individual or group.

There is some research to indicate that it is not as effective to require feedback from the performer of a task to an observer or comptroller. Pilecki found that when the individual was not subjected to the "harrassment" of a required, periodical "progress" report, there was greater evidence of task completion. Similarly, the results were the same in comparing the minimizing relay feedback requirement with task performers who had to give no feedback whatsoever.[22] This finding seems consistent with results of studies by Herzberg[23] and others[24] which stress the need for freedom of the worker to work on the task as he sees best. Some degree of mutual communication is necessary at the outset of a task, but after that a minimizing of feedback requirements, at least up to the point of task completion, seems to lead to greater motivation of the worker and appears to assure greater probability for task success.

Negative feedback, however, serves a vital system function, since by its "critical" nature such feedback challenges both the system and its actions. At least from the theoretical perspective, information which "opposes the direction of system action" is maximally evaluative and is most conducive to adaptation and change. The work of information theorists and cyberneticians indicates that for many purposes negative information is in fact more valuable than positive information. Also, evidence from these fields suggests both a higher accuracy and communicative value for negative information. But regarding "frequency," negative feedback, especially in social systems, has a real potential for depressing human beings and producing defeatist attitudes when it exists in great quantities. Positive feedback tends, of course, to counteract this effect.

In sum, we should observe that both positive and negative feedback have advantages and both are ultimately necessary—the first to support the system and its activity and the latter to challenge system direction and activity. Both are critical to system openness and to system vitality. Balancing positive and negative evaluations is the challenge, along with realizing sufficient but not too much (overload) evaluative information.

IMPLICATIONS OF FEEDBACK
FOR SYSTEM REGULATION AND MAINTENANCE

System regulation and maintenance are, as implied, vital functions in any system. In social systems, such as a school organization, the responsibility for this charge lies inevitably with the administration. It is the administrator's task to ensure that organizational regulation and maintenance are attended to. This, of course, is achieved through homeostatic processes of communication (feedback) and control.

Our examination of the concept "feedback," above, suggests two related considerations for educational administrators. First of all, the monitoring of system activity and the establishment of feedback mechanisms and their use have a cost factor which consists of time, energy, effort, and resources that could be expended on other pursuits such as goal-directed activities. However, it is obvious that if a system is to remain vital, relevant, and contributory, it must monitor its activities. In social systems, such monitoring ideally must have both internal and external sources. For example, with schools this means that feedback must occur internally between decision centers (administration) and work groups (teachers and committees). Also, external feedback must be established between the total school organization and parents, citizens, and other governmental units (the environment).

The second basic consideration for the administrator, then, is the question "How?" Here theoretical notions and empirical findings about feedback are of help. As has been emphasized above, the ideal of complete and continuous evaluative information is difficult if not impossible to achieve with social systems in the real world. Costs are great, "overload" inevitably results, and ultimately system breakdown might occur. In answering the "how" question, administrators must *realistically*, as opposed to ideally, confront the task of system maintenance and relevance. As they do so, some obvious guidelines from our discussion of feedback will emerge.

The nature, extent, and form of feedback must conform to criteria of functionality and relevance. There is little value in monitoring successful, operational programs in the school except at periodic intervals. For example, if the school's reading and science programs are effective, there is little need to establish continuous formal feedback channels to evaluate these programs. Rather, informal feedback and periodic (possibly yearly or biennial) formal assessments may well suffice. On the other hand, if a new program of health studies or an advanced placement program in the high school is being implemented, formal feedback mechanisms of a proportional, intermittent, or even continuous nature might be more functional at least until the programs become operational and effective. Also, the notion of relevance is important in that in the latter example the particular kinds of evaluative information deemed necessary for program success, such as pupil attitude or achievement data, as opposed to all data, should be identified and consciously sought.

When feedback is desired, a conscious, designed mechanism must be implemented. System monitoring requires strategies, means, and action devices; it cannot be left to chance. The system may be monitored through a citizen's committee to review the school district budget, an information exchange through the district office's telephone switchboard at bond-issue vote time, a teacher attitude checklist, or a testing of student achievement. But whatever the method, precise solicitation of evaluative information, means for processing such information, and plans for the implementation of the findings of this information are essential. In this way the school as a system can ensure that relevant, functional feedback will be obtained, processed, and used for the good of the system.

An appropriate balance of feedback is important. In this regard two kinds of "balance" are desirable. First, there needs to be a balance of feedback from relevant sources. For example, in assessing a new curriculum, feedback from both internal (faulty and students) and external (parents and citizens) sources is appropriate. In assessing a new organizational structure for the high school faculty, a balance between data from administration and that from faculty would be required. Second, there needs to be an appropriate balance between the two basic kinds of feedback—positive and negative. This is not an either/or matter; it is a functional balance that is called for. When dealing with feedback about the construction of a new school building, positive and negative feedback may be equally sought. When assessing the effects of a new administrative procedure, such as one reporting student tardiness and absences, possibly only negative feedback would be desired. In any event, the appropriateness and balance of feedback, though situationally determined, must be established.

Further, it may be added that yet another kind of feedback balance requires the administrator's attention. That is a workable balance between all kinds of feedback being sought and used at a given time. As both the generalist and the person sitting at the "controls," the administrator usually is the only one in the school setting who can monitor the entire organizational feedback process. It is his task to set priorities and, in turn, to guard against the extremes of either overload or lack of needed information. Most importantly, it is also his obligation to see that feedback is ultimately used to the best advantage of the school—the regulation and control of a functional organizational life state.

SYSTEM DYNAMICS AND CHANGE

The concepts of steady state and feedback as developed in the discussion of system regulation and maintenance are also important in the exploration of system dynamics and change. By definition, open and closed systems perform regulation and maintenance functions, but only open systems have the potential for dynamic and changing growth states: *Only open systems can develop, evolve, and adapt.* System change, therefore, is also inherently related to the system's environment.[25]

As we have seen, the open system is uniquely equipped with the potential to combat the universal tendency all systems have toward entropy. It does this in part through regulation and maintenance of its steady state, thus avoiding entropy and system degradation or degeneration. It also does this through processes of change, growth, development, and adaptation—the evolutional or dynamic characteristic of open systems. In this sense, as the open system grows or develops, its steady state is modified to higher levels of functional activity and an even more dynamic ratio of the system's components themselves.

Evidence of the evolution of systems is easily found. In the mechanical realm one need only look at vehicles, or "systems" for transportation. From the early sleds, wagons, and carts to modern conveyances, considerable change has occurred. If one looks at air travel in this century, the leap from lighter-than-air craft to the rocket-propelled space craft is astounding. The evolutional capacity of open systems can also be attested in the evolution of man himself, and in the social systems that man has created. For example, although it is fashionable to decry government, politics, and politicians today, one can easily establish the viability of the evolved democratic approach to governing a nation over the primitive structures used to govern cannibalistic tribes. And, if we look at public education in America today, even the sternest critics are compelled to admit that this social system and its many subsystems (schools) have come a long way. Further, and even more directly, since the days of Taylor's "scientific" management to today's "executive statesman" posture, the practice of administration has evolved to a more useful and contributing set of skills.

However, even though all open systems have the potential to change, system evolution, adaptation, and growth are not in any sense spontaneous. That is, it must be remembered that all systems tend toward entropy and, therefore, system growth, like system regulation or maintenance, requires constant attention. Too, it is ultimately the open system's choice as to whether it will maintain itself and whether it will change—grow, develop, and adapt. It should be observed additionally that since system growth is also related to the system's environment, the choice of whether or not to grow does not reside fully in the system. That is to say, an environment can cause a system (or one of the environment's subsystems) to grow, develop, and adapt despite the system's disposition in this regard. In such a case, if the system chooses not to rise to the stimulus, it may well encounter entropy and be replaced by a new system. On the other hand, if the system chooses to react positively to the stimulus, its existence can be enhanced.

System growth and adaptation are thus conditioned by system forces, environmental forces, the systemic tendency toward entropy, and the open system's potential for growth. This is illustrated in Fig. 3.1. An open system has ultimate but not full control over its destiny. Within the limits of this set of impingements, open systems also have the ability to extend both their control and change capabilities—but again they must choose to do so.

At this point two illustrations might be helpful, the first regarding whether or not the system chooses to fight the entropic tendency. Occasionally, persons who are so extremely ill that there is no medical hope for them do in fact, and miraculously, recover. This is often attributed more to

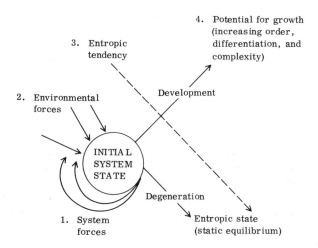

Fig. 3.1 The destiny of the open system.

the "will to live" than to the assistance of medical science. In other cases, despite the potential of medical science to facilitate recovery, the patient dies. In such cases the "will to live" can be, and is, questioned. This same phenomenon can be readily observed in social systems as well.

As a second illustration, the research and development (R & D) thrust in industry provides an excellent example of the potential of open systems to extend their capacities for growth and adaptation (or change). In our complex, every-changing, technological society, experience has shown that if industries are to stay alive, market research, basic research, and developmental activities are essential to ensure the relevance and contribution of such systems to the environment which they serve. Industries without R&D centers can exist but often succumb; those with R&D centers have evinced higher maintenance as well as growth potentials. Attesting to the value of R&D for social organizations is the increasing priority given to such activities in schools and other educational organizations over the past few years.

As Miller cogently points out, system growth is related to the availability of energy for input.[26] The exponential nature of this concept (as noted further by Miller) can well be seen in the above R&D movement as well as in instances in which system disposition is directed toward growth and adaptation. Witness as evidence here the comparison between thriving nations and primitive or backward nations, between corporate giants and businesses that have failed, and between certain churches today and religious sects that are all but fading from existence.

The matters of system growth and change do not present an entirely rosy picture. For, as Miller again has observed,[27] as systems increase in size the variables and subsystems which impinge on system activity also increase. This in turn can have a twofold effect on the system: it can benefit from increasing energy and resources, or it can suffer from the collapse or dysfunction of its proportionately more numerous subsystems and impinging variables. Thus, system growth or evolution adds still another infringement on a system's existence, the effects of size and complexity. To illustrate this, the efforts toward decentralization in mammoth industries or in large school systems such as in New York City, or in large high schools which move to campus or floor plan organizations, all appear to be instances of adaptation to the effects of system growth.

HOW SYSTEMS CHANGE

As Berrien observes in his recent book on social systems[28] and Marney and Smith imply in their discussion of adaptive systems,[29] analysis of the developmental processes of systems, or their progression from randomness and disorder to orderliness and complexity, offers an excellent perspective for understanding social systems. Also, for those concerned with social systems, these processes have a range of implications for working with social systems. How, then, do social systems change?

Four major determinants of system change are feedback, memory-learning, change-capacity, and system-environmental relations. In examining each of these determinants we can discover how systems change and what needs to be done to facilitate system change. Implications for the educational administrator can then be drawn.

Feedback, the concept developed in the preceding section of this chapter, is an obvious and basic determinant of system change. Just as evaluative information is essential to system regulation and control, so it is essential to system modification. As systems receive feedback regarding their activities, products, structures, processes, components, and effects, they are able to ascertain their relevance and utility. Positive information (feedback) supports systemic activity; negative information (feedback) challenges system activity and direction. The latter information is most helpful to a system's evolution in that it reveals system weakness, system irrelevancy, and may be used to point the way for system adaptation, growth, or development. Even if negative feedback results, in a sense, in tension or conflict, system activity in the growth sense is nonetheless facilitated. Therefore, *evaluative information is basic to system change.*

The system processes of learning and memory also are determinants of system change. Evaluative information, although it contributes to system change, is not in and of itself enough to cause dynamic system growth or adaptation. Systems must also develop memory and learning capabilities in order to be able to profit maximally from, and use appropriately, such information for system good. Memory comprises the system activities of storing, cueing, and retrieving relevant evaluative information. Learning is the system activity of rejecting irrelevant information, accepting relevant information, collating bits of information into useful units, and in general profiting from, building on, or extrapolating from the information available to the system. *For any system to change, its memory and learning processes require development and refinement.*

Systems must, however, go even further to develop their dynamic change potential; they need to extend and refine their change-capacities. Any system's change capacity is composed of two basic elements: a set of change-related or directed activities, and an action element. The R&D center as discussed above is one example of a system change-related activity. Training centers, resource centers, experimental groups, technological services, "think" tanks, "brainstorming" sessions, and participative decision-making and planning are all examples of change-related or directed activities. In other words, one part of a social system's change capacity is its consciously devised and implemented research, planning, developmental, and production or testing activities. The second important aspect of system change-capacity is its action element. It is not enough to think and talk about change; a system must ultimately activate it. In this regard the system must have implementation strategies, procedures, equipment, and personnel. *System energy and resources need to be committed and directed toward effecting change.*

Finally, the system's relations with its environment represent a determinant of growth and adaptation. Change—like feedback, a new school building, or devising a new curriculum—has a cost factor. Here are both the tangible or "out-of-pocket" costs and the substitution or replacement costs (that which might have been done if the change had not been brought about). System change, whether adaptation, growth, or development, requires energy and resources. If a system feeds on itself, it obviously will eventually be self-consuming. *Systems, then, must be able to attract and extract needed energy and resources for growth from their environment.* Basic in this regard is the functional relationship of the system and its environment, the system's ability to identify useful resources and energy in its environment, and its ability to use such energy and resources for the ultimate joing benefit of the system and its environment.

IMPLICATIONS FOR ADMINISTRATION

There are many implications for educational administrators in the concepts of system dynamics and change, and, considering the scope of educational change and adaptation of the decade of the 1960's as well as the continually snowballing tendency for an expanding role-function for education and demands for such in the future, these concepts are more relevant and timely than ever before.

At the outset, and of greatest importance, is the basic notion that *any system has the ultimate choice over whether it will grow, remain the same, or degenerate.* If schools are to be dynamic, relevant, and vital, they must first *choose* to be so. Although environmental forces will continually force public schools to grow and adapt, educational administrators face a monumental task in causing their faculties and staffs to seek a dynamic steady state in the face of entropic tendencies, and in the face of both internal and external impingements. Their counterparts in parochial and private schools often face an even more imposing task in this regard. However, in any event, before evolution and change can take place, commitment in this direction must be realized.

Secondly, *system change of any kind is costly.* Change is neither spontaneous nor natural. Just as children's growth is conditioned by and can be fostered with proper foods, exercise, rest, and intellectual, social, and aesthetic activity—all of which have a "cost" when maximized—so organizational growth is contingent on attention and provision for growth. This means the administrator must (1) identify what is necessary for his organization's development, (2) obtain and apply such necessities, and (3) guide in the overall process of system growth and evolution, being aware at all times of the full range of costs of such activity relative to the overall state of his organizational system. In this sense, system adjustment and adaptation are usually more reasonable than are sweeping, revolutionary changes. Change in the open system, unless in extreme situations, should be fostered and should be continuous in an adaptive, evolutional sense.

Thirdly, *the administrator needs to give attention to the determinants of open system change.* He must encourage feedback and develop mechanisms and procedures for obtaining evaluative information for control and change. He must also seek to increase his school organization's change capacity through change-related or directed activities such as research, development, experimentation, and planning, and through effecting action programs which will contribute to organizational adaptation and growth. And he must maximize the school's relationship with its environment in order to obtain the necessary resources for change and the dynamic evolution of the school as a functional system.

In this latter regard there are, of course, a host of implications. The educational administrator must lead in the identification of appropriate relevance for the type of education or schooling with which his organization is charged. He needs, further, to develop relationships with all related aspects of the environment. He needs to identify at the local, statewide, regional, and national levels the resources necessary for his organization's development and ongoing activity. Additionally, on his shoulders largely falls the responsibility for "orchestrating" an extensive, concerted effort toward the evolution of his school in its environmental setting. Since the many implications in this regard are so obvious, we can now turn to the final arena of important systems concepts, those dealing with system decline and breakdown.

SYSTEM DECLINE AND BREAKDOWN

A final set or category of system concepts with relevance for the educational administrator embraces the notions of system decline and breakdown. As observed earlier in the introductory remarks for this chapter, this general area of systems thinking has yet to receive the emphasis or in-depth consideration received by the other areas discussed above. This in no way negates or minimizes the import of such concepts. In fact, as one looks at the milieu

of the administrator with its stresses of civil rights, integration, teacher negotiations, student demands, and taxpayers' revolts of the past decade, such
concepts are of great importance.

The life space of the open system alone has a dynamic, evolutionary
growth potential. But as we have also observed, there are many forces or impingements on open systems that, in effect, challenge the life state of those
systems. These impingements, such as the universal entropic tendency (toward randomness, disorder, and death), internal system forces, environmental forces, and system size itself, all can affect or counteract the system's
steady state and dynamic existence. Actually, *anything that threatens the
open system's existence has a potential for contributing to eventual system
decline and breakdown.*

Thus any disruption, disturbance, or stress on an open system has potentially an immediate as well as long-range effect on the system. This effect
is easily illustrated with human illnesses. In the cases of the common cold,
chicken pox, pneumonia, and even headache, there is an immediate effect.
That is, the human system must counteract the forces affecting its steady
state. Obviously, in the case of pneumonia it is important to do this most
immediately and effectively, since the long-range effects are serious. It is
likewise important to tend to the common cold because, unchecked, such a
condition might lead to even more serious threats to the system. All of
these system strains have an immediate cost to the system. What the system
must do to restore a healthful, dynamic steady state represents effort, energy, and resources that could have been expended in other ways. When suf-
fering with pneumonia one must rest, secure medicine and medical advice,
and use one's time appropriately to recuperate. Without such a disruption
one would, of course, be able to use system effort, energy, and resources in
other ways, possibly even to improve the system's steady state. *But with the
threat to the system's existence, maintenance and survival are of greatest importance; steady-state development and growth are deferred until a normal,
healthful state capable of growth and development is resumed.*

In addition to the immediate effects of system strains and threats, all
disruptions and disturbances have potentially long-range effects on the system. To illustrate again with human illnesses: the complications of menin-
gitis from the mumps, the effects of radiation on reproductive organs, or the
paralysis of limbs can, in fact, affect the human being as a system for the re-
mainder of its existence. In these instances the system's initial steady state
cannot be restored and the system must achieve, at least temporarily, a
functional but less vital state. Thereafter the system is, as well, limited or
restricted by the effects of the particular disturbance on it. The paralytic,
for example, must adjust to a different life state and exist within the bounds
of the effects of paralysis.

Open systems—whether man, man-machine, or machine systems—are
vulnerable. Any system threat poses both immediate and long range problems for the system, and any disturbance or disruption to the system represents a basic cost for the system. Such threats may derive from the system

itself or from the system's environment. The sources of system threats are, therefore, numerous and varied.

In looking at the general kinds of system impingements that contribute to system decline and breakdown, one can observe that these impingements derive from two basic arenas and can be of two general kinds. As pointed out above, system threats come essentially from both within and without the system. Internal threats, or the "deterioration or depletion of the components of a system,"[30] can be categorized or classified as *system decay.* External threats, or "that which displaces, that which moves a system from one state to another,"[31] can be termed *system disturbances.* Further, the nature of system decay and disturbance may be either the effect of a single, powerful stimulus, or may result from a combination of forces (overload). Thus the gradual failure of the science department to teach material that would enable students to prepare for college work in the sciences is an example of *decay* in a school system. Citizen demands for vocational programs or work-study programs, on the other hand, are school system *disturbances.* The irate parent or board member, or the adamant teachers' association president in confrontation with the administrator illustrate *single, powerful threat* forces. Contrastingly, the administrator's classic in-basket full of "meaty" problems reveals *overload threat.* And as can be seen, there are various possible combinations of the internal, external, single force, and overload impingements on a system.

The reason why the administrator must be aware of the source and nature of threats that confront either the administrative or organizational systems is simply the same as why the physician must know what the illness is before he can treat it effectively. *To rid a system of a threat or stress one must deal precisely with what is affecting the system's life state.* Just as the physician cannot treat symptoms, neither can the administrator deal with symptoms when his social system is under threat or strain. To restore a system to normality, the precise disruption must be ascertained and relevant system adjusting action must take place.

In this regard, the educational administrator's activity relative to obtaining financial support for the schools can be used as an illustration. Assuming that the tax levy increase has just gone down to a resounding defeat at the polls, it behooves the administrator to get at the heart of the problem if he wishes to maximize or even maintain the school's current life state. He cannot just assume that this is a system disturbance caused by the older voters and private school patrons. Even if it is basically such a disturbance, there might well be other causal factors such as that the citizens do not know why they were asked for more money, or parents are unhappy because their children are not getting into the colleges of their choice. Possibly even system decay may be present. Maybe the school board has been unable to communicate the relevancy of additional programs to the voters, or maybe the teachers have been disgruntled over working conditions and have accordingly worked against the levy. Further, maybe the proposed increase was too much for the taxpayers all at once, or in the light of mounting municipal, state, and federal taxes an overload effect caused the negative reaction. Or the problem may involve several or all of these kinds of things. In any event, until the administrator gets beyond symptoms to the real threats, little can be done to alleviate the system's problem of securing additional funds.

The central concept in the systems literature that is most helpful in understanding system decline and breakdown is that of stress. Stress is a generic term that can be used to embrace all of the events, forces, or processes which threaten a system's stability or life space. Also, it is a concept about which research findings can be discussed particularly in terms of their relevance for their educational administrator.

SYSTEM STRESS

From the classic work of Hans Selye,[32] stress can be typified as a state of (homeostatic) imbalance characterized by a departure from order (disruption of normality or routine beyond tolerable limits; deviation from normative conditions) and a specific reaction syndrome. Two things are important in this definition. First, stress is a condition of substantive imbalance, a departure from normal order; in other words, it is any system state wherein threat or disruption has been perceived and a stimulus has affected the system. It is, in another sense, an abnormal system state. Second, stress is a state wherein a generalized reaction takes place; that is, where system reaction and compensation are not idiosyncratic or happenstance, but rather are a predictable syndrome consisting of threat appraisal, activation of protective or corrective mechanism, and restoration of order.

By definition, stress represents a generic system state that includes the effects of all the events, forces, or processes that in the perceiver's interpretation present a threat to the system's existence, and it is the state in which system adjustment occurs. For until the system restores its former life state or reaches a viable (lower or higher) ordering of itself, the system is still experiencing stress. The generalized stress reaction syndrome is variously referred to in the three stages of threat appraisal, system activation, and employment of appropriate energy and resources to restore order.

Miller is most helpful in dealing with the matter of open system stress. In drawing on Selyes' work, *Miller has advanced the notion that living or open systems respond to stress first by a lag in response, then by overcompensatory response, and ultimately by catastrophic collapse of the system.*[33] This is illustrated in Fig. 3.2. This is to say, when stress initially disrupts a system, it lowers the system's effective capacity. If in deploying reaction or compensation efforts the system is not successful in restoring its initial state, it then expends more and more energy and resources to restore a normal state of activity (overcompensation). If all of this fails, and the system is without energy and resources, or is unable to deploy these appropriately, the system collapses. This underscores, of course, the earlier point relative to system disruption: threat diagnosis is important and concerted system action toward threat disposition is imperative. One of the real, long-range

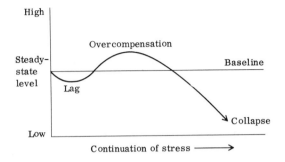

Fig. 3.2 The effects of stress.

consequences of stress is total system degeneration.

Miller further notes (relative to open system response to stress) that *systems which survive tend to employ the least costly defenses first and increasingly more expensive ones as time goes on.*[34] The logic here is clear. Obviously system cost is minimized when easily replaceable or least expensive defenses are used as much as possible to counteract stress. If stress is always met with overcompensation and energy and resource drains, this may inevitably become a system stress in and of itself and system depletion will render the system useless. When a system is threatened, it must be both efficient *and* effective in restoring normalcy.

Although research on stress has not been extensive or operationally definitive, there are a number of findings from the study of stress that are relevant to our discussion. For example Selye's notion of a generalized stress reaction syndrome—but particularized interpretation and, therefore, idiosyncratic appraisal of what is stressful—has been upheld in other research. Put another way, whether looking at paratroopers or people in education,[35] what is threatening or distrubing depends on the perceiver. What is stressful for one is not necessarily so for another. To illustrate this point we need only to look at administrators—conflict is stressful to some, not to others; a full schedule is stressful to some, and not to others.

Also the lag, overcompensation, and collapse reactions to stress illustrated in Figure 3.2 are generally reinforced by writings in this field. When some encounter stress, their performance drops; others are motivated to higher levels of activity; and still others collapse. Since stress is idiosyncratically perceived and its ultimate effect on a system's life state depends on the nature and duration of the stress, it is relatively impossible to predict the full extent of the immediate or long-term consequences of stress. It follows that the notion prevalent in much of the organization literature that people should be subjected to stress and tension in order to maximize their drive and movement forward is somewhat erroneous. For some people stress may be a motivator, but for others it may do nothing (not in fact be a stress), it may hinder, or it may result in collapse. And even in the motivation instance, it might be difficult to ascertain the full spectrum of long-range positive and negative effects. The long-range effect, however, of overcompensating and using costly energy and resources at its gravest extreme is one of "burning out" or "using up" a system in highly inefficient ways. The cost of "effectiveness" over efficiency is well documented in the organizational literature. Efficiency, particularly in the arena of forces that threaten a system's steady state, is an important concern for system existence, development, and, of course, contribution.

Some studies such as Brown's have revealed stress as a motivator,[36] but others such as Lasell's[37] suggest that before one can predict the ultimate effects of stress in social or work contexts, one needs comprehensive knowledge about those receiving the stress, other impingements on those stressed (re overload), and comparative data on the effectiveness-efficiency balance.

Stress, as revealed by Robert Kahn's pioneering work with organizations,[38] does have an imposing potential for negative effect in the organizational setting. For example, in his study of organizational stress, Kahn found that communications and communication structures are affected (impeded and, in a sense, distorted) as well as are the power relations in the organization. Applewhite similarly has noted the effect of stress on communications and the effect of stress on status structures in the organization.[39] In this regard (according to Applewhite) pressures (or stress) increase the frequency with which colleagues consult each other, and this in turn affects informal status by indicating superior skills and competence in particular group members.

The sum total of stress effects on people, or on people in a setting such as a school organization, is the immediate and potentially long-range threat to their existence as systems. Although open systems are unique in their ability to combat entropy, stress on both the individual and the organization (overload), and stress from within and without the system, are continued challenges to system vitality, growth, and contribution.

IMPLICATIONS FOR ADMINISTRATORS

The implications of stress and concepts of system decline and breakdown are numerous, in part because of the failure noted in much of the literature on systems dealing with such matters, and in part because as such systems as schools become larger and open to full view, the forces affecting them tend to increase in scope and frequency. Magnifying the import of these concepts for the educational administrator are the increasing number and variety of stresses that he faces from internal tensions such as student and teacher militancy, environmental disturbances from overburdened taxpayers, to societal strains of civil rights, integration, and the "new" morality. Many such relevancies have already been stated or implied; the major ones can now be set forth explicitly.

First, a significant implication from our discussion of system decline and breakdown is that the administrator, and all those responsible for an organizational system, must accurately perceive and diagnose the forces, strains, and stresses that threaten or distrub the system. It is not enough to deal with symptoms or to approximate those things which affect a system's steady state. Rather, dysfunctions, disturbances, decay, and disruption must be accurately assessed and consciously dealt with.

Second, anyone responsible for system survival must give attention to the costs of system disruptions. Inherent in restoring order and activity after disruption is cost: cost in terms of righting the system, cost in terms of realizing a renewed, functional system state, and cost in terms of what might have been accomplished had the threat or disturbance not occurred. Although we have emphasized the negative aspects of cost in our discussion (and this is important), there can also be a positive side in system disruption. For instance, if the school is not doing as good a job as it should and the state department or citenzenry is critical, this circumstance may cause the school to adjust and move more appropriately to a higher level of existence and contribution. Also, in times of disturbance and decay, systems are able to identify their most useful and vital parts and to identify useful components and processes that normally would not be so obvious. This positive range of outcomes is not always forthcoming, however, and may as well be a "costly" (in another sense) route to finding system relevance and strength. The point is, nevertheless, that system disruption can produce a range of positive and negative consequences; that these may be difficult to predict and costly is another implication.

A third consideration is that administrators ought, in dealing with personal or organizational stress, to employ first the least expensive and then increasingly more expensive means to restore system order and a functional system life state. To avoid wasting all of the system's energy and resources on "maintenance," easily replaced or readily available defenses should be used. Obviously, if these defenses are not effective, more and more costly ones can be employed. This is a basic concern for efficiency when the system's existence is threatened. However, there is need for a concern for an appropriate balance between efficiency and effectiveness. Effectiveness, as implied above, is equally relevant because of the fact that systems under prolonged and uncompensated-for stress ultimately collapse.

A fourth important implication for the administrator, as well as anyone who works with people, is that stress or system disruption, although producing a definite reaction, have a variable effect. That effect is that stress to one is not stress to another, and the effects of stresses as seen in our examples of illnesses are potentially both immediate and long range. Before keeping colleagues or employees "on their toes" or "attentive" through the use of strategies employing tension and stress, it is imperative to know those with whom one is working, their reaction to such stimuli, the other forces or factors impinging at the time, and the overall significance of the induced stress for all concerned. In cases of emergency, or in crisis, one does what is needed; in the normal range of affairs one needs to proceed rationally and situationally where stress, tension, and strain are concerned, always aware of the final or ultimate effect of system disturbance and disruption. Even within tolerable ranges of steady-state disruption, system balance is threatened and overload is at least probable.

Finally, administrators need to be aware of the nature and range of events, forces, and processes that threaten the systems with which they work, since ultimately system growth and development are related to the matters of decline and breakdown. *If a system must devote all of its efforts, energies, and resources to maintenance or prevention of decline and breakdown, little will be left for system adaptation and growth (or, for that matter, functional productivity).* A key to an open system's ultimate "openness," then, is its ability to regulate itself and handle at minimal cost the disruptions that threaten it. As systems become self-controlling, self-correcting, *and* self-generating, their relevance (to both the system and its environment) will be maximally ensured. Since the latter cannot be realized without both of the former, conscious, purposive system activity as circumscribed by the open systems concepts in this chapter are all necessary for the open system wishing to improve itself. As such they are most relevant concepts for the practicing school administrator.

NOTES

1. O. R. Young, "A Survey of General Systems Theory," *Gen. Syst., 9* (1964), p. 61.

2. *Ibid.*, pp. 61-62.

3. *Ibid.*, pp. 61-90.

4. *Ibid.*, pp. 65-66.

5. *Ibid.*, p. 62.

6. R. R. Grinker, (ed.). *Toward a Unified Theory of Human Behavior.* New York: Basic Books, 1960, p. 149.

7. H. J. Bremermann, "Optimization Through Evolution and Recombination," in M. C. Yovits, G. T. Jacobi, and G. D. Goldstein, (eds.), *Self-Organizing Systems.* Washington, D.C.: Spartan Books, 1962, pp. 93-106.

8. See J. G. Miller, "Living Systems: Structure and Process," *Behav. Sci., 10,* No. 4 (October 1965), p. 367.

9. *Ibid.*

10. J. O. Wisdom, "The Hypothesis of Cybernetics," *Gen. Syst., 1* (1956), p. 112; also, O. R. Young, "A Survey of General Systems Theory," *Gen. Syst., 9* (1964), p. 72.

11. J. G. Miller, "Towards a General Theory for the Behavioral Sciences." Indianapolis: Bobbs-Merrill, *Reprint in the Social Sciences,* No. 528, p. 244.

12. P. J. Rusche, "A Study of Selected Aspects of the Communication Flow Between a School and a Community." (Unpublished doctoral dissertation; University of Rochester, 1968), p. 139.

13. G. Hearn, *Theory Building in Social Work.* Toronto: University of Toronto Press, 1958, pp. 47-48.

14. F. J. Pilecki, "An Investigation of the Predictive Value of Intermittent Feedback and Relay Feedback in Task Accomplishment." (Unpublished doctoral dissertation; University of Rochester, 1966).

15. C. L. Hull, *Principles of Behavior.* New York: Appleton-Century, 1943.

16. See J. S. Brown, "A Proposed Program of Research on Psychological Feedback and Knowledge of Results in the Performance of Psychomotor Tasks," in *Research Planning Conference on Perceptual and Motor Skills.* U. S. A. F. Human Resources Research Center Conference, Pre. 31 (1949), No. 49-52, pp. 81-87.

17. J. McNeil, "An Educational Effort to Improve Instruction Through Visual Feedback," *J. Educ. Res.,* 1962, *55,* No. 6, 283-285. Also, J. Lesner, "The Effect of Pupil Corrected Tests and Teacher Comments on Learning to Spell in the Upper Elementary Grades," *Dissertation Abstracts,* 1967, *28,* No. 2, 542-A.

18. D. H. Jenkins, "Feedback and Group Self-Evaluation," *J. Soc. Iss., 3-4* (1948), 50-60.

19. H. J. Leavitt and R. A. H. Mueller, "Some Effects of Feedback on Communication," *Hum. Relat., 4* (1951) 401-410.

20. Cited in B. M. Bass, *Leadership, Psychology and Organizational Behavior.* New York: Harper & Row, 1960, p. 128.

21. L. E. Bourne and R. B. Pendleton, "Concept Identification as a Function of Completeness and Probability of Information Feedback," *J. (expl.) Psychol., 65* (1958), 413-420.

22. Pilecki, *op. cit.*

23. F. Herzberg, B. Mausner, and B. Snyderman, *The Motivation to Work.* New York: John Wiley & Sons, 1959.

24. A. Zalesnik and D. Moment, *The Dynamics of Interpersonal Behavior.* New York: John Wiley & Sons, 1962, p. 295.

25. M. C. Marney and N. M. Smith, "The Domain of Adaptive Systems: A Rudimentary Taxonomy," *Gen. Syst., 9* (1964), p. 113.

26. J. G. Miller, "Toward a General Theory for the Behavioral Sciences," *Am. Psychol. 10,* No. 3 (July 1955), p. 529.

27. *Ibid.*

28. F. K. Berrien, *General and Social Systems.* New Brunswick, N. J.: Rutgers University Press, 1968.

29. Marney and Smith, *op. cit.,* pp. 107-134.

30. Young, *op. cit.,* p. 80.

31. *Ibid.*

32. H. Selye, *The Stress of Life.* New York: Longmans Green, 1957.

33. Miller, *op. cit.,* pp. 527-528.

34. *Ibid.,* p. 528.

35. See, for example, W. Lasell, "An Examination of the Interrelationships of Stress, Dogmatism, and the Performance of a Stressful Task." (Unpublished Ed. D. Dissertation, University of Rochester, 1969).

36. A. F. Brown, "Conflict and Stress in Administrative Relationships, *"Administrator's Notebook, 10* (March 1967).

37. Lasell, *op. cit.*

38. R. L. Kahn, D. M. Wolfe, R. P. Quinn, and J. D. Snoek, *Organizational Stress.* New York: John Wiley & Sons, 1964, pp. 67-71.

39. P. B. Applewhite, *Organizational Behavior,* Englewood Cliffs, N. J.: Prentice—Hall, 1965.

Chapter 4 / Process conceptions of systems

The best known, and thus far possibly most useful, system conceptualization is that of the input-output model. In fact, the fundamental premise of all systems thought is rooted in the input-output processing relationship. A number of process system models and theories have been devised with relevance for both the analysis and functioning of systems. Such conceptions have import for the educational administrator since they are basic to his understanding of the systems movement as well as to his ultimate ability to capitalize on the movement. In this chapter we will explore more fully the process conception of systems, illustrate several process system models and theories, deal explicitly with input, output, and input-output linkage, and finally, indicate the relevance to school administrators of three important system processes.

THE INPUT-OUTPUT MODEL

The basic notion of system, as revealed by all forms of systems theories, is built on the input-output relationship. Process conceptions are concerned with this aspect of the open system, the action-processing dimension of a system's ongoing life space. Most directly, *process conceptions of systems deal with the transformation of inputs through processing subsystems into outputs and the resulting effect of output on subsequent input and action through feedback and output evaluation.* The classic "black box" model of an open system illustrates this idea graphically (see Fig. 4.1).[1]

According to process conceptualizations of systems, inputs in the generic forms of *operands* (those inputs which are to be processed) and *operators* (those inputs which are to do the processing)[2] are transformed through functional subsystems into output (outcomes or products of system action). Results of system action are invariably evaluated in open systems and such information, as "feedback," is channeled back into the system and affects future system activity. To some extent output includes products, affectivity, and feedback. Output in continuous time-space, in effect, becomes system input relative to future system activity.

The above simple and somewhat abstract model fails, however, to reveal fully either the dynamic or potential of process system conceptions. Within the context of a system such as, for example, a school organization, numerous input-output processing subsystems exist and in essence consti-

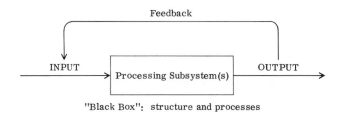

Fig. 4.1 The "Black Box" model of the input-output system.

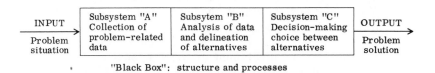

Fig. 4.2 Subsystem activity in administrative decision-making.

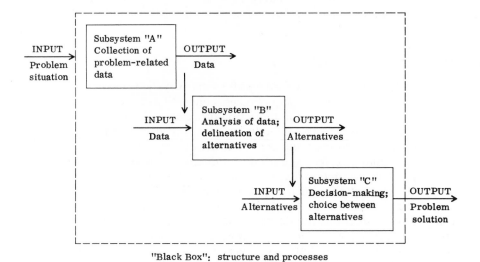

Fig. 4.3 The linkage of subsystem input and output relative to the basic input-output system model.

tute the system's structure and processes. Often more than one subsystem is used in transforming input into output. Figure 4.2 illustrates how several definitive subsystems might well be linked in an organizational system activity such as decision-making. Each of the processing subsystems is, in fact, an input-output system in its own right. This in turn is represented in Fig. 4.3.

All but the most restricted system activity can, therefore, be subdivided into definable and linked input-output processing subsystems. Further, as seen in Fig. 4.3, all subsystem or system output is linked directly to, or becomes, input for new subsystem or system functioning.

Also, as noted above, there are both operand and operator categories of input. *Input is, in fact, multifaceted.* Therefore, in an administrative decision situation, for example, input consists of a problem, data, and alternatives which must be operated on, as well as people, analysis and evaluation procedures, and thought processes which do the operating. Likewise, *output is also multidimensional* and can be categorized generically in terms of productivity and affectivity. In other words, decisions are productive outcomes of decision-making activities, just as work done is a resultant of work activities. In each case, system activity affects the people in the system (or in its subsystems) and those in the system's environment. That is, decision-making or work is successful or unsuccessful and people from the system or the environment feel good or bad about the outcomes of such activities. This is illustrated in Fig. 4.4.

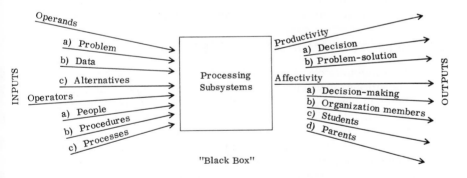

Fig. 4.4 The multidimensionality of input and output in the decision system model.

Feedback, which can logically be considered an output of system activity, can also be viewed in greater detail in terms of its overall effect on system functioning. Not only is there internal system feedback or evaluative information occurring within a system, but also, since they exist and function within an environment, open systems characteristically receive external feedback resulting from environmental evaluation of system action. Further, both internal and external feedback affect future system action in terms of effects on (1) input, *and* (2) system or subsystem structure and

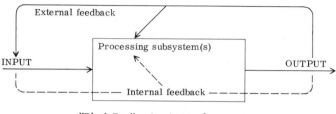

"Black Box": structure and processes

Fig. 4.5 The input-output system model, showing internal and external feedback and their effect on input and subsystem processes.

processes. Figure 4.5 illustrates these kinds and functions of feedback.

Since the potential forms of input and output are for·most open systems infinite in scope, and a finite but extensive variety of processing subsystems can be identified in any sizable open system, analysis of a system like a school in terms of process system concepts offers a fruitful approach for understanding the functioning of such systems. Through this perspective an extensive number of aspects of attributes of the system in action can be focused on along with their linkage and relationships. Process system concepts provide both a comprehensive *and* detailed means for viewing open systems and their activities. The approach is essentially microscopic (as contrasted to the macroscopic notions presented in Chapters 2 and 3) and descriptive. As such, it can contribute not only to the understanding and evaluation of a system but also to efforts to improve a system and its activities.

SOME PROCESS SYSTEM MODELS AND THEORIES

In order to illustrate more clearly and demonstrate more fully the relevance of process conceptions of systems it might be best to examine some examples. The human being's life processes clearly exemplify the input-output process system model described above. For example, the human process of food consumption (actually a subsystem of the larger human being's life system) graphically portrays the process system model. In order for the human being to continue to live, energy is needed to replace that used up in prior activity. Thus food is consumed to provide energy in order to maintain the human system and to sustain future activity.

In this analogy the human being is the "black box" of processes and structure which acts on "inputs" designed for system survival and to facilitate system functioning. Food and liquids are the "operand" inputs (as are vitamins, when needed!)—and appendages such as arms and fingers which convey food and liquids to the "black box," the mouth which is a receptacle for raw materials, the teeth and jaws which operate on food commodities, the esophagus which transfers food and liquids to the digestive center, and the digestive center itself which processes food — all represent "operator" inputs. The "productive" output of system and, as implied, subsystem activity, is usable energy which is transmitted to organs, the bloodstream, and the nervous system. (This output is, of course, "input" for subsequent system activity.) In addition to such "product" output, there is also the output of eating and drinking, which has an affective component with social, physical, and aesthetic effects as well. That is, the human being enjoys or does not enjoy that which is consumed, and the nourishment either makes the person feel better or, if contaminated, may make the person feel ill. Additionally, as is inevitable, there is a certain waste factor in the body's use of food and liquids, and that which is not usable or which exceeds the operand input is expelled from the system.

Throughout the human system's nourishment process, feedback likewise occurs. If the operand input is palatable, the feedback is positive. More may be desired, or memory information about the food's pleasantness is stored for the future. If the food is tainted, feedback mechanisms in the input receptacles, the mouth and the stomach, may trigger other mechanisms to expel the "operand" input immediately. Or if food cannot be processed by the chewing mechanism, feedback is used to trigger a discharge mechanism. Further, if the input is of marginal value, such as food with a large proportion of cellulose, feedback triggers the production of greater quantities of waste. If the input for any reason is dysfunctional to the stomach or digestive center, it is quickly repelled as a result of feedback.

In a most obvious and visible sense the human life process offers an input-output processing model and illustrates clearly the totality and detail of the abstract open system input-output model.

In a similar way the increasingly prevalent negotiations mechanism in school systems today provides an illustration of the process system model. In this case, as teachers' associations and school boards negotiate teachers' contracts and employment conditions, an array of inputs are channeled through a processing mechanism (the negotiation procedure) into output or the settlement of differences. Here "operand" inputs are teacher needs and demands, fiscal data, school-board policy and decisions, and available resources, to name but the most apparent. Negotiators, legal restrictions, formalized procedures, and negotiating sessions represent "operator" inputs. Output is revealed in such productive resultants as negotiated contracts, improved wages, and better working conditions, as well as in such affective outcomes as staff morale, teacher-school-board relationships, and school-board members' feelings toward employees (teachers and administrators).

In this system process model analogy, the interrelationships of subsystems, and of output and subsequent input, can readily be seen, as can be the dynamic quality of feedback. The success of any negotiations process is centered in the functional and facilitating linkage of all relevant subsystems in the process, and the quality of subsystem output at every stage of the process is a determinant of the quality of eventual process output. Throughout the complex maze of linkages of subsystems and their activities, feedback or system and subsystem evaluation are crucial to maintaining productive and effective relationships in order to ensure optimal negotiated outcomes.

Therefore, both human beings and human groups offer excellent examples and models of the process system concept. To better understand such open systems, the process system conception can be used for descriptive and prescriptive purposes. Systems can be viewed globally and in great detail in this way, and system improvements can be generated by explicitly focusing on the processing of inputs into output. In this latter regard, for example, if board of education and teacher demands in negotiations are unrealistic, if feedback is minimal in the negotiation process, and if the relevant subsystems in the process are not functionally linked, system process analysis will both reveal precisely where the dysfunctions are, and provide a basis for suggesting corrections deriving from established principles of system process functioning.

The computer further provides a useful and easily grasped model of the system process conception. The computer is itself the "black box" of processing subsystems. If we look at student accounting or attendance reporting in a school using computerized technology, daily attendance data and a computer program are inputs which, when processed by the computer, result in output in the form of monthly attendance reports showing absence, tardiness, and changes in enrollment. In this instance a machine system is used to transform input into relevant output for the school organization. In this illustration the internal and external aspects of feedback can be graphically illustrated. When the computer bogs down and will not process the data because of faulty input (such as wrongly punched cards or inadequate programming), that is internal system feedback. When the users of the output find that the data as processed reveal inaccuracies or are not what is desired, external feedback occurs. In either case, modification of the machine system processing activity is called for before system activity can be functional.

Before moving to a more detailed treatment of the major dimensions of the process system concept, two process system theories with relevance for school administrators will be briefly described in order to further establish the viability of the process systems conceptual approach. First, we will look at Stogdill's theory of individual behavior and group achievement;[3] then, we will turn to Easton's model of the political process.[4]

Stogdill has developed a process theory of organizational achievement which conceptualizes inputs in the group context as member behaviors and outputs as group achievements.[5] In his theory, member inputs are acted on through group structure and operations or are mediated through two categories of variables — formal group structure and operative role structure. This theory can be represented simply and graphically in model form as appears in Table 4.1.

The theory provides a powerful and viable analytic framework for looking at and assessing group activities. It focuses on the major aspects of the process whereby individual behavior in an organizational system is transformed into group achievement; it also links input, process, structure, and output variables in a meaningful way. Using the Stogdill model to analyze, for example, a faculty meeting, the activities of a curriculum committee, or

Table 4.1 Structure of Stogdill's theory of organization achievement

Member Inputs	Mediating Variables		Group Outputs
Behaviors	Formal structure	Role structure	Achievement
Performances	Function	Responsibility	Productivity
Interactions	Status	Authority	Morale
Expectations	(Purpose, norms)	(Operations)	Integration
	Group structure and operations		Effects

a parent-teacher conference focuses attention on the major categories and determinants of output for such system processing activities. Further, the theory allows relationships between input, output, and processing subsystems to be established and examined. One way to better understand complex systemic activity is through the use of such a model, which systematically pinpoints attention and links effects to the processing of stimuli or initial conditions.

This theory has a number of implications for administrative practice. For example, Stogdill reveals the importance of "expectations" as input. Thus, regardless of whether or not a member of a group is actively performing or interacting in group activities, his expectations represent a vital input. The group member "going through the motions" will not contribute as much as another group member whose expectations are positive and goal related. Also, if a group member has little faith in the "group process," this can well condition his effect in the group context. If the group member's expectations are essentially negative, this too will have a limiting or hindering effect on his contribution, whether the group is a curriculum committee or a group of teachers planning for the next faculty meeting.

Stogdill's theory also underscores an important relationship in the organizational and operative role structures. In this sense, this theory causes the analyst to look at both the general and the particular aspects of structure impinging on the processing of inputs in terms of extent and balance. Facilitating and inhibiting factors can be ascertained, along with functional and dysfunctional effects of subsystems on outcomes. If, for example, there is little flexibility (in the operative role structure) for action, system "openness" and the range of alternatives are restricted. If, on the other hand, little formal structure exists, little control can be expected relative to the processing of inputs or relative to outputs and organizational goals. (It can also be seen here that in addition to practical, analytical applications, the Stogdill theory has a potential for generating explicit hypotheses for predictive, research, or clinical purposes.)

Finally, the theory has implications for leadership and group achievement. Achievement is, in this sense, directly linked to the quality of inputs and system processes as well as to leadership. In fact, according to this theory it is the challenge of leadership to maximize inputs, structure and processes, and subsystem activity in order to optimize output. Further, output comprises several dimensions – productivity, group integration, and group morale – all of which are important to group stability and viability. In Stogdill's theory all categories of ourput are important effects necessary to group survival and development. When any category is emphasized to the detriment of others, the system is potentially in trouble. Realizing output balance in an organization is the leader's task. For example, it is the administrator's job to see that all of these things come about: that schools are effective, that the members of the school staff work together (in a functional subsystem sense), and that individual staff members are motivated to do their best.

Another process systems theory with relevance for the educational administrator today is Easton's model of the political process. Although some few may still wonder about the import of such a model for the school administrator, given the current state of affairs in education with teacher and client negotiations, increasing competition for the tax dollar, and more governmental and private invasions into the educational arena, the political aspects of educational administration are most apparent.

According to Easton, the political process can be viewed practically and heuristically as an input-output system model. His theory, in its basic terms, says that the political process is simply one in which a political system processes inputs, in the forms of demands and support, into outputs, in the forms of decisions and policy. Such outputs are in turn monitored by the environment and the political system itself, and this evaluative information is fed back into the system and becomes input for further system action. The Easton model is pictorially presented in Fig. 4.6 and its similarity to the abstract system process model can easily be seen.

This theory offers a viable framework for analyzing political behavior, whether it be in the society at large, a particular community, or within an organization. The theory has had a major impact on the discipline of political science; it also has implications for educational administrators.

The model of Easton's theory graphically points out that political policy and decisions are the results of *demands* on the political system per se. Thus, if educators fail to articulate and express their desires in terms of explicit demands, they cannot expect favorable policies or decisions except to the extent that others who make demands hold similar wishes and desires. For example, if state certification changes for teachers are needed and edu-

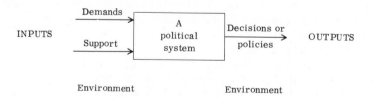

Fig. 4.6 The Easton model for the analysis of political systems.

cators do not make known their wishes to state legislators, they are subject
to the desires or apathy of others, or to a continuation of what is currently
in effect. Relatedly, since "demands" in the political system are "negotiated," it is imperative that demands be well formulated, effectively presented, and authoritatively supported.

The Easton model pinpoints the importance of the concept of "support" as an input in the political process. Since demands here are negotiated
in an arena of scarce resources, and since not all demands on a political system can be met, *support for demands* is a strategic necessity. Educators cannot go alone to the political arena with their demands (or wishes) and hope
that logic and their professional competence will ensure that the demands
are met. Rather, support in the political context must be mustered and
brought to bear in attempts to affect the political system. The obvious result of powerful coalitions or, at the other extreme, lack of support or
"party splits" on political policy and decisions can be readily seen. It therefore behooves educators wishing to affect public policy and the availability
of resources for education to make demands *and* to mount sufficient and
compelling support for these demands.

The relevance of Easton's theory for educational administrators is not,
however, limited to the external, or larger, political environment. Within
communities and even within the school organization itself, political activity
takes place. Whether the object is to project new school facilities, design a
new curriculum, negotiate a new teachers' salary contract, devise a code for
student dress, or establish school transportation policy, "political" activity
is inevitable. And here the Easton political process systems theory is applicable for purposes of analysis or for devising action strategy.

In sum, the process conception of the open system provides both a
popular and a useful approach toward the analysis and understanding of
these systems. The conception offers an analytic framework which is descriptive in both a global and detailed sense, and which forces the analyst to
consider the full range of linkages and relationships between input, subsystem processing, and output. *The process system model helps one to move
toward "cause" and "effect."* Additionally, process systems conceptualizations have predictive capacity; as a result of their use in system evaluation
they can be used to predict outcomes, to hypothesize about system action,
and to anticipate system deficiencies.

We can now turn to the three major dimensions of process system conceptions — input, output, and the input-output relationship — and suggest
the relevance of these for the practicing educational administrator.

INPUT

Input can be defined in a number of ways. In one sense, it can be defined as
the state of a system at some initial time. In another sense, it can be conceived as action stimuli (variables) — events, occurrences, or forces — which
prompt system action. In still another sense, it is that which is acted on by

a system. However, *in the process system conception, input is everything that is "put into" any given system processing activity.* It is held by process systems theorists that the key to all system activity (processing) resides in the nature of input and output, and in their relationships. It is imperative, then, that the full range of inputs, outputs, and their relationships be used in analyzing, evaluating, or dealing with a system.

For anyone such as the administrator who wishes to use the process system approach to better understand, or to improve, the organizational or social system with which he is working, an analysis of inputs relative to system action is a logical beginning place. To illustrate both the extent and potential complexity of such an analysis, given the basic operand and operator subcategories of input, a scheme for the analysis of input in an organizational context such as a school or school district might well include the following hierarchically ordered breakdown of input:[6]

Input

A. Operand Input	B. Operator Input
Information	Control structure
Message	Formal
Inquiry	Informal
Expectations	Operations (processes)
Strategy	Decoding
Energy (behavior)	Advisory
Rational behavior	Decision-making
Performance	Communication
Interaction	Memory
Irrational behavior	Work
Performance	Rectification
Interaction	Personnel
Resources	Individual
Material	Individuals
Human	Small Group(s)
Fiscal	Large Group(s)

This scheme, which is, of course, only one of many possible ways to characterize input, reveals the range and nature of input in the organizational context and therefore the kinds of inputs that are basic to organizational activity. It should be noted that this classification scheme can be broken down into even more specific categories,[7] and that input specification may vary depending on the nature of the system or system activity at hand. In this latter regard, computer input differs from social system input, and organizational context input varies from small or primary group context input.

The basic implication from the process system conception of input for the school administrator is twofold: it involves the multidimensionality of input and the inherent complexity of input in the organizational context. *Input can vary not only in kind and substance, but also in amount, degree, and mix.* Input may range from simple combinations from the above illustrated categories to the most complex combinations of more specific inputs. It behooves the administrator to know the kinds, nature, and extent of input for system activity at any given time, and to take this knowledge into account in working with his organization.

For example, if the administrator wishes to move effectively toward a favorable voters' decision on a tax levy increase, it is important for him to know whether the messages and inquiries directed toward the school really convey the concerns or expectations of the citizens who will vote at the polls. It is also important for him to know whether or not messages from school people to the public are consistent, accurate, and congruent. Further, he must know to what extent behavioral input is rational (purposive) or irrational (expressive). He must be concerned as well with decoding, communication, and rectification (clarification) processes in detail. All in all, to effect desired outcomes (a favorable vote *and* support for the schools) an administrator must monitor and utilize effectively all categories and kinds of input which can contribute to successful system action. Likewise, he must control, redirect, and overcome input which would contribute to the failure of system activity. The administrator's knowledge of the nature and range of relevant system inputs and the system's ability to deal with them, especially when inputs are heterogeneous, is basic to the ultimate success of system action.

Another fact that educational administrators may determine from the process system concept of input is that inputs, of whatever type, originate both inside and outside the system. Therefore, the implication is that the administrator desiring to direct system action most efficiently must seek resources and energy both within the system and outside it, and should attempt to link inputs in the most effective ways. Since system input and output are directly and causally related, the best way to optimize output and improve the existence of the system is through careful monitoring of the quality and use of input.

Other important implications of the input aspect of process systems concepts center around the matter of whether inputs are routine or unique. To the extent that inputs are typical, common, or routine, and the system has built up experience in dealing with such kinds of input, system action is facilitated. Not only does the system develop and refine strategies and procedures for handling these inputs, but also the system is better able to predict the consequences of its actions when dealing with that which is familiar. On the other hand, *unique, crucial, or critical inputs pose special problems for the system.* Prediction is often less possible, and coping with these kinds of input can be costly. However, the greater the extent to which a system can devise heuristic strategies and procedures, and adapt these to peculiar and unique circumstances, the better will be the system's response to, and processing of, such inputs. The implication here is clear: preventive administration and the development of flexible subsystems (processes and procedures) maximizes an organizational system's ability to confront and cope with the unique. Rather than solve problems one at a time, mechanisms that facilitate a range of problem solutions need to be operationalized. And this as well frees the system to cope more adequately with the peculiar and the unique when these arise.

Input into an organizational system such as a school is indeed complex. System action is, in no small way, related to the administrator's knowledge of input and his ability to use and capitalize on it wisely.

OUTPUT

As is true with input, output too can be defined in a number of ways. It is conceived as the resultant of system activity, the state of a system at some terminal time, system products, and as the full range of outcomes of system action. The latter definition is that most often used in system process conceptions and has been implied throughout this chapter. In other words, *output is the sum total of the effects of outcomes of systemic activity.*

We have already noted two generic categories of output, *productive* and *affective,* and have suggested that *feedback,* at least in the process systems concept sense, is in reality output. Productivity refers to the tangible results or substantive outcomes of system action. The productive output of an organizational system like a school may be a decision, a policy, a report, a new curriculum, a budget, or the plans for a new building. Affective output is the sensed impact or the intangible effects of system action. Here the affectivity may be the feelings or reactions of teachers or staff, of students, of parents, of citizens, of other educators, or of the board of education to such productive outcomes as decisions, policies, or programs. Feedback as a form of output refers to all evaluation of system action. It is after the fact and may derive internally or externally and be of a positive (supporting) or negative (challenging) nature. Thus output is, like input, multidimensional. In order to understand and analyze system action using the process systems approach, it is also necessary to develop a detailed conceptualization of system output. A hierarchically ordered breakdown of output, similar to that set forth for input, using the three major subcategories of output mentioned above, would be as follows:[8]

Output

A. Productivity

Products	Performances
Information	Behavior
Decisions	Decision transmission
Policy	Information transmission
Rules	Policy enforcement
Resources	Rules enforcement
Planning	Arbitration
Records	Consultation
Research	Work
Contracts	

B. Affectivity
    Organizational
    Clients
    Interstitial groups
    Supra-educational
      organizations
    Extra-organizational

C. Feedback
    Internal
      Positive
      Negative
    External
      Positive
      Negative

This scheme reveals (1) the range and nature of output that may result from organizational system action, (2) the kinds of outcomes that are typical of organizational system action, and (3) the kinds of outcomes that are typical of organizations such as schools. As with input, output can, of course, be specified in greater detail,[9] and the degree of classification specificity used to analyze output must be related to the kind of system or system activity under scrutiny.

The obvious relevance of output for the educational administrator (as revealed by process system conceptualizations) lies in its multidimensionality and potential complexity. For example, the administrator may, in his zeal to make a decision or set policy for the good of his organization, minimize or even forget about affective outcomes. Regardless of how good such a decision or policy is, if it is ill-timed, if those it affects are unprepared, or if it has a differential effect (that is, if it's helpful to staff but irritating to parents), the ultimate effect of system work may well be minimized or even dysfunctional. Thus the administrator must be aware of the full range of outcomes of system action and must be sensitive to the ultimate possibilities of differential outcome effect. Also, the administrator must be aware of the need to maximize all kinds of output and to ensure that outcomes are constructively and functionally related to system goals and purposes. Possibly one of the most traumatic and persistent effects of administrative action is the unexpected, and unplanned for, consequences of using a restricted conception of output to guide system activity.[10] As was noted in the discussion of Stogdill's theory, *conscious attention to all aspects of output and a balancing of system effects is essential to maximizing system activity.*

For the administrator, a second implication of output in the system process sense can be drawn from the internal-external effect of open system action. The effects of open system activity impinge ultimately (more or less) on *both* the system and its environment. Outputs, whether productive or affective, can affect people within the system (and its subsystems) differently from those in the system's environment, and product and affective outputs can range from little to much, from useful to not useful, and from positive to negative. Since feedback as a form of "evaluative" output is ultimately based on this differential effect, it too is variable. The administrator's task in facilitating useful and functional output and in maximizing evaluative information is a difficult one due to the multifaceted outcomes of open system action. *System activity must be consciously directed, and those directly and indirectly affected must be considered appropriately if the positive and contributing outputs of system activity are to be maximized.*

A third important implication of output from the perspective of process conceptualizations of systems is that some "loss" between input and output is inherent in system activity.[11] Just as there is some "loss" from apples in preparing them for applesauce or an apple pie, so there is some "loss" potential in all open system activity. The systems point of view does not blindly accept supersummation (the whole is greater than its parts), but realistically conceives that output can be equal to, greater than, or less than input — but most often, in action processing systems, output roughly approximates input. Therefore, *there is a cost in all system activity and a potential for waste.* To reduce waste and to maximize outcomes for inputs used requires explicit attention and designed system action. Conscious, effective system activity, the responsibility of the administrator in an open organizational system, must be planned and designed to optimize outcomes for costs committed.

The concept of output, in the process systems sense, has much relevance for the educational administrator. Thus far we have but begun to reveal its significance. However, since Chapter 5 will deal with output analysis, this important aspect of systems thought can be most completely handled there. The last implication derived from process theory output and the general discussion of input and output leads to a most crucial aspect of the process system conceptualization, the linkage of input and output or the input-output relationship.

THE INPUT-OUTPUT RELATIONSHIP

The third major aspect of process systems conceptualizations is the matter of input-output linkage. Although all open systems operate according to the property of equifinality (that is, a given terminal state can be achieved by a variety of means), in terms of maximizing system effectiveness the input-output linkage is, as implied, critical. There is more than one way to "skin a cat"—or to organize groups, teach reading, or change cirrucula. However, there are obviously better and more efficient ways to do each of these. *To ensure most functional output, attention must be given to input-output linkage, or to the processing of input variables.*

In open systems, inputs are linked to, or processed into, outputs by the structures and processes of these systems. These structures and processes (the contents of the analogous "black box") are appropriately conceived as functional subsystems. As such, subsystems are input-output processing systems in and of themselves, but as linked in functional activity they are the components of the larger system of which they are a part. As noted earlier, *open systems operate and maintain themselves through the functional interplay and interrelationships of their subsystems.*

In an organizational system such as a school there are numerous subsystems. There are human subsystems such as teachers, administrators, and clerks; there are material subsystems such as buildings, textbooks, and facilities; there are machine subsystems such as motion picture projectors, computers, and typewriters; and there are man-machine subsystems such as records systems, transportation systems, and teaching systems. There are then a vast number of discrete and overlapping "functional" subsystems in any system as large as a school or a school district, and these subsystems may be conceived in a number of ways. One such breakdown follows, as an example which may be used for analyzing the input-output linkage in a school system:[1][2]

School Subsystems

A. Administrative
   Decision-making
   Communications
   Policy
   Rules and regulations
   Arbitration
   Research
   Work

B. Supervisory
   Control
   Development
   Advisory

C. Instructional
   Teaching
   Program
   Extracurricular
   Materials
   Facilitation

D. Purpose
   Goals
   Objectives

E. Personnel
   Organizational staff
   Pupil services

F. Record keeping
   Staff
   Student
   Fiscal
   Facilities

G. Client Constituent Relations
   Information
   Participation

H. Business Management
   Fiscal affairs
   Physical plant

I. Negotiations
   Employees
   Community
   Other

Using this subsystem categorization, inputs and outputs as classified in the two preceding sections of this chapter can be linked in terms of their functional relationship according to the organizational subsystem or subsystems used to process the input. Through such analysis the full "process" picture of system action can be ascertained.

More important, however, than specifying in precision and detail all of the functional subsystems in a system such as a school or school district, are the notions that subsystems are overlapping, may be temporary or of long duration, and are ultimately functionally determined. Although any system has certain finite, definable subsystems or components, certain other components or action elements are situationally or purposively developed. In a school, for example, there may be guidance, mathematics, and English departments (subsystems), but members from each of these subsystems might join to form a temporary subsystem to alleviate a single student's problem. *Ideally and practically, subsystems must be conceived and utilized in open systems in terms of how they can functionally contribute to particular or general system action.* This negates against the viability of a formal rigorous classification scheme but does not minimize in any way the importance of input-output linkage. Rather, it suggests the need for flexible, planned, and intelligent utilization of action-processing subsystems in order to optimize the input-output relationship.

In addition, the linkage of subsystems *themselves* is an important matter. Whenever more than one subsystem is utilized in processing system work, a functional linkage between the subsystems (beyond individual subsystem functionality) is necessary. There are three general ways in which subsystems may be related. At the first level there is the *necessary* relationship between them. When subsytems are dissimilar or serve different functions, and an effect is based on the cooperative or linked activity of the subsystems, a necessary relationship exists. For example, the school band director and the student band members exist in a necessary subsystem relationship in musical performance.

At another level, when diverse subsystems replicate each other's roles or when they tend to assert authority over their own behavior—even though the organization is moving toward a precise goal—the relationship is *contradictory.* This type of subsystem relationship is basically dysfunctional, since it at least causes a duplication of effort, and at worst can be disruptive and even destructive to the system in which it occurs. Examples of this kind of relationship would be a situation in which the guidance staff and teaching staff of a school independently strive to establish homework policy, or when the teachers' association attempts to determine and effect personnel standards and policy relative to the length of the teachers' work day while the school is preparing for an accreditation visit.

The third level of subsystem relationship, and the most desirable, is the *complementary* or *synergistic* relationship. Here, although any and all subsystems can exist separately or be linked necessarily, the result of the linkage of subsystems is greater than any of the subsystems could effect alone, or by working independently. In other words, *in this kind of relationship, subsystems augment each other and the results of their coordinated activity are more than could be realized if they operated independently.* When the departments of a high school work together to establish general building objectives and interdisciplinary or core courses, a synergistic relationship is realized. Obviously, relative to the kinds of subsystem linkages possible, a challenge for the administrator is to build necessary relationships, avoid contradictory ones, and foster complementary or synergistic relationships of subsystems as he works with his total organizational system.

There are numerous implications from the process system input-output relationship for educational administrators. Most basic is simply the matter of functionally linking input and output. It is true that a lot of time in schools is spent with inputs and outputs, but unfortunately, attention is seldom given to the full spectrum of the functionality of their relationship. The in-service education of the professional school staff is a case in point. Administrators typically insist that teachers keep "updated" by taking college courses, attending workshops, reading professional materials, visiting other teachers, and numerous other means. The output hoped for is an "improved" teacher who is "in tune" with the times, who uses modern materials and methods, and who does a better job than before. However, little is done to diagnose teacher shortcomings or weaknesses, or to relate "in-service" activities to particular teacher needs. It is assumed rather that *all* teachers need a given workshop or in-service session, that *all* teachers need two college courses every other year, and so on. Such approaches ensure a great deal of wasted time and effort, and since little attention is given to input-output linkage, they can promise very little more in terms of real output than happenstance might offer. Relative to in-service education there is little, if any, evidence that the input of a particular activity (e.g., a workshop or course) will, in fact, have the same or desired effect on *all* teachers involved. *But since outputs are directly and causally related to inputs by the processing subsystem(s), this linkage requires conscious consideration.*

A second implication is that realistic organizational or subsystem goals ought to be pursued. Since system activity "costs," and since system energy and resources are not overly abundant, most open systems have little energy to use for pursuing either nongoals or goals that cannot be realized. Hence it does not seem wise for schools to educate teachers for wise use of their leisure time or for other occupational pursuits through in-service activities, any more than it is wise to try to make every teacher a truly "great" teacher. Optimizing *reasonable* outputs is enough of a job; reaching *realistic* goals maximally is a sufficient challenge for any open system.

Another implication here is that output maximization and optimal input-output linkage demands planning. In administrative literature, planning is an often-used word but it remains in practice and underdeveloped concept. Actually the systems movement, particularly through PPBS and system design concepts, is most promising for helping administrators to alleviate this deficienty. It seems unnecessary to belabor the point that *if the input-output relationship is crucial, planning of appropriate system or subsystem activity for the processing of inputs into purposive output is essential.*

An additional and related implication of the nature of the input-output relationship is that the administrator must select and use appropriate subsystem activity relative to the inputs at a given time and the output deemed desirable. As suggested above, system processing activity involves the selection and development of a subsystem or subsystems to process system work. Particularly, when either inputs or outputs are unusual, critical, or difficult, the design of appropriate subsystemic activity is important. While routine or usual input can well be handled through tested, regularized processes, new and challenging situations or variations in desired outcomes dictate the adapting or developing of particular processing subsystems. For example, usual procedures can be used to transform typical pupil attendance data into monthly or annual reports. However, if an epidemic or drastic population influx were an input, the normal processing treatment might need some attention. Or, if a proposal to obtain funds for a project for one element of the pupil population required detailed data (an output variation), the processing procedures might need modification. A real task of the admininstator is to select the subsystem or subsystems for the processing of input into functional system output. This is, of course, graphically underscored in such present challenges as seeking equal educational opportunities and negotiating the demands on administrators in schools today. No matter how complex the subsystem(s) activity required, it is the charge of the person responsible for the overall system and its activities—the administrator.

Finally, there is a cost implication in the nature of the input-output relationship. The administrator often conceives of cost in a dollars-and-cents frame of reference. Systems thinking, on the other hand, forces one to think of cost in a broader perspective. Costs in this sense are all matters of consumption relative to gain. This includes expenditures, substitution values, and replacement for all energy and resources used (fiscal, material, *and* human). In organizational systems like schools there are, then, costs in time, personnel, facilities, materials, money, and even of feelings. Therefore, in order to maximize output, one must optimize the input-output relationship in a broad cost-benefit sense. *All categories of gain and loss or waste must be related to their costs.* For example, in changing the curriculum, all matters of cost—teacher time, morale, teacher efforts in this direction vs. attention to ongoing classroom activities, and so forth—must be evaluated against gains (e.g., a new program) and losses (e.g., teacher resignations or dissatisfaction) or wastes (e.g., duplication of efforts or existence of an already good program).

Ultimately in the process systems framework the input-output relationship must be assessed along with input and output per se. Such an analysis of the activities of an open system will contribute to a comprehensive and detailed understanding of the system and its action processes. This kind of analysis has a real potential for the administrator who must work with complex open social systems. To conclude the discussion of process system conceptions we can now turn to three specific processes (or functional subsystems) with particular relevance for system action in open social systems.

THREE SYSTEM PROCESSES:
SUBSYSTEMS WITH RELEVANCE IN SOCIAL SYSTEMS

Subsystems can, as observed above, be construed in a number of ways; in fact, in any way that is helpful. In an organizational system such as a school (actually a social-work system), three important functional subsystems, in the process systems sense, are those of *work-action, communication,* and *monitoring.* All of these "subsystems" contribute in a vital way to the inter-

relationship of subsystem activity and to overall system input-output linkage. The goal here is not to delve into these three concepts or their full relevance in detail. Our concern is only to focus on these subsystems in the process system perspective and to note their primary significance.

Work-Action Subsystems

These form the essence of the operational structure of organizations and task groups. Social systems of this kind exist for precise purposes, and their operations represent the means used to fulfill those purposes. As such, then, work-action subsystems are those organizational components that do the "criterion work" of the system—or what the system is supposed to do. Our breakdown of subsystems in the preceding section (on the input-output relationship) is, in effect, a work-action subsystem breakdown for the typical school organization. As implied, this subsystem of the larger organizational system has its own subsystems and can be analyzed in terms of these. In traditional organization theory, work-action subsystems are equivalent to the organization's division of labor, departmentalization, and assignment of function.

From the process systems point of view, the relevance of this subsystem concept for the educational administrator is precisely that the work-process subsystem represents the operational aspect of his total organization. Thus, in order to realize an organization's *raison d'etre,* work-action subsystems must be designed, developed, and maintained at both a responsive and a functional level. In the process systems sense, the functionality of these subsystems is the basic determinant of overall system contribution. In school organizations these subsystems—whether teaching, administrative, or guidance—process the majority of output that has effects on the system and its environment. Such subsystems ought not to be established as *ad hoc* arrangements, or allowed to develop by happenstance, nor yet permitted to "just grow," like Topsy. Instead, they require conscious and constant attention to ensure their relevance and functionality to the system's work load; *"organization for work" is crucial.*

The Communication Subsystem

In an organizational system like a school, the communication subsystem is also of vital importance, since it functions like the neurological structure in a living organism. Miller has observed that "no one has yet demonstrated a species which failed to survive because too much of its total mass was neural tissue."[13] Almost everyone who has worked in a bureaucratic organization has wished for more information, facts, or data in order to operate more effectively. However, we also know of the effects of too much communication—overload, noise, distortion, and "problems of sorting out the relevant." (Pilecki's study of feedback relative to communication overload and distraction, as noted in our discussion of feedback in Chapter 3, is also relevant here.) *The task of an organizational communication subsystem is then to*

process and provide appropriate amounts of information for and about all phases of system (and subsystem) action. This involves capturing, decoding, collating, storing, transmitting, and otherwise processing and clarifying sufficient, but not excessive amounts of information.

In social systems where the human members have a maximal and creative capacity to communicate, when such needs are not fulfilled by system mechanisms, the potential problems of communication—false or inaccurate information, nonrelevant information, overload, and no information at all—are magnified. If an organization is to function properly an adequate communication subsystem is necessary to support and facilitate organizational activity. The implication for the administrator is clear: the organizational communication subsystem (structure and processes) needs to be designed, implemented, maintained, evaluated, and corrected when necessary if the organizational system is indeed to function as a system. Essential to the linkage of all subsystem activity is a communication capacity which is functional to the organizational work-action process.

The Monitoring Subsystem

Finally, since the monitoring subsystem increases in relevance as the size of the system itself increases, the implication of this concept for today's school administrator is underscored. The basic function of the monitoring subsystem is that of system *control* over subsystem activity and subsystem *accountability* to the total system. If all subsystem relationships were necessary or synergistic, and none were contradictory, and if all subsystem functioning were relevant, the need for such control would be minimized. But in the social system, people who are both rational (purposive) and irrational (expressive), who are motivated by numerous forces, and who are organized in many ways, require a certain level of control in order to ascertain the purposefulness of their actions in the context of the system. Although this is not a one-way street (that is, we hopefully realize today the rights, as well as obligations, of organizational members), for organizations to maintain themselves as systems and to continue their functional action, the activities of their subsystems inevitably need to be monitored. Again, this concept is parallel to one in the traditional organizational literature—that of the hierarchical ordering of authority.

It seems obvious that the administrator should see the relevance for monitoring in terms of his organization in the subsystems sense. In fact, part of the rationale behind the administrative or leadership position per se is that of monitoring and controlling the social group at hand. This, of course, does not imply monitoring in the negative, absolute, complete-control sense: rather *it means conscious attention to sufficient accountability and control in order to ensure that subsystem activity contributes functionally to total system action.* This challenge is assuredly magnified as the organizational system increases in size.

SUMMARY

In conclusion, the process systems conception offers a viable analytic frame-work for the educational administrator. It is descriptive and analytic in both a generic and detailed sense, and provides a heuristic means for assessing what organizations, as open social systems, do. Especially this perspective is helpful for "cause and effect" analysis. This thought perspective has useful linkages to more traditional organizational concepts and contributes to the detailed evaluation of organizations as open systems.

We can now turn to the final consideration in our theoretical explo-ration of systems: to output analysis, another systems frame of reference with analytic value for practicing administrators.

NOTES

1. W. R. Ashby, *An Introduction to Cybernetics.* New York: John Wiley & Sons, 1956, Chapter 6.

2. F. Kopstein, "General Systems Theory as the Basis for a Theory of Instruction." Paper presented at the Annual Meeting of the Society for General Systems Research, December, 1956, pp. 17-18.

3. R. Stogdill, *Individual Behavior and Group Achievement.* New York: Oxford University Press, 1959.

4. D. Easton, *The Political System.* New York: Alfred A. Knopf, 1953.

5. After Stodgill, *op. cit.,* p. 13.

6. G. L. Immegart, "Systems Theory and Taxonomic Inquiry into Organi-zational Behavior in Education," in D. Griffiths (ed.), *Developing Taxono-mies of Organizational Behavior in Educational Administration.* Chicago: Rand McNally, 1969, Chapter 6, pp. 177-178, 182.

7. See *Ibid.,* p. 182.

8. *Ibid.,* pp. 177-178, 184-185. By permission.

9. *Ibid.,* pp. 184-185.

10. See, for example, "The Gouldner model of anticipated and unanticipated consequences," in J. G. March and H. A. Simon, *Organizations.* New York: John Wiley & Sons, 1964, pp. 44-47.

11. See Stogdill, op. cit.; and J. G. Miller, "Toward a General Theory for the Behavioral Sciences," *Am. Psychol., 10* (1955), pp. 513-531.

12. Griffiths, *op. cit.,* pp. 182-184. By permission.

13. Miller, *op. cit.,* p. 530.

Chapter 5 / Output concepts and outcome analysis

There are indeed many ways to examine and analyze systems using systems concepts. Systems may be viewed in terms of system properties, characteristic states, and their processes. Still another way to assess systems and their activities is through the analysis and evaluation of the results of systemic activity in terms of output systems concepts.

Many have noted society's propensity for focusing on the "finished product." The hallmark of much social system work is, in fact, the drive to get the job done. The evaluation and assessment of organizational outcomes and achievement are of particular import to those in executive or administrative positions. For example, the school administrator *is* interested in how well children are being educated, the executive of a shoe factory in how many shoes are being produced, the administrator of a hospital in how well patients are being cared for, and the head of a department store in the number and value of purchases being made in his store. Each of these executives has an output concern and this interest is related rather obviously to organizational purpose.

Outcome concerns are not, however, solely related to the matter of organizational purpose. They can as well be related to the personality of the organizational executive expressing them. To illustrate, some school administrators are most concerned with the outcome of making children better citizens, others with providing adequate preparation for college, others with developing "the whole child," and, unfortunately, still a few with promoting winning athletic teams.

Also, perceptions of organizational outcomes are somewhat a function of specific executive or administrative jobs. To the personnel man, the on-the-job performance of organizational members is focal; to the customer relations executive, the level of client satisfaction is important; to the foreman, the harmony and cooperation of his workers are crucial matters; to the plant supervisor, the level of production is central; to the production engineer, cost efficiency is vital; and to the corporation president or organizational executive head (who must work with the trustees) profits are a basic consideration.

There are, of course, many others who have a concern for output. In particular, those who support or fund organizations—whether taxpayers for schools or foundation agents associated with developmental or research projects—also ultimately express output concerns or a precise interest in the gains to be realized as a result of their investment in a system. Further, the clients of a system are vitally interested in how they can benefit by availing themselves of the services of the system. For money expended, college students are interested in what they can learn, sick people in what relief they will realize, and purchasers in the amount and usefulness of products. Both employees of an organization and the directorate, or policy-making body, guiding an organization have output concerns. Workers seek to produce products worthy of their involvement, teachers desire to help children as much as they can, and policemen attempt to maintain civil order as well as possible. Likewise, bank trustees hope to ensure the fiscal stability of their banking institutions, advisory councils provide ideas and advice for the groups they serve, and school board members seek to develop viable policy and directions for education, all on the basis of the results of prior organizational activity and achievement and the organizational effects desired or valued.

Thus the concerns relative to organizational output are determined to some extent by (1) organizational purpose, (2) executive personality, (3) the nature of specific executive jobs (or positions), (4) those supporting an organization, (5) the organization's clients, and (6) employees and directors of the organization itself. This conclusion suggests that conceptions of organizational results or outcomes might well be somewhat idiosyncratic and to an extent characteristically biased or distorted. *Not only may the various assessors of organizational outcomes tend to emphasize certain aspects of output, but they also may ignore or be unaware of certain other outcome dimensions.* The assessment of organizational effects can potentially be somewhat less than systematic, let alone scientific.

But there are definable dimensions of outcomes. In the foregoing examples there are concerns about *products* and *benefits* (materials and services), *people* (organizational members and clients), and *consequences* (sales, profit, and client attitudes). All of these are potentially useful indicators of organizational output and represent valid dimensions for use in analyzing the results of organizational activity. If social organizations exist for purposes and are to do something, one of the best ways to assess an organization would be to analyze its outcomes—in terms of both significant dimensions and totality.[1]

As derived from the systems movement, outcome analysis (or achievement or output evaluation and analysis) has some rather important advantages over other modes of organizational assessment. This approach allows for a quantitative, qualitative, or mixed (quantitative and qualitative) evaluation of an organization and its activities, and focuses on what happens as a result of organizational (system) activity. It is also behavioral in nature and based on the broader concepts of systems thought. Outcome analysis is not hampered by the pitfalls of structural analysis (the fact that organizations do not behave as they appear on paper), goal analysis (that many goals are verbalizations and are unreal, others are inappropriate, others are "hazy," and still others are impossible to achieve), process analysis (that there are many ways to reach a given end state), or interaction analysis (the facts that many interactions are irrelevant, and that it is difficult to truly assess all of the significance of behavioral interchange).

SOME OUTPUT CONCEPTS

Organizational literature has tended to be preoccupied with the structural and process aspects of the operations and functioning of organizations. Less obvious has been attention to the outputs or results of organizational activity. Certainly the early organizational theorists, the efficiency experts and the organizational engineers, had an outcome orientation; however, this was evinced primarily in terms of productivity. Disenchantment with early approaches to organizational analysis led first to the human relations movement, which has in turn prompted a number of organizational scholars to become increasingly interested in various kinds of outcomes of organizational activity.

For example, as discussed in the last chapter, Stogdill has in his theory of individual behavior and group achievement focused explicitly on the multidimensionality of output.[2] His theoretical scheme conceptualizes output according to three major dimensions — productivity, morale, and integration. Bennis[3] has advanced a theory of organization in which *organizational health* is viewed as a critical dimension of organizational functioning. According to Bennis, organizational health itself has several aspects — adaptability, sense of identity, and capacity to test reality.

Explicit attention to output has also been expressed in the writings of Optner, Etzioni, and Parsons. Optner[4] has explicated an analytic approach for business and industrial problem-solving that is premised on a careful, systematic assessment of output. Etzioni, in a discussion of the viability of the systems model vs. the goal model for evaluating organizational achievement, expresses an obvious concern for rational assessment of organizational outcomes.[5] Likewise, Parsons, in his classic treatment of organizations, has dealt explicitly with the dual aspects of productivity — product utility and services utility.[6] Further, in our discussion of the open system in a processing sense (Chapter 4) another relevant categorization of output can be noted.

To some extent, the increasing interest in systems approaches and operations research has contributed to recent attempts to conceptualize more viable schemes for output assessment. Although the human relations movement took the first step in this direction, systems thought seems to have provided the impetus necessary for increased conceptualization and analysis of output.

Perusal of existing organizational output conceptualizations or analysis schemes such as those identified above reveals that these approaches to systems analysis have a potential ranging from highly quantitative procedures at one extreme to qualitative or subjective strategies at the other. But regardless of the qualitative, quantitative, or mixed approach to output analysis, the problem-solving perspective is precisely outcome-oriented. In this sense, such methodologies seek through the enumeration and evaluation of effects to provide a useful structure for solving organizational problems and maximizing organizational activity. Qualitative output analysis, used in instances when quantification is not feasible or appropriate, offers a heuristic structure for judgmental or subjective situations where problem solutions are awkward, intuitive, and often tenuous.[7] Since many of the problems of the educational administrator are of this nature — and since educational outcomes and output, at least at the present time, are not highly amenable to quantification — it may well be best to focus our attention here on a model for output analysis that is both subjective and practical. For the quantitatively inclined reader, or those wishing more information on other kinds of approaches, a number of the writings referred to throughout this chapter suggest appropriate materials.[8]

It is hoped that the heuristic approach will at this time best introduce the reader to the potential and utility of output concepts and analysis. We will develop an output analysis framework, illustrate how it might be used, and finally discuss the implications of the framework for educational administrators.

AN HEURISTIC FRAMEWORK FOR OUTPUT ANALYSIS

There are numerous ways to generate analytic frameworks, ranging from empirical investigation to deductive reasoning. However, as Stogdill has noted, the collation of existing concepts into more workable and broader conceptualizations is a most powerful way for deriving an analytic scheme.[9] It is therefore the intent here to draw together certain existing notions about organizational outcomes and systems output concepts into a viable, subjective, and practical framework for output analysis.[10]

What are the outcomes of organizational activity — operations, work and behavior? Clearly the first category of outcomes, and the most obvious, is that of *productivity*.[11] Organizations exist to produce, whether their products are material or nonmaterial. Most pointedly, productivity is the attainment of organizational goals or the fulfillment of organizational purpose. In this sense, productivity involves the relationship between an organization and the relevant parts of the external system or environment (e.g., with schools, between the school and children) in which it acts or operates. This relationship can be visualized as the maximization of the conditions (such as costs and benefits) of some category of organizational output in relation to objects, or groups of objects, in the external environment. Relative to schools, productivity is the behavioral change(s) that takes place in children as a result of the educational experiences the school provides. This may be in terms of content mastered, skills acquired, attitudes fostered, or even readiness level achieved relative to future educational activity. Such outcomes represent a maximization of teaching behavior relative to the client system (children from the external environment) which a school serves; the outcomes are the fulfillment of school organization purposes.

Productivity as emphasized above is not, however, the sole category of outcome for organizations. As the members of an organization, such as a school, work together and behave organizationally, other things result as well.

Another category of output of organizational activity is organizational *integration*. [12] When people interact and joing forces in common causes such as organizational work, interpersonal bonds tend to increase. (There are exceptions to this phenomenon, since understanding likewise can produce cleavages.) Not only do people tend to band together, but also they tend to identify more strongly with the social organization as such and to internalize it — its purposes and concerns. Organizational integration, then, is the meshing of the needs of the individuals and groups within the organization to organizational goals, and the linking of individuals and groups in the pursuit of those goals. Integration is, in another sense, organizational "adhesive" — it holds organizational members together and unifies individual and organizational purpose. Such an output dimension has apparent import for the organization; the organization must be staffed and continue to exist in order to continue to do something. Relative to schools, this kind of output can be illustrated through the commitment of department members in a high school to departmental concerns (e.g., attendance at conventions on their own time, and sometimes even at their own expense) or through the commitment of the teachers in an elementary building to unified effort and action (e.g., working together after school hours to improve either the total school program or particular grade level courses of study). Further, the degree to which school objectives and the objectives of staff members of the school become congruent illustrates organizational integration. (In this latter example, it is not necessarily the identification of member to organization goals but is, rather, a mutual agreement on goals and implies the possibility for shifting on the part of either.

Another outcome of organizational activity is that of *organizational health*. [13] Just as the human being's personal behavior habits result in a certain condition of "health," so does organizational activity result in a state of organizational health. This category of output represents an index of the ability of an organization to maintain itself and its productivity in terms of the dynamic interaction of the organization and its environment. A parallel can be drawn between the potential of the healthy person and that of the healthy organization. Healthy individuals tend to be more productive, resilient, and dynamic than do unhealthy ones. Likewise, organizational health indicates a dynamic organizational state, one which has growth potential and is capable of purposive action. Interestingly, schools as organizations or systems seldom exhibit much concern for this kind of output. Possibly public educators assume "a captive audience" and "enduring existence" and thus tend to care less about the "health" of school organizations beyong the bothersome effects of an extremely intolerable condition such as the blatant dissatisfaction of teachers or some similar major disorder. In general, it seems that educators cater to minimum "health" standards as opposed to maximizing such standards in school organizations. But some schools, such as those in Flint, Michigan, express a real concern for organizational health and the ability to grow and increase their contributions to their environment. Not only must the organization have people working together for shared goals (integration), but also the organization must be able to maintain a dynamic relationship (a state of reciprocal exchange) with its environment.

A final general category of organizational output is evaluation or *feedback*.[14] This is the inspection and modification of organizational resources, processes, procedures, or activity (inputs or structures) based on all other kinds of output or the results of system action. Organizations cannot just keep on producing; eventually (or horefully, continually) they must inspect and evaluate the impact and value of their products and activities. Relative to the school setting there is a need to evaluate the school's products to see whether they are indeed desirable. For example, are children what teachers and citizens want them to be as a result of (educational) organizational activity? Also, in terms of integration outcomes, is the congruence of teacher and organizational goals real or merely verbalization? And in regard to "health," is the school functioning maximally in contributing to the real needs of its community and society? The careful assessment or evaluation (monitoring) of all categories of organizational outcomes is an integral part of continuing and improving organizational performance.

There are, in summary, four categories of organizational output: productivity, organizational integration, organizational health, and evaluation (feedback). This leads then to a second question: how can these outputs be assessed — analyzed or measured?

In the case of productivity there are two potential measures — *product utility* and *service(s) utility*.[15] Product utility represents the usefulness to the organization or the external environment of results or goods which are either consumable or which serve as instruments for a further phase of production by the organization or the environment. Such utility for schools lies in the skills a graduate acquires that enable him or her to be employed in a gainful occupation, and the knowledge and skills that a student acquires which enable him or her to pursue advanced education. Service utility is the usefulness to the organization — or the external environment — of capacities, or assistance potential, or task-completing-potentiality, which serve as instruments for a further phase of activity by the organization or the external environment. Relative to schools, this is "productivity" as exemplified by children's developed ability to read, to manipulate numbers, or to think analytically.

Organizational integration, the second output dimension, can be measured or assessed in three ways. The first way to view integration is to examine the potential for *self-actualization* within the organization. That is, to what extent are individuals as members of the organization able to realize their highest personal goals (attained or attainable through the acceptance, willingness, and encouragement of the organization)? A second way to measure integration is by examining the extent to which the individual employee (teacher) or group of employees (teachers) is involved with management in making decisions regarding the achievement of organizational goals. This is a measure of *group decision-making.* Do the members of an organization have a voice in matters relating to them and what they do? A third way to indicate integration is by assessing individuals' (or organization members') *flexibility to change.* To what extent do organizational members, or members' groups, willingly attempt and accept innovation? This rests primarily in the security of the organization member in his position in the organization.

The third dimension of output, organizational health, can also be analyzed in three ways.[16] The first measure of organizational health is the organization's *capacity to test reality.* This capacity represents the extent to which an organization searches out, accurately perceives, and correctly interprets the real properties of the environment, particularly those which have relevance for the functioning of the organization. For the schools, this would be their ability to properly assess the educational desires and monetary support potential of their client-constituent environment. Another way to assess organizational health is through the measure of *identity sense.* Identity sense is the extent to which an organization evinces knowledge and insights into what it is, what its goals are, and what it is to do. Pertinent questions in this regard are these: To what extent are goals understood and shared widely by members of the organization, and to what extent is self-perception on the part of the organization members in line with the perceptions of the organization by others? A final measure for organizational health is organizational *adaptability.* Adaptability is the extent to which an organization solves problems and reacts with flexibility to changing environmental demands. For example, do schools change with societal demands, such as requirements for vocational and occupational training in an advanced technological society?

Lastly, organizational evaluation or feedback, the fourth output dimension, can be assessed in two ways, in terms of *desirability* and in terms of *penetration.* Desirability of feedback or evaluation is the degree to which feedback and evaluation are encouraged and wanted by the organization, as reflected by those directly involved. Or, in practical terms, to what extent does an organization such as the school want to know how it is doing? Penetration of feedback or evaluation is the degree to which, or distance which, feedback gravels from the point at which it re-enters the organization until it reaches all persons responsible for and holding commensurate authority for implementation. For example, does external and internal evaluation of teaching get to the teacher or is it stopped someplace short of the target?

From the four output dimensions and suggested means for assessing each discussed above, a viable scheme or framework for output analysis can be posited. Table 5.1 is a graphic representation of the analytic scheme and

Table 5.1 A framework for organizational output analysis

Dimension	Measure	Degree of Presence
		(None) (High)
		0 1 2 3
1. Productivity	a) Product utility	+——+——+——+
	b) Service(s) utility	+——+——+——+
2. Integration	a) Self-actualization	+——+——+——+
	b) Group decision-making	+——+——+——+
	c) Individuals change flexibility	+——+——+——+
3. Organizational Health	a) Capacity to test reality	+——+——+——+
	b) Identity sense	+——+——+——+
	c) Adaptability	+——+——+——+
4. Evaluation (Feedback)	a) Desirability of	+——+——+——+
	b) Penetration of	+——+——+——+

shows how each aspect of output can be rated according to its degree of presence. The result is an output profile for the outcomes of organizational activity.

Although many of the assumptions underlying this output analysis framework are implicit in the foregoing discussion, all such assumptions should be noted explicitly. First, it is held that the scheme covers the entire range of organizational outcomes[17] and focuses on the major, significant aspects of organizational output. Also, it is held that the measures provided in the scheme are adequate for subjectively evaluating the outcomes of organizational behavior or activity. Further, the scheme is deemed applicable to all kinds of organizations (schools, hospitals, clubs, etc.) and to any part of them that produces outcome(s).

Beyond these somewhat ambitious and lofty assumptions there are other basic premises. First, organizational output or outcomes are multidimensional and more than products or work done. Second, and not as obvious, this analytic framework is grounded in the notion that all aspects of outcome must be present to some degree in the results of organizational work. If they are not, the organization is in trouble.[18] For example, if an organization is unable to test reality (to know what is relevant for its environment) the ultimate effect is apparent. Mass production of buggy whips today is a quick road to bankruptcy. Thus all aspects of output must be accounted for in organizational activity and zero amounts of output in any aspect must be regarded as serious system pathologies.

A third premise underlying the scheme is that "openness" or dynamic potential (in the systems sense) is revealed by the scale. An organization exhibiting all aspects of output to some degree is more open (and dynamic) than one with several "zeros." Also, the greater a profile "leans" to the right on the scale the more open is the organization. Since open systems are those that exchange matter and energy with their environment (are most dynamic), and since to do this maximally requires a high degree of "presence" of all categories of outcome, the logic here is evident.

It follows that to maximize (as contrasted to Herbert Simon's notions of "satisficing") in an organization, conscious attention must be given to increasing or maintaining at a high level all aspects of output or outcome. To do less implies undue reliance on the status quo and the safety, but ultimately disastrous consequences, that a closed or "less open" system affords. However, an increase of any of the outcome aspects is ultimately at some expense to the others. If, for example, organizational health is to be increased, some energy expended toward other outcome dimensions must be diverted. It is impossible to pull resources and energy "out of a hat." Of course, it is recognized that increased efficiency and effectiveness in one area may allow the diversion of now-surplus energy to other and equally important aspects of output. Too, it is possible to attract more energy and resources for system work, but most schools are limited in this respect by the nature of their fiscal support. In any event, increasing or maintaining outcomes at a high level is difficult and requires constant attention; it cannot be left to chance. Organizations must give conscious, planned, calculated attention to all aspects of output.

The heuristic outcome analysis framework or scheme presented above has a number of cogent implications for practicing school administrators. To increase the potential relevance of such considerations it might be helpful to turn to a brief indication of some of the applications of this framework in the field of education.

APPLICATION OF THE
SUBJECTIVE OUTPUT ANALYSIS FRAMEWORK

The subjective output analysis framework sketched above has already had several applications to organizational phenomena in education. Its most extensive use to date has been in the research project for which it was developed. In that taxonomic study of organizational behavior in education, the scheme was used to classify some 90 units of educational organizational behavior.[19] Also, the scheme was tested in that project with a wide range of behavioral units extending from very small ones (e.g., a phone call) to much larger, more complex units of behavior (e.g., the five-year history of an organization). In another instance, and illustrative of other potentially practical applications of the scheme, it was used as a framework for the diagnosis and remediation of problems in a school organization. As such it functioned both as an analytic vehicle and as the framework for redirecting organizational operations and activities. The scheme has, additionally, been used in several studies of organizations in education and in other related fields.

Table 5.2 Output analysis scheme: Profile For 90 Classified Units of Behavior.

Dimension	Measure	Degree of Presence
		(None) 0 1 (High) 2 3
1. Productivity	a) Product utility	
	b) Service(s) utility	
2. Integration	a) Self-actualization	
	b) Group decision-making	
	c) Individuals change flexibility	
3. Organizational Health	a) Capacity to Test reality	
	b) Identity sense	
	c) Adaptability	
4. Evaluation (Feedback)	a) Desirability of	
	b) Penetration of	

Detailed discussion of all applications of this mode of output analysis is beyond both the scope and intent of this chapter. It will, however, be possible to show briefly the results of the application of the scheme in the above-mentioned situations. Relative to the taxonomic research, as noted, 90 units of behavior were classified according to the scheme. Analysis of the 90 resulting output "profiles" assisted in the generation of "taxonomic" groups or "species" of organizational behavior, and provided a basis for determining the similarity and dissimilarity between the classified units of behavior. Also, by summing these 90 profiles, an "averaged" or mean profile for the sample was generated. This output profile, for behavior from two educational organizations (a public school district and a private university), is reproduced in Table 5.2 From this profile a number of generalizations can be drawn which illustrate the potential of the framework for organizational analysis. (Caution must be used here due to the restricted sample in the study, the way the units of behavior were obtained, and the fact that the research was essentially exploratory in nature.) The profile, for example, indicates a greater concern for productivity than for any other category of output. Concern for integration and organizational health is revealed as rather low and, although feedback is reputed to be desired, it is not seen as being realized to the extent desired. Thus, not only can one generalize about given units or segments or oganizational activity using this analytic framework, but also "profiles" can be developed to obtain "domain" or cumulative profiles. Further, as can be seen in the next example, these profiles can be used for diagnostic and remediation purposes in seeking organizational improvement.

A second application of this scheme was its use with the staff of a relatively new vocational high school. This school was composed of a group of teachers drawn mostly from business and industry with little experience in, or knowledge of, working with youth of high school age, particularly those with learning or adjustment problems. The school's administrative officers were, however, experienced administrators with varying public school backgrounds. Although the school's opening year was evaluated as successful by the staff, students, parents, and "feeder" schools, there was a growing awareness of problems.

For one thing an obvious communications problem existed between those experienced with public education and those on the staff from the business or industrial world. Also, many members of the staff were ill-prepared to cope with the learning problems encountered in their classrooms. And there were organizational problems, beyond communications, which were symptomatic of any new, fast-growing, and relatively undefined organization. The school's principal decided first to help his staff cope with the instructional problems that were facing them. Once this program was under way and producing visible results, the principal turned his attention to organizational problems.

In attacking the organizational problems of this somewhat unique school staff, the subjective output analysis framework was used to assess the outcomes of the school's operations to date, and the effectiveness of faculty meetings. All staff—teachers and administrators—assessed their school. These data were then collated and discussed. The data from the teachers resulted in a profile not unlike that in Table 5.2. There were, however, noticeable discrepancies between the teachers' profile and that of the administrative staff. In this regard, teachers saw much less "group decision-making" and "feedback penetration" than did the administrators. This latter fact is worthy of note, especially in that both groups saw "desirability of feedback" quite similarly. Also, the levels of productive output—product and service utility—were generally agreed on. Other items such as "identity sense" and "self-actualization" (scored higher by administrators), and "individuals' change flexibility" (scored higher by teachers) revealed differences in assessment.

As a result of this evaluation and analysis, the staff then began to discuss the "merits" and meaning of such profiles, and the desirability of continued operations along existing lines. It was decided in the discussion that the organization was not as "healthy" or "integrated" as it should be, and that feedback from the teaching staff to administrators was not effectual. On this basis the group began remediation, or the redesign of the system, along several lines. First, they sought to devise ways to improve internal communications. Second, they decided to explore more systematically how members behave in organizations and how each member of the organization could maximize his efforts, particularly in group activities.

In this latter respect one of the tangible outcomes of the group's self-output analysis was the modification of staff meetings. It was decided that faculty meetings would be chaired by a teacher, not by the principal. Faculty meeting agenda were to be determined by a teachers' committee rather than by administrators. Administrators could, of course, participate in faculty meetings, but instead of dictating to teachers they were to make proposals and discuss relevant matters as a part of the group. Administrators were further charged to be receptive to teachers' ideas and proposals (especially those resulting from formal group activity), and were requested to keep the faculty up to date on action and disposition of important matters.

Although no systematic study was undertaken to ascertain all of the effects of this exercise in output analysis, the results were operational—staff-administration relations and communications improved, a number of organizational problems have been alleviated, and the school is today a growing, expanding enterprise.

Several other uses of the output analysis scheme have been in studies of educational or related organizations. For example, Thompson used a modified version of the scheme in his study of the effects of group self-evaluation feedback on school-board groups.[20] In this study the output analysis scheme was used to provide data about school-board groups which was "fed back" to the group in order to see if such evaluative information affected subsequent group behavior. Similarly, a modified form of the output analysis scheme was used by Buckley to analyze a YMCA organization.[21] This study resulted in the identification of several organizational problems (e.g., disagreement over goals and level of organizational productivity) and provided a basis for a change strategy for use in the organization. Finally Schuttenberg, in an outcome analysis study of an electronics parts plant, used the output analysis scheme to test several hypotheses.[22] Again using a modified form of the scheme, Schuttenberg tested several correlational hypotheses (between scheme dimensions), and identified variables (such as age, time in company, time in present job) that affect responses in organizational output analysis. He further generated a number of questions and hypotheses for subsequent study. Such investigations as these reveal both the empirical and practical utility of outcome analysis for social systems like schools.

It is hoped that from these brief and sketchy illustrations of the applications of an heuristic output analysis framework to the educational scene, an indication of the viability of output analysis concepts and procedures is revealed. The discussion of output concepts and analysis can now be concluded by focusing on the implications of this systems approach for the practice of educational administration.

THE IMPLICATIONS OF OUTPUT ANALYSIS FOR PRACTICE

It is interesting that this avenue of systems thought has led directly to a number of "cautions" revealed, and being increasingly voiced, in the organizational literature at large. In fact, these cautions—or more positively, implications (as drawn from the basic output analysis scheme)—have a wide range of relevance for organizational practice beyond import for output maximinization in and of itself. The implications which follow apply to practically all aspects of organizational activity and merit careful consideration by anyone interested in optimizing the full range of organization functioning.

1. The first implication, and possibly the most important, is that *organizations as open systems must engage in conscious, long-range planning.* An important question in this regard is: Does the organization have a five- or ten-year plan? And further, is this plan written and in the hands of all of the organization members? It can be suspected that administrators of school organizations would give few affirmative responses to such questions. But, if increasing or maintaining all dimensions of output at a high level is a difficult task as implied above, planning is a prerequisite for proper attention to all operational and output dimensions. At least it is necessary to ensure that no aspect of output is overlooked by the organization, or that any exists in a zero quantity. Just as the administrator must schedule his time and program his day to cope with the numerous and diverse problems that confront him, so must the organization schedule and program attention to the numerous and diverse aspects of organizational outcome. For example, too much exercise may be dysfunctional to an individual's health, and similarly, too much attention to productivity by an organization may be dysfunctional to the organization's health. It is imperative that organizations at times be a bit selfish and attend to their *own* well-being. Possibly organizational service or productivity is stressed too much and thereby unhealthy, unintegrated organizations result; such a preoccupation is, of course, circular and ultimately self-defeating.

2. Another implication that can be drawn from this analytic approach is that *social organizations like schools, which are open systems, must pursue real goals and objectives.* Sociologists have focused our thinking on the problems of ends (goals) and this set of output analysis concepts clearly indicates that organizations can ill-afford to waste energy and resources in processing unwanted materials, providing useless services, or moving toward unattainable goals. Since energy (and resources) are not unlimited for organizations such as schools, wise use must be made of all available resources and energy. As has been observed, to attend to all dimensions of outcome requires a give and take, improved functioning, or more energy. Since realizing the latter has obvious limitations, *the members of any organization must be certain of both the "realness" and "usefulness" of organizational goals.* One might ask in passing, does the organization have an explicit set of goals as well as behavioral, operational objectives? Further, are these periodically monitored, reviewed, and changed?

3. *Relatedly, the organization heeding the relevance of the concept of output multidimensionality must be concerned with waste reduction and generally adequate allocation and use of all resources and energy.* This follows and is inherent in the foregoing implication regarding the necessity for

real operational goals and objectives for the organization. Organizations, in fact, have little to waste. What is wasted on production, for example, might well be expended on organizational health or integration. The wisdom of conscious, systematic choice (good decision-making) in regard to the allocation and use of energy and resources is basic to maximizing all dimensions of organizational output.

4. *Also, organizations need to be concerned with attracting and utilizing appropriate and adequate resources—human, financial, and material.* Since output is dependent directly on input and its processing, and since super-summation (the resulting whole being greater than contributing parts) is an ideal not often realized in organizational work, the quantity *and* quality of resources determine the quantity and quality of realized output, and ultimately the full range of effects of system activity. This is true in regard to all output dimensions and is not limited solely to the production of goods.

5. Another implication of the output analysis concept is that *the organization needs to attract and use competence soundly.* If productivity were the only concern, competence utilization would not be such a crucial matter, beyond at least a rather obvious point. But output is more than products and, with fixed resources (or at least relatively fixed resources), *the appropriate deployment of special skills and abilities is central to organizational maximization.* The organization must be able to identify the competencies required (in terms of professional, human, or organizational skills), have them at its disposal, and use them wisely.

6. An important relevancy for organizational communications can be derived from the output analysis framework. Not only must ways be found to enhance information exchange about all aspects of organizational operations and activity related to outputs, but also organizational information exchange must be both accurate and relevant. *As the basis for interaction and the data for evaluation, organizational communications are central to what an organization does and, in fact, how well it does it.*

7. The outcome analysis approach also implies that *involvement is a key concept relative to organizational activity in an open system.* To attend to the numerous and diverse outcome considerations posited, organizational authority must be dispersed to specialists, internal power in the organization must be balanced, delegation must be manifest to an extensive degree, and commitment to the full range of outcomes needs to be realized by more than just the chief organizational administrative officer. *In other words, every organizational member needs to be related to, and concerned with the totality of outcomes.* For example, the rank-and-file employee needs to be involved with more than just his task or production-related work. Obviously, task and product preoccupation and focus must at times be discarded for a new view of what happens as a result of organizational behavior, including the "selfish" interests an organization must have for itself as an entity (to be fostered and valued per se).

8.   Further, it is implicit in the output analysis mode of thought that *organizations must continually monitor or evaluate the results of their work.* This continuing assessment and processing of "feedback" is essential if the organization is to be cognizant of its outputs and contributions as well as trends in its effects.   Certainly such assessment must go beyond products and effects on clients, and include the totality inherent in a global output conceptualization. *Unless systematic monitoring occurs, only conjecture can be made as to the real utility, viability, status, and value of an organization.* Also in this regard, evaluation must be translated into action programs. For example, the smoker who knows of cancer probabilities from his own smoking behavior is not immune to the effects of smoking until there is an actual change in his behavior. So it is with organizations.

9.   Finally, *the outcome analysis logic suggests that organizations should be change-oriented.* This is obviously true relative to the outcome of productivity, but also it is of great import to overall organizational operations and structure. Unfortunately, many organizations are, or become, quite tradition-bound. This is not necessarily bad, as such, but the degree to which tradition pervades the thinking of many organizational members is inhibiting. Organizations can be change oriented (adaptive) and still serve valid traditional or enduring ends. *What is required is a concern on the part of organizational members to assess critically the changing context and environment of the organization, and to be receptive to modifications that are dictated.* To continue to serve antiquated ends is an obvious deterrent to improve organizational functioning. Some traditional ends might, on the other hand, remain as goals but to maximize all outcome dimensions, organizations as open exchange systems must be disposed to change.

In conclusion, output analysis reveals that there is more to organizational output than productivity. As such, output analysis, whether quantitative or qualitative, offers a viable approach to understanding and improving social organizations like schools.[23] Its relevancy extends beyond mere outcome concerns to the full range of open system functions and operations.

NOTES

1.   This is, essentially, the approach advanced by S. L. Optner in *Systems Analysis for Business Management.* Englewood Cliffs, N. J.: Prentice Hall, 1960; see also G. L. Immegart and F. J. Pilecki, "Assessing Organizational Output: A Framework and Some Implications," *Educ. Adm. Q.,* (Winter 1970), pp. 62-76.

2.   R. Stogdill, *Individual Behavior and Group Achievement.* New York: Oxford University Press, 1959.

3.   W. G. Bennis, "Toward a 'Truly' Scientific Management: the Concept of Organizational Health," *Gen. Syst., 7* (1962), pp. 269-282.

4.   S. L. Optner, *Systems Analysis for Business and Industrial Problem Solving.* Englewood Cliffs, N. J.: Prentice Hall, 1965.

5. A. Etzioni, "Two Approaches to Organizational Analysis: A Critique and a Suggestion," *Admve. Sci. Q., 5* (September 1960), pp. 257-278.

6. T. Parsons, "Suggestions for a Sociological Approach to the Theory of Organization," *Admve. Sci. Q., 1* (June 1956), pp. 64-67.

7. See Optner, *op. cit.,* p. 10ff., in this regard.

8. See, particularly, Optner, *op. cit.;* and F. W. Banghart, *Educational Systems Analysis.* Macmillan, 1969.

9. Stogdill, *op. cit.,* pp. v-vii and 3-12.

10. The framework or scheme presented here was primarily developed and applied in a large-scale research project. See D. E. Griffiths (ed.), *Developing Taxonomies of Organizational Behavior in Education Administration.* Chicago: Rand McNally, 1969, pp. 175-176.

11. Parsons, *op. cit.*

12. See Edgar H. Schein, *Organizational Psychology.* Englewood Cliffs, N. J.: Prentice Hall, 1965, pp. 97-98.

13. Bennis, *op. cit.*

14. Stogdill, *op. cit.*

15. From Parsons, *op. cit.*

16. Based on Bennis, *op. cit.*

17. Or at least it can be used to classify the full range of outputs in assessing of organizational activity.

18. After Stogdill, *op. cit.*

19. Griffiths (ed.), *op. cit.,* Chapter 6.

20. C. W. Thompson, "The Effect of Selected Feedback on Member Inputs and Group Outcomes in Public School Board Groups." (Unpublished Ed. D. dissertation, The University of Rochester, in process.)

21. C. A. Buckley, "Output Analysis of Halifax YMCA." (Unpublished report, Department of Educational Administration, Boston University, May, 1969, 10 pp.)

22. E. M. Schuttenberg, "An Organizational Outcome Analysis of an Electronics Parts Plant." (Unpublished study, Department of Educational Administration, Boston University, August, 1969, 11 pp.)

23. See also G. L. Immegart and F. J. Pilecki, *op. cit.*

Chapter 6 / A brief summary of the relevance
of systems for administrators

In the space of relatively few pages an attempt has been made to introduce the practicing school administrator, or the administrator-to-be, to the systems movement. Thus far we have looked at the potential of the movement quite generally and have examined in more depth the theoretical aspects of systems. Throughout, the relevance and implications of systems thought for the practice of educational administration have been emphasized. Before moving to specific systems approaches and procedures that can be used by administrators to facilitate their practice of administering educational organizations, the major relevancies from the discussion so far might well be underscored.

That systems exist and exhibit certain universal properties is of significance per se. The real value of the systems mode of thought is that the same rules which are applied to one situation can be applied to other situations (systems). Moreover, the prognostic and prescriptive value of systems thinking, especially as evidenced by systems concepts and theories, provides potentially great and heuristic value as an analytic framework.

For example, Miller's notions about system response to stress—that is, undercompensation, overcompensation, increasing lag, and ultimately total collapse — are applicable to a wide variety of situations from small social group activities to large organizations, as well as for the basic organisms studied by Miller and others in developing this concept of system response to stress.[1] Obviously, Miller's concept has value for "preventive administration" in that his notion on the course of stress response can guide an administrator in curtailing stress before its ultimate and dysfunctional consequences are manifest.

Just as systems notions are applicable to many areas of practice, the systems modes of thought heretofore described employ theories from many disciplines. This is, in fact, the heart of the systems movement. Scholars from a wide variety of disciplines — sociology, psychology, medicine, engineering, and the natural sciences, to name but a few — have all joined forces in the development of a common set of principles which apply to a variety of particular disciplines. Likewise, practitioners in a number of fields are applying the products of systems thinking to their areas of practice.

Although it is impossible to exhaust the implications of systems concepts for the educational administrator in a brief introductory statement, the writers would be remiss if they did not point in explicit terms to the major relevancies of systems thinking for the educational administrator. This summary will be brief and generic, but it should reinforce for the reader the viability of systems thought for administrative analysis and practice, and hopefully encourage him to explore the literature for even more useful ideas.

First, *administration — the administration of an organization — is a system in and of itself.* It is an open system that takes inputs and converts them via system processes into outputs which have consequences for the system itself and for the environment of the system. To illustrate, the administrative system replenishes itself by selecting new or replacement members (input) and orients the new administrators to the system (via system processes); the new members of the administrative staff then affect the administrative system per se, as well as the larger organizational context of which it is a part. Thus the administrative system — like the organizational, computer, machine, or whatever kind of system — is concerned with the processing of inputs into outputs. As such, the system is governed by, and can be conceptualized in terms of, the systems notions that are relevant to all open systems.

Likewise, *the administrative system is in actuality a subsystem of a larger organizational system and is a suprasystem to subadministrative systems.* For example, subadministrative systems in most school systems would typically include the following definable groups: elementary school administration, secondary school administration, and central office administration. As is true of all open systems, administrative systems have both sub- and suprasystems. *Therefore, administration does not exist in isolation; rather it is functionally related and necessarily contributory to a larger context (system), the school district.* It is an entity made up of components (subsystems), each of which may be more or less effective and contributing to basic, overall system purpose. System action (of an administrative system) is both a function of subsystem performance and a function to a suprasystem.

The administrative system is, further, an *open* system that exchanges matter and energy with its environment and other relevant systems in its environment. In processing inputs, the administrative system draws and capitalizes on its environment (e.g., replacement members are sought from the teaching ranks or from other school organizational systems) and its outputs affect the environment (e.g., administrative policy and action in schools impinges on teachers, students, and parents alike). Therefore, the administrative system is a *performance system*[2] that is inextricably and functionally related to larger contexts (the total organization and the environment). *It is, in essence, an "exchange" system that processes wanted goods and services.*

But, as is true with all systems, the administrative performance system is subject to certain system forces that either facilitate, or mitigate against, its effects. Illustrative here (from systems concepts) are the tendencies of systems toward progressive segregation and progressive mechanization. Obviously the ability of any system to regularize a division of labor (segregation) and the processing of work (mechanization) can serve to enhance system action and production. However, such regularization can become seriously dysfunctional. If a system uses only "regularized" structures and mechanisms to process work, and does not consciously modify these as time and circumstances dictate, then the system tends toward closure and the lessening of its "open" qualities. It is then "less" healthy. The ultimate effect in this direction is the loss of the real viability of the open system — dynamism — and an increasing uselessness of the system to its clients (e.g., students) and environment. Witness only the problems that so often accrue from an increasingly large number of rules and regulations.

It is to this end that systems such as administrative performance systems must be concerned with more than the processing of work, and concomitantly productivity, as the sole outcomes of system activity. As pointed out earlier, there are other categories of system outcomes: namely, integration, health, and feedback. For systems to remain open (dynamic) they must realize more than productivity per se. *Simply, an organizational system such as a school must stay together and function in a unified way (integration), must remain alive and viable (health), and must monitor, evaluate, and assess its actions (feedback) in order to continue to contribute.* Only as organizations are able to optimize this full range of outcomes can they maximize their basic contributions to their clients (students) and environment.

This brings us to another important contribution of systems thought which runs contrary to more popular beliefs such as the organismic approach. Inherent in the Gestalt point of view and many popular organismic conceptions is the concept of "supersummation." Supersummation is a concept embracing the notion that the whole is greater than the sum of its parts. It is granted that a human being might be more than the sum of a skeleton, organs, skin enclosure, and so forth. However, it does not necessarily follow that, if a group of people or a faculty committee get together, their solution to a problem will be better than any solution an individual can formulate; or that by using a great quantity of resources (people, materials, and energy) the results will be enhanced. Everyone is aware of the failures of groups, the lack of creativity of some committees, and the waste of multitudes of resources when brought to bear on certain problems. *Thus, the systems notion that output may exceed input, be equivalent to it, or be less than input is often borne out by experience.* The lesson is, most pointedly, that output may be less or greater than input but usually approximates input in a somewhat lesser quantity. One cannot blindly hope to get *out* more than is put *into* system activity *unless* the system and its activity are consciously directed to maximizing output through a synergistic relationship of subsystems. One way to consciously do this (to maximize output) is to be aware of all categories of output and capitalize on them to enhance a single output category, such as production, when this is dictated in system action. However, systems theory, and experience, indicate that system optimization is neither necessarily inherent in purposive activity nor solely a matter of chance. More appropriately it is the consequence of conscious and rational planning.

Another important implication for administrative practice that emerges from a review of systems thought is that an objective consideration of resources is necessary in formulating system strategy and action. It is not only the nature and quantity of resources that is of concern (e.g., people, money, commitment, etc.), but also the potential value and impact of such resources. Since resources are, in a sense, the "grist for the mill" of system action, they are direct determinants of the quality of system outcomes. Relative to the perennial problem of educational administrators, that is the hiring of the last teacher before the fast-approaching opening date of school, the *qualitative* and quantitative aspects of resources (teaching candidates and orientation procedures) come to bear. Does the administrator accept the sole candidate for the job if this prospective teacher is undertrained, inexperienced, and obviously unable to cope with a classroom? Many administrators might be disposed to hire such a candidate. But if attention is paid appropriately to resources and their qualitative aspects, other solutions may well emerge. For example, there may be an available substitute teacher who could better be employed for a year or semester, or temporarily for a few weeks, until such time as an adequate search for a qualified candidate would yield more desirable results. In other words, *systems thinking draws attention to the fallacy of rationalizing away the qualitative and quantitative aspects of resources that are crucial to a system.*

Central to systems notions is the inherent loss of energy in all systems action. Whether the system is a machine such as an automobile engine or a human organization such as a school staff, there is some loss of energy through system activity. Obviously, just as gears in a machine wear out, people in an organization get tired out. Systems, even open systems, are not infinitely enduring entities. They are, rather, subject to wear and tear, to abuse, and to nonpurposive action. Thus, school administrators can expect members of their school staff to "tire out" and also to engage in nonfunctional activity as well as to be abused by others as they go about their work. Attracting energy and resources, maintaining and directing them wisely, and retooling and rejuvenating them when necessary are crucial challenges confronting any administrator.

Systems thought also emphasizes the importance of evaluation or the monitoring and controlling of the system and its activities. *Feedback is a central concept in all open system conceptualizations. Only as a system such as the school is able to assess its activity and output can it effectively modify and redirect its efforts in more meaningful ways.* In this way appropriate system controls can be effected for channeling system action toward the accomplishment of goals. Feedback enables a system to profit maximally from past experience and to capitalize on such experience in charting future action. These monitor and control mechanisms do not necessarily limit system action but rather set appropriate boundaries for action and help the system to avoid pitfalls and impediments revealed in past action. Schools constantly need to evaluate their effects and project future action accordingly. In this sense, control is not so much a restriction as it is a guide to future purposive, goal-directed activity.

Projecting this notion further, schools, like all open systems, need to establish "governing" or "homeostatic" mechanisms. *Homeostatic balance or regulation is a key systems concept and refers to the procedure by which systems adjust to impingements and recover from a normal range of strains and stresses.* To illustrate, grievance procedures currently represent an important homeostatic mechanism in school organizations. As teacher demands for increases in salaries and improved working conditions are brought to bear on school boards and administrators, formalized grievance procedures serve to keep the actions and reactions of employee and employer in balance. Through this homeostatic mechanism differences are resolved and system efforts (of teachers and administrators) are coordinated for action toward basic organizational goals. School policy along with rules and regulations also represent homeostatic "controls" for certain of the impingements and strains that confront schools.

As indicated earlier, information and communications are crucial aspects of system functioning. Implications of communications and information flow, structures, and overload abound in the systems literature. In a classic article, Miller[3] draws attention to problems of information overload. His concept "7+ or −2" points out the fallacies of long lists of announcements at faculty meetings or extensive, detailed rules governing the behavior of teachers. *Similarly, other systems ideas point to the need for a communications structure that (1) maximally permits the exchange of necessary information in an organization, and (2) provides for information flow in all directions − up, down, and horizontally.* The implications for the educational administrator here extend beyond the school organization itself to the school-community context as well.

Lastly, systems concepts indicate that although open systems can achieve increasing openness (dynamism), they still tend toward entropy, a state of disorder, or ultimately, death. *Thus, if an open system does not consciously seek a dynamic existence, if it is left to the natural tendency of all systems, it will become increasingly useless.* Although schools with their captive clientele (public education for all youth) probably would never achieve a true entropic state, they can nonetheless resort to minimally contributing states. It is important, then, that schools seek to keep their purposes, plans, and programs viable and in tune with the dynamics of an ever-changing society. School objectives and curricula must be constantly reviewed and modified accordingly if education is to achieve its purposes. Should the relationship of the school and its environment be left to chance, the school would tend to contribute less and less. Only through attention can the school as an open system continually ensure its evolution and development as a dynamic entity.

These, then, are some relevant implications of systems concepts for the practice of educational administration. As indicated in the introductory chapter, this heuristic mode of thought or approach to practice has also spawned a number of specific notions, devices, and procedures of an essentially practical or applied nature; notions (etc.) that have most direct relevance for administrative practice. In the final chapters some of these tools, or the application of systems approaches in the administration of education, will be the subject of attention.

NOTES

1. J. G. Miller, "Towards a General Theory for the Behavioral Sciences," *Am. Psychol., 10,* No. 3 (July 1959), pp. 527-528.

2. A concept well articulated by L. E. McCleary and S. P. Hencley, *Secondary School Administration.* New York: Dodd, Mead, 1965, pp. 94-102.

3. J. G. Miller, "The Magic Number—Seven Plus or Minus Two," *Psychol. Rev., 63* (1956), pp. 81-97.

Part III / Toward the application of systems approaches in education

Chapter 7 / The concept of
the administrative support system

A salient feature of virtually all organizations today is growth. Whether one is looking at educational, industrial, political, civic, or religious organizations of either voluntary of involuntary nature, current organizations reveal the presses and effects of organizational growth. Growth, whether in size, expanded programs, increased developmental activities, or a combination of these, places attendant problems on all aspects of an organization. (This is really a basic systems notion: Any change in any part of a system affects the system as a whole and all of its components.) One aspect of an organization which is vitally affected by growth is the organization's administration, which in function can be likened to the nervous system in a living organism. If this analogy can be drawn—and the planning, control, communication, decision-making, and evaluative functions of organizational administration all attest to its validity—then in all growing or developing organizations attention must be given to administration, its structure and function.

Anyone connected with school systems today is well aware of the growth in these organizations, whether this growth results from more pupils, improved curricular offerings, expanded programs of studies, state mandated programs for exceptional students, or just plain trying to do a better job. Also, anyone familiar with the task of administering an educational organization is aware of the effects of these kinds of growth or development on administration. Schools, already the *largest* organizations in many communities, are also, in many communities, among the *fastest growing* organizations. Although some today are prone to criticize administration or blame bureaucracy (and, of course, administration) for the ills of the organization, it is possible that administration is, in fact, merely a most visible and overworked scapegoat. It has been noted earlier (Chapter 1) that administrators are often entangled in a web of "brushfires." This may or may not be of their own doing, but in either case the systems movement can facilitate the educational administrator's job—hopefully in such a way that the administrator can focus on the more substantive situations and impingements, such as the effects of organizational size and growth, that confront him.

The systems movement provides the administrator with a perspective for viewing his task, organization, and problems that is helpful in and of itself. Certain conceptual and theoretical frameworks have been set forth in the preceding chapters and also some specific contributions which are generally denoted as *administrative support systems* have been identified. The latter can facilitate the administrator's job but before looking in more detail at examples of administrative support procedures or devices, the effects of organizational growth and development on administration ought first be considered in order to establish the growing need for administrative support. Then the concept of the *administrative support system* can be more precisely developed. This is at the heart of alleviating administrative problems in organizations; it provides a practical framework and approach to conceiving administrative structure and functions for facilitating the practice of administration. Additionally, the administrative support system concept will be illustrated relative to the school administrative organization, and ways will be suggested in which this concept may be employed in school organizations.

THE EFFECT OF ORGANIZATIONAL
GROWTH ON ADMINISTRATION

For some time now, organizational theorists have observed the developmental stages of the organization just as the child psychologists have analyzed the developmental stages of the growing child. Until recently, however, little was done to translate the meaning of the developmental maturation of the organization into practical considerations that could serve as a basis for improving the organization. Earlier descriptive approaches revealed how things were, and, at best, suggested implications for "organizational leadership." However, little attempt was made to relate organizational growth to more tangible and meaningful matters such as organizational communications, employee morale, improving operations, or to administrative structure and function.

Recently, however, some organizational theorists have sought explicitly to identify the effects of organizational growth on administration. Haire, for example, has pointed out that organizations cannot and do not grow in a simple linear or additive fashion.[1] He cogently advances the relevance of the Square-Cube Law from geometry for considering the effects of growth and development in organizations. When applied to organizations, this law suggests that *as the mass of an organization grows, the structure supporting that mass is subjected to increasing strain.* Unless the supporting structure of the organization is maintained in terms of the degree and amount of support the growing mass requires, the organization is in trouble and may ultimately collapse. If the "mass" in an educational organization is pupils and teachers as well as school program operations and the supporting "structure" is administration (including allied procedures and supportive personnel), then this structure—administration, its personnel and procedures—must be continually and consciously designed to support the mass (pupils and teachers and attendant operations).

Haire further notes, in applying the logic of the Square-Cube Law, that *mass increases as a cubic function while structure increases as a square.* Therefore, if mass triples while structure doubles, structural development lags and will progressively fail to keep pace with the support required by the mass. Many prevalent administrative staffing philosophies which dictate that new administrators should be added sparingly as an organization grows are consonant with this structural lag notion.[2] Or if, even as is common in some educational organizations, mass and structure (or administration) grow in a linear fashion, there is still the question as to whether the structure in such a case is adequate for the mass it is intended to support. For example, it is commonly assumed that when a 600 pupil school with 20 teachers and *one* administrator grows to a 1200 pupil school with 40 teachers it would have roughly *two* administrators. Such growth indicates a fixation on a constant structure-mass ratio with little real attention to the structural requirements for a growing organizational mass.

This, however, is contrary to Haire's notion that the supporting structure *must* increase proportionately in terms of the mass it is to support. Haire bases his conclusion on findings from the study of industrial organizations. His idea is further supported by data from a parallel study of the growth of a school district over a 60 year period.[3] In this study it was found that, in one particular educational organization, "structure" (that is, administrative and allied supporting personnel) grew at an uneven (*and* less than linear) rate in comparison to the organizational "mass." This study revealed that "structure," or structural elements, typically lagged, then showed a rapid growth spurt, lagged again, spurted, and so on, but *increasingly fell behind the linear growth of "mass"* (defined as numbers of teachers and pupils). The common assumption that fewer administrators are required as school organizations grow was revealed in this study. However, some facts of life that are common knowledge to most who administer schools argue in the opposite direction: *the larger the organization, the proportionately greater the structure (administrative and service or support personnel) needed to support it.*

In looking at Parkinson's notion (that there is a pressure and necessity to increase supervision at a rate faster than an organization is growing), Griffiths and Davies indicate that supervisory (support) services seem to be spread thinner as organizations grow in size.[4] These authors point out that, at worst, educational organizations should keep a constant ratio between supervisory staff and district size, and that *at best they should seek to add proportionately more supervisory personnel as they grow* "both because the organization becomes more complex, and because education stands a better chance of improving with more adequate supervision."

The demands on supporting structure—administration and allied personnel—change markedly as organizations grow and develop. In this regard Lippitt and Schmidt[5] note that early in the life of an organization the task of administration is one of "development" and "getting started." Risks here are relatively few, and administrative energies need be expended primarily in terms of getting the organization moving. As the organization grows, however, the administrative task becomes more complex. Questions of how to organize, how to evaluate, how to stabilize, and other similar matters *must be* considered. More risk is then encountered and greater effort and energy are required of administration. As organizations reach maturity the task is even more difficult; organizational administration must *also,* in addition to ongoing concerns such as the above, consider and contend with matters of organizational reputation, pride, uniqueness, adaptability, and societal contribution and demands. Obviously, increasing *and* additive demands are placed on administration as the organization grows and develops.

Therefore, as the organization grows, not only must administration see that the organization continues to operate, but also it must:

1. Face increasing challenges relating to control, coordination, and articulation;

2. Cope with a greater challenge in the organizational maintenance area (e.g., holding the organization together and keeping it moving);

3. Provide a structure capable of handling a larger range of communication, decision-making, and morale problems;

4. Perform an increasing number of tasks, functions, and services (staffing, negotiating, planning, program development, and budgeting); and

5. Deal with the demands for adaptation and change from the environment outside, and from within the organization, as well as from growth itself.

Organizational growth does indeed increase the task of, and demands on, administration, and it does make the administrative task more tenuous. This has magnified the need to find ways to facilitate the administration of growing, complex social organizations like schools. The *administrative support system* concept which draws both conceptually and practically on the systems movement offers one approach toward relieving the pressures of organization growth and development.

THE ADMINISTRATIVE SUPPORT SYSTEM CONCEPT

There is nothing magical or new in the concept of the *administrative support system.* It is not a cure-all for administrative problems and represents actually a refinement of the notions underlying the old line-staff concept replete in the organizational literature. The terminology comes from the systems movement, and from the label "management support system" that is used to categorically embrace a number of systems devices and procedures used in the operations research and systems analysis tradition. In this sense, administrative support system(s) has been chosen over management support system(s) in that the former is more general and is not restricted by any connotation to the purely quantitative approaches or "service to management alone" that can be attributed by some to certain of the management support system notions. Actually, "administrative support system" avoids the quantitative, mechanistic, and restricted bias of the other terminology and enables us to look more broadly at man, machine, and man-machine systems that support both organizational administration itself and organizational operations. (The latter point, the administrative support of operations, is important as well as consistent with our discussion of organizational growth. Administration not only directs, coordinates, and controls operations but also supports operations in many ways, such as through exercising supervision, providing resources, making decisions, planning, and providing for employee and client welfare.)

An administrative support system can be defined as any subunit of an organization (albeit human, machine, procedural, functional, or any combination of these) that facilitates, assists, provides resources, or otherwise *serves* line administrators *and* operational personnel. Put another way, operationally for educational organizations:

> An administrative support system is any subunit of a school district organization (albeit human, machine, procedural, functional, or a combination of these) that facilitates, assists, provides resources, or otherwise serves (a) line administrators such as the superintendent, assistant superintendent(s), and principals, and (b) operational personnel such as the teachers.

The administrative support system thus can be differentiated from the line administrative system which directs the school organization and its personnel, and from the operational system (e.g., teachers and counselors) which does the work of the schools—instructing and working with children or students. It is recognized that all organizational personnel, in fact, have some line, service, and operational functions. For example, the superintendent, who is primarily a line administrative officer, also has some service or support functions and does some organizational work (operations). And the teacher, basically one who does organizational work (operations), likewise has service or support functions to other teaching personnel and, at least, line authority over students. These three dimensions are then relative for any member of the school organization, but the line, service, and operational position emphases of all organizational jobs can be differentiated.

To illustrate this, if we look at administrative jobs as those which direct activities and view operational jobs as those which do work, but also realize each has some aspects of the other, the superintendent's and teacher's jobs in a typical school organization can be differentiated as in Fig. 7.1. Further, the line and support services aspects of administrative positions can as well be differentiated for two typical administrative positions in school organizations, as seen in Fig. 7.2.

Such clarifications are more helpful than the traditional line-staff dichotomy which casts line administrators in authority relationships and staff administrators in supervisory relationships and which, in fact, ignores operations except in implicit terms of subservience. In the past, staff or

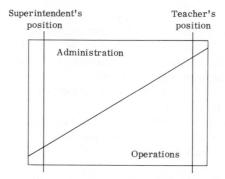

Fig. 7.1 Relative administration-operation aspects of two positions in a school organization.

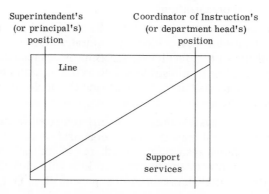

Fig. 7.2 Relative line-support services aspects of two administrative positions in a school organization.

supervisory positions were also either vague or fuzzy in conception, or too authoritative in practice. It seems more reasonable at the present time to view organizational positions relative to each other and in the light of major functional emphases, rather than as absolutes or fuzzy attempts at differentiation (e.g., the line position of director and the staff position of supervisor). Fig. 7.3 illustrates several typical educational organization positions in the three-dimensional space of the line authority, operations, and support services functions.

Along with the notion of administrative support systems is the corresponding idea that personnel in such systems or positions work from a base of competency rather than authority. Thus, if the coordinator of audiovisual services for a school district is the head of the administrative support system that facilitates teaching by providing technological and media support, when he works with teachers he will influence them by his competence and the in-

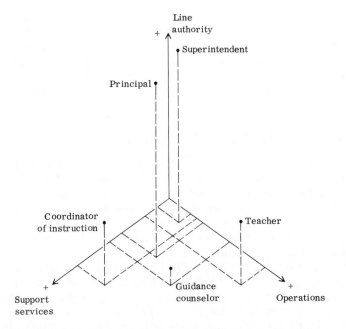

Fig. 7.3 Relative location of typical education organization positions according to three job dimensions.

herent worth of his ideas or techniques, instead of by telling them what to do or how to do it. The coordinator's basis of influence and license to invoke action would be his skills and competencies, his ability to work with people, and the relevance of his ideas and approaches for teaching. Knowing what we do about morale, how to bring about change, and how to work with people, this competence or "clinician" approach is superior to the authoritative, dictatorial, or laissez-faire approaches of staff supervisors or coordinators who, in the past, used authority of position or status to put teeth into their admonitions or did little to effect change.

Administrative support services are, then, what the definition implies—they are not authoritative directives or hazy supervisory suggestions. Rather, they are supportive services of a broad range, from people with specialized information to techniques such as computer programs, that facilitate organizational work and direction.

Finally, we should underscore the notion that administrative support systems function in a service capacity to line administration, operations, *and* other administrative support systems as well. To illustrate, the pupil personnel support system might be used as an example. This typical administrative support system in a school organization has many functions, one of which is pupil or student accounting. Data produced and organized by this support system are also used by line administrators to project district building needs, by other administrative support systems such as that of business management in projecting budget expenditures, and by operational personnel such as teachers in planning and developing district and classroom curricula. In other words, *administrative support systems serve the entire organization, horizontally as well as vertically; their service is based solely on the criteria of relevance and assistance potential.*

ADMINISTRATIVE SUPPORT IN AN ORGANIZATION

We have thus far talked only generally of the concept of the administrative support system in the educational organization. Our discussion has been focused toward clarifying the line-authority, support-service, and operations aspects of organizational positions and to indicate how the administrative support services concept in this scheme eliminates some of the confusion surrounding the older line-staff concept and contributes to the task of administering an educational organization.

In practice there are, even in the smallest of organizations, many administrative support systems, or, probably more accurately, administrative support *sub*systems. In order to avoid semantic confusion and the complexity of sub- and supra-system terminology, we will term any administrative support service subunit, no matter how small or large, simply an administrative support system. Since any bounded definable entity is a system in and of itself, and since all administrative support systems function as entities in and out of themselves, they are systems in the true sense of the word.

As indicated in our definition of a support system, administrative support systems exist in a variety of forms. In the management support system tradition of operations research or systems analysis, PERT (program evaluation and review technique), a computer accounting system for school district pupil attendance, or a linear program to allocate custodial or maintenance crews throughout a school district over the summer months are, of course, administrative support systems. But by our definition, people such as the reading specialist, the instructional coordinator, the primary grade level resource teacher, or the data processing specialist can also be conceived of as administrative support systems. And so may procedures, such as PPBS (the planning program budgeting system) for district planning and budgeting; man-machine combinations, such as a testing specialist and the computer for analyzing pupil achievement test results; even functions, such as negotiations procedures for teacher contractual conditions, or research design assistance for teachers applying for Federal or State funding of special developmental projects—all can be viewed as administrative support systems. Also, major divisions of the school organization, such as the business management division, the staff personnel office, or the audiovisual center, can be thought of as administrative support systems. In fact, by construing all human, machine, procedural, functional, or unit activities other than line administration and operations as administrative support systems, the relative focus and emphases of these other aspects of the school organization are clarified, particularly regarding their internal organizational functioning. Such a conception is in tune with modern organization thought and practice.

There are in the school organization, then, the following definable kinds of administrative support systems:

1. The task area or service area administrative support system (a major division or subunit in the organization).

2. The human administrative support system (the incumbent of a particular position in the organization).

3. The machine administrative support system (a technological vehicle for performing service tasks or support activities).

4. The man-machine administrative support system (a combination of human and machine components).

5. The functional-administrative support system (a general set of duties or responsibilities for a general organization process or task).

6. The procedural-administrative support system (a process or set of techniques devised to solve a specific problem or category of problems).

Examples of each of these kinds of administrative support systems as found in typical school organizations can be identified as follows:

Administrative Support System	Examples
Task or Service area	The Division of Business Affairs, The Pupil Personnel Office, The Staff Personnel Division, The Audiovisual Center, The Office of Pupil Accounting, etc.
Human	Coordinator of Instruction, Fine Arts Coordinator, Remedial Reading Specialist, Manager of Cafeterias, Supervisor of Building and Grounds, etc.
Machine	Computer, Card sorter, Calculator, etc.
Man-machine	Records retrieval systems, Data processing, Test scoring and analysis, etc.
Functional	Planning, Personnel records, Communication, Policy and rules and regulations, Decision-making, Negotiating, Liaison with state department, Evaluation, etc.
Procedural	PPBS, PERT, Maintenance deployment, Transportation scheduling, Inventory control, Purchasing, etc.

Obviously the above categories overlap and intertwine (in fact, some of the examples, depending on how they are implemented, might change categories), and so this categorization scheme and the illustrations of administrative support systems in education are necessarily arbitrary and somewhat forced. This does, though, reveal the scope of such support services, the range of the various forms they might take, and their complexity in any large organization such as a school or school district. However, complexity in scope and form, as well as the attendant problems of meshing supporting services and avoiding duplication and segmentation, *underscores the necessity for an organization to be cognizant of its support service requirements, and, in the systems perspective, to view and design administrative support for the organization as a total entity.* Further, the full range of potential support systems from the human to machine, the quantitative to qualitative, the comprehensive to the delimited, all should be assessed for their relevance and potential contribution. The potential of the systems movement for educational administration is great in this regard.

TOWARD A MACRO—CONCEPTION OF ADMINISTRATIVE SUPPORT SYSTEMS FOR SCHOOL ORGANIZATIONS

The complexity of administrative support systems for the large organization reduces the possibility that these aspects of an organization can be graphically represented in a single chart or model to pictorially portray an organizational support service scheme. However, through some illustrations we can more graphically represent this concept for a typical school system. To do this we will look at the total administrative support system in terms of a typical "organization chart" and in terms of a systems support services model.[6] Then, in the next section of this chapter, we can turn to the discussion of one particular support system.

Since most administrators are familiar with the classic (or common) organizational chart this is a good place to begin with the support system concept. All are, of course, aware of the organization chart pathology—that is, that organizations just *do not* behave as they appear on paper. On the other hand, it is not always possible to determine whether this is because of the chart, a given group of people, or a combination of these and other factors. Although the organization chart does not solve all of the problems of organization, it is a good place to start in designing an organization. In addition, any such chart can indicate the configuration of an organization, the intended flow of authority, the respective spheres of decision responsibility, and the organizational division of labor. Also, the organization chart can graphically differentiate positions in terms of the three component dimensions discussed earlier (line authority, support service responsibility, and operations). Figure 7.4 is a typical organization chart for a suburban school district today. This chart is based on sound principles of staff organization and sets forth the line, service, and operational aspects of a school district staff. For example, the organization is "flat" and avoids overlapping jurisdictions. It accounts for individual and group (council or advisory committee) activities. And the administrative support systems in the form of divisions, positions and functions are explicit.

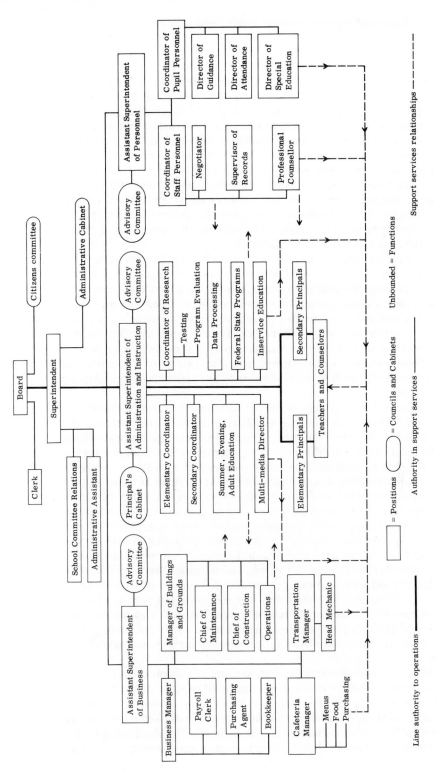

Figure 7.4

Line authority to operations ——————

Authority in support services ——————

Support services relationships — — — —

▢ = Positions ◯ = Councils and Cabinets Unbounded = Functions

In the organization chart shown in Fig. 7.4 each assistant superintendent heads a major support services division (which is an administrative support system) and under each are several definable administrative support systems in and of themselves. Only the assistant superintendent for administration and instruction, however, has line authority over principals and teachers. Of course, none of the other personnel in his administrative support system of instruction or administration have line authority over principals or teachers since they function in a support service capacity. In this way, the line authority and operations (connected by the heavy lines) are differentiated from the administrative support system aspects of the organization. The administrative support systems are, in effect, free to *serve* the organization, as opposed to directing or muddling its operations.

This somewhat traditional way of viewing the administrative structure of a school organization and its administrative support aspects can be clarified further through the use of a systems model. In a "systems" conceptualization of a school organization the organization can be subdivided into two basic kinds of systems. The first of these is the *criterion* system (or systems) —that is, the system or systems where work is done, such as in the instructional system in a school. The second category of systems is the *support* systems—those subunits of the organization which support or facilitate the work of the criterion system or systems, such as curricular or materials systems in schools.

The basic criterion system in the educational organization is the *instructional* system. This system includes teachers, guidance personnel, and all others who work directly in an instructional or developmental way with students. There are other possible criterion systems in the school organization since other kinds of work are done also, such as administration, program development, or purpose and policy determination. But, since these all (in a real sense) support, serve, or facilitate the criterion system, they can equally well be considered in the systems sense as support systems. Regardless of where one puts such activities, a systems model can be generated that views the criterion system (direct work—instruction) and its related support systems. In such a scheme, personnel, fiscal, business, facility, audiovisual, transportation, cafeteria, data processing, and all other "services" are support systems. And such support systems function in one of two ways: they contribute directly to instruction—e.g., the hiring of personnel, purchasing of supplies, or services to teachers (supervisory) or to children (health)—or they facilitate the other support service systems. Figure 7.5 is a systems model for administrative support services for a typical school organization.

In the administrative support system sense of this model it can be seen that certain administrative support systems directly serve instructional activity, such as is the case with the staff personnel, fiscal affairs, or administration support systems. In addition all such systems can likewise be broken down or subdivided into subsystems. For example, the fiscal affairs support system can be broken down into accounting, purchasing, and payments

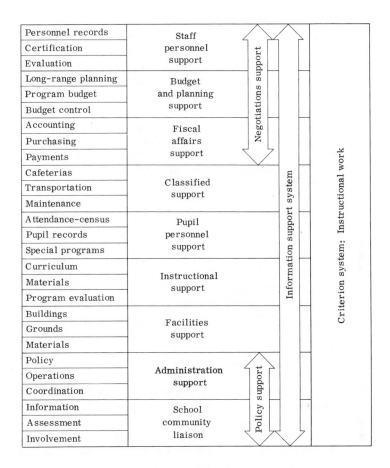

Fig. 7.5 A systems model of administrative support systems.

subsystems, or the pupil personnel subsystem can be subdivided into attendance-census, pupil records, and special programs subsystems. Other administrative support systems such as the information, policy, or negotiations support systems function directly toward some or all of the support systems themselves and relatively indirectly to the criterion system, instruction.

Obviously, only imagination (and, ultimately, feasibility) limit the detail of a systems conception of administrative support in the organization. There are an infinite number of ways in which support systems can be conceived and structured, and an equally infinite number of ways they can be operationally subdivided into workable subsystems. The illustrations thus far have been indicative and generic. To make the administrative support system most relevant in real organizations, detailed attention must be given to each support system and its components (subsystems, people, machines, procedures, and functions). Before discussing in greater detail a single support system and finally the design of administrative support systems, an important concept in the macro-conception of administrative support systems —that of *interfacing*—should be noted.

Since administrative support systems are, as observed earlier, actually subsystems in a larger (organizational) system, they are linked, related, and meshed (in an operational sense) in many ways. The points of tangency between support systems, along with their linkage and effect on each other, are called *interfaces.* As systems thinking points out, all systems are composed of interrelated parts and the quality of system action is contingent on the *functional relationships* of these parts. Thus the interconnections or "relatedness"—interfacing—of administrative support systems is an important consideration in their design, implementation, and operation. To avoid duplicative efforts, to ensure that everything that needs to be done is done, and to link vital support aspects (of one support system to another) proper attention to support system interfacing is required. The interface concept applies also to the criterion system relative to its support systems, and a continuing and contributing exchange between all of the definable subsystems is needed in any total organizational system.

A MICRO—CONCEPTION OF ONE ADMINISTRATIVE SUPPORT SYSTEM: THE INFORMATION SYSTEM

Few administrators have ever been in the position where they have had too much information, although too much *irrelevant* information is a luxury the administrator often enjoys. However, the need for relevant information is quite common—in order to respond to the questions of clients or constituents, to reduce ambiguity about a problem, to facilitate making a decision, to aid in planning or forecasting, or even just to satisfy curiosity. Information—in the form of data or hard facts—is most important to the educational administrator regardless of whether he is preparing next year's budget, filling out a state report, considering a disciplinary action, or developing a recommendation for curriculum change.

Possibly the first definable support system required in any organization, by either accident or design, is the *information support system.* In fact, few organizations of any size or complexity exist without an information system of some kind. The information system in a simple but conscious sense predates the "systems movement" by several decades. Whether it be the random personal files of the administrator, the personnel folders of teachers, the accounting registers of the business office, the budget request forms used in building the budget, or the cumulative folders of students, schools have long had information systems. Although the typical information system in most schools (or organizations) is somewhat less sophisticated and functional than the systematically and consciously designed information support system of the systems movement tradition, these have, in fact, served good and valid purposes. All organizations have information needs and develop ways to fulfill these needs. At a general level these are information systems. An organizational information system is simply an organization's arrangements for facilitating functional communications or data and information exchange.

The school organizational information needs are extensive. A complete listing of such needs would exceed the capacity of this chapter, but we can identify some of them to illustrate the range, nature, and scope of the information requirements in an educational organization. Boards of education, for example, need information about the kind of educational program their community wants, the willingness of people to pay school taxes, the performance and effectiveness of school personnel, the achievement of (or effect of the educational program on) pupils, the available revenues for supporting the school, the state mandates regarding the schools, and so forth. Administrators need such information as the relative achievement levels of pupils, the needs of teachers for supplies and help, the attendance of students and staff, the census data and enrollment projections for class planning, the research on educational methodology, the viability of new and innovative practices in education, and so forth. Teachers likewise need information about their pupils, about the school policies and curriculum, about new methods and procedures, about psychological and aptitude testing of students, about individual student progress, about parental feelings about the children in the teacher's class, about teaching materials, and so on. In all, the information needs in most educational organizations are indeed encyclopedic!

The information support system, then, is the conscious and planned system comprised of people, machines, procedures, and data which is designed to fulfill the information requirements of an organization, It is a support system in that while work is done in this regard, the prime focus of the information system is service and support to other organizational or work systems. It is, further, both a basic and complex support system—the former because information is a fundamental necessity in doing so much of the work in an educational organization; the latter because of all of the conceivable support systems this one interfaces with virtually all of the other components (support systems as well as the criterion system) in an organization like the school district. In temporal proximity and priority, the information support system is of prime importance.

An information support system consists of a number of components. It has *people* (administrators, clerks, technicians), *machines* (typewriters, telephones, card sorters, computers), *materials* (files, filing supplies, data cards, memo forms), *procedures* (keypunching, recording, collating) and *data* (about staff, students, buildings, and finances).

The complete, modern information system, cutting the pie another way, may be in part automated, partially automated, and nonautomated (hand operation as opposed to machine). But regardless of the arrangement, extent, or range (automated vs. nonautomated) of its components, the information support system ideally serves three basic functions: [7]

1. Transactions
2. Control
3. Planning

Although these functions were used to classify automated information processing by their conceivers, the categories apply equally well to partially automated or nonautomated systems or aspects of systems. They are applicable to the full range of information support activities.

In this sense, *transactions* can be conceived as operations such as record keeping, payroll preparation, bill paying, test scoring, or other routine business or processing functions. *Control* functions of the information system are those that ensure that other systems are operating properly and within appropriate bounds. Posting operations (inventory and requisition), accounting, calculating test performance norms, and similar operations illustrate "control functions." The *planning* function fulfilled by the information system, regarded by many as the system's most important function, is realized (1) through the availability and compilation of data necessary for long range projections of building or space needs and pupil population projections, and (2) through the techniques of simulation and modeling, possible only with the use of computer speed and facility, for analyses of transportation or student program scheduling.

From another perspective the information support system embraces several distinct operational phases. First, relevant or useful information is *selected* for processing or storage in the system. Once selected, the information is *codified* for purposes of the system (e.g., recorded verbatim on a cumulative folder, reduced to a symbol system such as report card grades, or keypunched onto IBM cards). Next the data are *stored* on an appropriate record medium in an appropriate place such as a file folder in a filing cabinet, a computer tape in a tape rack, a microfilm in a film file, or on cards in a card file. Some data are then programmed into analysis operations (collation, reduction, and/or synthesis) of continuous or periodic nature. Finally, data are re-called, "unstored," through the employment of a *retrieval* scheme. whereby relevant, requested information is made available for whatever use a support subsystem or the criterion system intends. Sophisticated information systems also have self-monitoring or *evaluation* devices and a *removal* capacity for ridding themselves of outdated data.

In building an information support system, an organization must first identify its information needs or requirements and then design a system with components, functions, and appropriate operational procedures in order to provide the precise kinds of data or information required at the time they are needed. An overview of the process of support system design and a brief example will help to illustrate this. The reader interested in looking further into the nature and function of the information system is referred to the Winter 1968 issue of the *SDC Magazine* (System Development Corporation) for a discussion of three case studies.[8]

DESIGNING AN ADMINISTRATIVE SUPPORT SYSTEM

A number of guidelines, procedures, and approaches for use in implementing the support system concept have resulted from systems analysis approaches to practical orgnizational problems. There is general agreement on the overall approach to support system design and guidelines for organizations desiring to develop systematic support components. However, precise steps in the process vary somewhat in overall practice and also relative to the nature and kind of support system under consideration. Thus we cannot describe a process or series of steps universally applicable to support system design and implementation. We can, however, discuss generally a strategy for the development of a support system, indicate more specifically the precise steps involved in the design of one particular support system, and then provide an example of an information system. In this regard the design of an information support system can appropriately be used for illustrative purposes since it is a most crucial support system in any organization, and since such a discussion will further help to describe it.

An important consideration in the development of any support system is that the design of such systems should be a cooperative process in the organizational context. That is, people need to be involved—both those in the organization and external "experts." Those within the organization include, first of all, anyone who will be a part of the support system. Also, all "clients" of the support system's service, appropriate administrative personnel, and allied personnel within the organization should be involved. "Clients," as used here, refers to people in the organization who use or profit from the system's service, such as administrators, teachers, or personnel from other support systems themselves. In another sense, organizational employees whose work interfaces in any way with the support system being designed can and should be involved in the systems' design. As Goer has noted relative to the information system, it is important

> . . . to give central consideration to the human components and the way they relate to each other. You don't limit the scope of your attention to pieces of paper and reports without thinking of people and how they interface.[9]

In addition to the involvement of organization members, support system design calls for certain kinds of *expertise* which is seldom found in the school organization. External competence must be sought, particularly in regard to the systems approach itself and the special nature of the support system under consideration. For example, in designing an information support system for a school district, a systems analyst, an information analyst, a communications engineer, a data processing specialist, and a records system expert might be employed to help the district's staff. Or, in developing a business affairs support system, a systems analyst, an accountant, an economist, a data processing specialist, and a business procedures analyst might be used in system design and development. In any event, just as systems theory is inherently interdisciplinary, so the systems approach, whether in research or in solving practical provlems, draws on competence and expertise from all relevant fields or disciplines, as well as the people of the organization itself.

Also a vital part of the strategy of support system design is the notion that support systems need to be based on knowledge of the organization, its structure and procedures. Here, since the support system is actually a subsystem of the larger organization and is intimately and functionally related and relevant for the larger organizational system, it is important that the system be designed with adequate knowledge of the larger organization. And only by knowing the needs and requirements of the larger organization can adequate and contributing support systems be devised. Thus, in designing any support system it is important to look at the system being considered relative to the total organization and its potential contribution to the organization.

In support system design, relevant aspects of existing personnel, procedures, and function are all evaluated and considered for inclusion, modification, or revision relative to the support system being considered. All existing, related aspects of the organization are evaulated in addition to the total organization and ideal support system functioning. Put another way, in designing an information support system, existing information elements (e.g., personnel files, data processing records, or cumulative folders) are not discarded. Rather, their value and contribution are assessed in terms of both past and future consequences, and these components are built upon in designing more viable and functional information support and service for the future.

Finally, in designing support systems, the emphasis is on the *functional* nature of such systems. The system is not viewed as an entity in and of itself but instead is seen as a contributing component of the larger organization. In designing an information system, for example, the ideals of the information system *qua* system or of information handling per se are, in fact, secondary to the function of such a system for the organization of which it is a part. Functional aspects of system performance are primary concerns in support system design.

The above guidelines, procedures, and approach strategy are generally applicable in the development of organizational support systems. To look in more detail at the overall matter of support system design.we can now turn to the steps in the design of an information support system. The following nine steps, in chronological order, indicate the major categories of activity for an organization such as a school district wishing to design an information support system.

1. *Analyze organizational information needs and requirements.* First, a detailed analysis of who needs what information, when, how, and why should be determined for the total organization and each of its definable subunits (e.g., offices, officers, support systems, school buildings, individual teachers, etc.). Included in this analysis would be the determination of: (1) what is adequate information, (2) whether it is needed in a raw form or must

be collated or analyzed, and (3) the relative importance or priority of informational needs.

2. *Review existing information support.* Next, a functional review and evaluation of all existing organizational information and information services should be undertaken. Such a review would hopefully establish the effectiveness and potential of "givens" for use in designing an optimal, comprehensive information support system.

3. *Develop criteria and standards for information support system design and evaluation.* After assessing information needs and existing services, and thereby determining information support system goals and priorities, specific criteria or performance specifications for the support system should be formulated. These criteria or standards for the support system function in subsequent design steps and later in support system performance evaluation. Part of this activity involves defining what is included in the information support system and setting forth system exclusions (what is not a part of the support system). Here the linkage or interfacing with all other organizational subsystems also receives consideration.

4. *Plan and design alternative systems.* Once system performance criteria and inclusions and exclusions are determined, several alternative support systems can be developed and modeled. These alternatives should be worked out in specific and operational terms, and subjected to both cost and feasibility·analysis.

5. *Test functional consequences and operational consequences of each alternative.* After alternative solutions (systems) are developed and modeled, their relative payoffs or outputs (functional results) and operational consequences for the organization need to be explored. In this phase, modeling, simulation, field testing, or expert *and* internal organizational review should be employed to determine what can be expected of each alternative. Testing then can be done for the total organization and for each of its subunits with attention to the interfacing of the alternatives with other support systems. Here nonproductive alternatives are eliminated from further consideration.

6. *Assess the workable alternatives in terms of min-max criteria.* Review of all alternatives in terms of the support system criteria and standards used in their design represents a final step before selecting the most desirable alternative for testing or implementation. Systems should be reviewed in terms of minimum and maximum performance specifications and in terms of their cumulative potential and shortcomings.

7. *Select the desired alternative and operationalize it in detail.* Whether for full-scale testing (if deemed appropriate) or implementation, the best support system design can then be selected and operationalized in detail. Here total organizational structure, personnel, procedures, and equipment must be considered along with how the plan will become operational (e.g., through testing, phasing in through several stages, or immediate, full implementation).

8. *Train personnel for testing or implementation.* It is obvious that for any organizational operation to be successful, personnel need orientation and training. This includes personnel within the support system, personnel in other linking or interfacing units, and all "users" of the system.

9. *Evaluate and review system performance.* Whether testing an information support system or implementing one, evaluation of the system at periodic intervals using the performance criteria established for the design of the system (in step 3 above) is necessary to ensure that the system is functioning as intended, that system performance is adequate, and that system revision or adaptation is not necessary. Due to the dynnamic qualities of growing, developing organizations, constant and conscious surveillance is needed to maintain functional relevancy and operational success.

To illustrate further we may look briefly at the budget item request procedure used annually in most school districts as a small but concrete information system. Although the process of making requests for supplies and materials by teachers is actually a subsystem of the larger budgeting system or the information system required for budgeting purposes, it can be, as is the case with all subsystems, conceived of as a system in and of itself. In the illustration, we may start from the common point of a school district's administrative staff typically reviewing its budget request forms prior to duplicating them for staff to use in building the next budget.

Assume that the superintendent, the business manager, and one or two principals feel it is time to take a hard look at the existing forms which require teachers to simply list items needed along with the price, quantity desired, and supplier on a mimeographed form. Also assume that the business office wishes to move to computerized processing of budget data in the next year and that several suggestions for improving the forms (e.g., putting textbooks on one form and consumable supplies on another or indicating priority relative to various requests) have been voiced over the years.

At this point the superintendent might well call on the services of a management specialist and a computer specialist to sit down with the district's administrators and assist in designing a budget request information system. At such a meeting, the objectives of the designed information system would be identified, the information needs would be specified, and procedures used in the past would be reviewed and analyzed. Together the members of the administrative staff and external specialists would design (using the above steps) an information system to meet the requirements for budget building in the district.

For example, in this process principals might express the need for teachers to justify or indicate why they are making their particular requests and to indicate the relative priority of their requests. The business official may indicate that some scheme is needed to differentiate between categories of requests such as textbooks, audiovisual supplies, equipment, and consumable materials. Also he may wish that use location and unit quantity be specified on the forms. The management specialist might indicate the need

Services Personnel	Textbooks	Supplies	Field trips	Equipment	Repairs and renovation	Miscellaneous

(Check one category)

Teacher_____ Location_____   Worksheet No._____
Year _____ Subject _____   Account No. _____

Justification:_____
_____
_____
_____

Short justification (for key punching):

A	B	C	D	E	F	G	H	I
Line No.	Prior. *	Rank order	Quan.	Unit	Description	Supplier (use code no.)	Unit cost	Total line cost
1.								
2.								
3.								
4.								
5.								
6.								

* Priority:
    1. Essential
    2. Desirable

Work sheet number by justification:

Page_____ of _____

Fig. 7.6 Budget worksheet.

for the use of NCR paper forms to avoid the problems of messy carbon copies that have plagued administrators in the past. The computer specialist might suggest the use of a supplier code number for use in computerizing the system, as well as the use of page and item line numbers for computer retrieval purposes. Together the group might arrive at a process for submitting, reviewing, and processing the forms that permit better feedback to teachers on the disposition of their requests.

As a result of the information systems design work on the budget request, a budget worksheet such as that in Fig. 7.6 might result. The worksheet (on

NCR paper) would be filled in by teachers, checked by department heads, and reviewed by the building principal. After the principal analyzed the requests and made necessary additions of deletions, the requests would be forwarded to the central office. Following initial screening and review, all data would be keypunched and printed out to facilitate, both in terms of speed and accuracy, the process of administrative and board-of-education analysis of modifications needed in the projected budget. At this point, copies of the budget request forms as keypunched would be returned to building principals and the teachers making the requests. When final budget decisions were made, a computer printout would be provided for all members of the administrative staff in order for them to know of the action taken relative to all budget requests.

Following implementation and use of the procedure, the system design group would reconvene to evaluate the system in terms of actual use relative to the objectives set for the system. Modifications or adjustments would be made to refine the system as needed.

In this way, the administrators of a school district can design administrative support systems or subsystems more efficiently, which in turn enable them to cope more effectively with important tasks confronting them. The design of an administrative support system, whether as common or simple as in the terse example noted, represents a systematic approach toward management improvements in education and has the potential for contributing to the overall operation and mission of a school idstrict.

NOTES

1. M. Haire, "Biological Models and Empirical Histories of the Growth of Organizations," in *Modern Organization Theory.* New York: John Wiley & Sons, 1959.

2. D. E. Griffiths and D. R. Davies, "Is Parkinson Right?" *Executive Action Letter.* New London, Connecticut: Croft Educational Service, *4*, No. 9 (April, 1965), pp. 1-4.

3. G. L. Immegart, "Organizational Growth in an Educational Organization." Unpublished study, College of Education, The University of Rochester, 1965.

4. Griffiths and Davies, *op. cit.,* pp. 3-4.

5. G. L. Lippitt and W. H. Schmidt, "Crises in a Developing Organization," *Harv. Bus. Rev., 45,* No. 6 (November-December 1967), pp. 102-112.

6. The authors appriciate the insight of colleagues at the University of Rochester (particularly Professors Howard Bretsch, Lloyd DuVall, and Milton Pullen) regarding the organizational chart conception which derived from the study of school organizations, and the notions of Professor James Manwaring of Syracuse University which were helpful in the systems support services model.

7.   J. Cuffrey and C. J. Mosmann, *Computers on Campus.* Washington, D. C.: American Council on Education, 1967, pp. 34ff

8.   K. Profet, "Information to Manage Public Programs," *SDC Mag., 11,* No. 1 (Winter 1968), pp. 12ff.

9. M. Goer, "The Human Element in Management Information Systems," *SDC Mag., 11,* No. 1 (Winter 1968), p. 26.

Chapter 8 / PERT

It would be difficult to conceive of a discussion of systems approaches and systems applications without a mention of one of the most popular of all systems schemes. We are referring to PERT, the Program Evaluation and Review Technique, or the Critical Path Method, which was originally devised a decade or so ago in the coordination of development of U. S. Navy missiles.[1] Since that time, PERT has been rather widely adopted by industrial firms, governmental agencies, and educational institutions for use in planning projects.[2]

At the risk of oversimplification, the generic function of PERT can be tersely set forth. Given a desired outcome, or a completed event, or state of affairs, the PERT planner traces backward through all of the steps necessary to reach the final state. The steps are depicted on a flow-chart type of device which permits a visual scrutiny of the interrelationship of the events. Estimates of time are calculated for achieving each step in the network of events. That is, it is determined that step C will require "x" days or weeks, to which must be added the time estimates for preceding steps A and B.

Assuming that project completion is to be reached by a specified deadline, the path of those events requiring the most time is outlined. This becomes the *critical* path, and its time consumption is contrasted with the limitations or circumscriptions relative to the final deadline. Slack times from other events which are not included on the critical path are examined as well. Then decisions regarding the deployment of resources in terms of the critical path may be made in order to complete the project on time.

Through PERT, one is able to gather the information necessary for efficient appropriation of human and material resources, to detect obstructions in achieving desired goals, and to estimate project and subproject time requirements. But, and perhaps most significantly, the PERT network application, consistent with other systems techniques, is a means of reviewing the logical steps *and* their interrelationships in achieving a desired outcome.

It might be best in developing and describing the PERT concept to use an example of a project germane to the field of educational administration and then to follow the steps necessary for an application of the PERT technique to the project.[3]

A PROJECT AND APPLICATION

Project: Inservice Day

Each year the Shady Valley School District holds a Spring In-Service Workshop day for its teachers. Speakers of various specialties are selected by the Superintendent's Cabinet to address the assembly of faculties. Within the organization, various subcommittees are established to facilitate the program. Among these are included the preparations subcommittee, which is responsible for teacher registration, lunches, programs, publicity, and some personnel who will participate in the program. Typically, the preparations subcommittee is composed of one man who is free to enlist as much assistance as he needs.

This year the preparations subcommittee chairman is Mr. Brown, and he has one month—20 working days—to complete his responsibility. Mr. Brown decides to begin by PERTing the processes and events necessary to accomplish his goals. The results of Mr. Brown's use of PERT are summarized in the following section.

An Application

Step 1: Identify the desired outcome.

All events in a PERT scheme are first stated in terms of completed outcomes. In contrast, activities are stated in terms of performing an event. The contrast is seen between:

a)   closing the door—an activity; and, door closed—an event; or

b)   preparations completed— an event; and, completing the preparations—
      an activity.

It is essential to differentiate these since the time between events is contingent on the time required for activities.

In this example, the desired outcome, or final event, is the completed, total preparation for the inservice program.

Step 2: List the events necessary for completing the final event.

This means that a list is compiled of those significant subactivities, or events leading to the desired outcome which must be accomplished before the final outcome has been reached. Such a list need not be in proper or chronological order. In fact, when groups initially project the subactivities (process) toward a desired goal or outcome in a "brainstorming" type of session, it is hardly likely that the listing of events will be in the actual sequence. And if any events are omitted, PERT application readily permits their insertion. This is one of the features of PERT which commends its use: it can be adapted and modified, or revised with ease to handle additional data.

Once the events are listed, two questions must be answered: What event or events *immediately* precede each event? And what event or events *immediately* succeed each event?

Table 8.1 Events and their predecessor events for preparing In-Service Day.

Reference Number	Event	Preceding Event
1	Preparations committee chairman appointed	0
2	Registration supplies ordered	4
3	Registrar-hostess appointed	1
4	Building preparations planned	3,15
5	Luncheon ordered	4
6	News releases mailed	10
7	Group discussion leaders selected	1,3
8	Information coordinator appointed	1
9	Programs designed	15,8
10	Public news releases prepared	9
11	Materials typed	9
12	Materials transmitted to printers	11
13	Materials printed	12
14	Materials delivered	13
15	Group discussion rooms selected	7
16	Registration supplies delivered	2
17	Preparations completed	6,14,16,5

It can be assumed that Brown, in the example, developed the chart shown in Table 8.1. In it are contained the events necessary for *preparations completed* (the desired outcome event). These events are preceded by a reference number in order to handle the data easily. They are followed by the notation of which events precede the listed event. Note that the listing of events is not in any particularly logical order. The order or process chronology is derived later, as the PERT network is drawn.

In examining this listing, it can be seen that events 1 and 17 are the initial and terminal events. Also it can be noted that Mr. Brown felt that assistance—in the form of a registrar-hostess, an information coordinator, and group discussion leaders—would have to be involved in the building preparation and room selection, as he saw it.

Step 3: Diagram the events into a network.

The more common method of drawing a PERT diagram is to place the reference number of each event in a circular node and array the events in a chronological flow from left to right on a chart. The node is then connected to the preceding event by an arrow. When simultaneous events occur, there is a branching of the arrows, as seen in Brown's diagram (Fig. 8.1).

Before proceeding to the next step, it is necessary to review the diagram carefully. One must ascertain the accuracy of the transcription of the listing

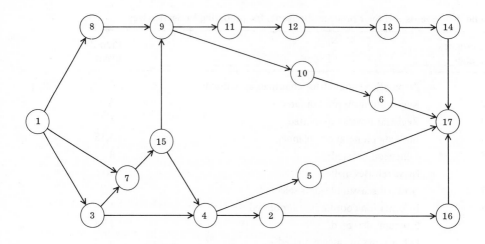

Fig. 8.1 Network of events.

of events to the network diagram. Also, it is important that each event be studied to determine its magnitude. If many subevents seem necessary to constitute an event, these should be PERTed separately in a subPERT diagram. That is, events should be within the same general hierarchical genus. One need not list the steps necessary to deliver program copy to the printer as part of this diagram, but, if one did so, these minor events are more appropriately included in a subPERTing of the event and it would therefore be displayed separately. Thus, just as all but the smallest systems have subsystems, so all but the smallest events in a PERT chart can be PERTed in terms of their "subevents." And, just as systems are understood by looking at their components or subunits, so events (or processes) are better comprehended.

Note in this diagram the full consistency with the previous listing of events. Event 15, which must immediately precede events 4 and 9, must itself be immediately preceded by event 7. Similarly, event 17 is immediately preceded by events 14, 16, 6, and 5. It is seen that the zero precedence of event 1 is inferred only, but not entered in the diagram.

It can be observed that if Mr. Brown had stopped after completing even this diagram, actually only the critical initial phases of PERT, at least some of his planning would be facilitated.

Step 4: Estimate the times for each event.

In completing a PERT chart, three different time estimates are calculated for the PERT diagram. There is first the *optimistic* time estimate *a* which answers the question: If everything goes as well as possible, how long will it take to complete the event? Also, there is the *pessimistic* time estimate *b* which is a guess of ultimate time required if everything which could possibly go wrong actually happened. Then, there is the educated guess, often based on experience, as to how long the completed event is *likely* to require *m*. The final time estimate *te* is derived from these other three estimates by applying the formula:

$$t_e = \frac{a + 4m + b}{6} \cdot$$

It is assumed that while the best *a* and worst *b* time estimates have an equal chance of actually coming true, the educated guess, or most likely time *m*, has twice the probability as the other two combined. The mean of these three times is derived to yield the *estimated time* t_e.

However, when there is a wide discrepancy between the optimistic time *a* and the pessimistic time *b*, there is apt to be a greater uncertainity associated with t_e. Thus, a variance measurement is usually used in calculating the probabilities associated with the estimates. When variance yields a small result, t_e will be fairly precise. Inaccuracy in t_e is indicated by a large variance between *a* and *b* estimates. In a case where the variance is large, one would re-examine the time estimates ascribed to both optimistic and pessimistic times in order to reassess the initial conjectures. The formula for variance, stated consistently with previously used symbols of PERTing, is:

$$\sigma^2 = \left(\frac{b - a}{6} \right)^2 \cdot$$

Table 8.2 shows the optimistic, likely, and pessimistic times established by Mr. Brown for completing his In-Service Day planning, the t_e derived from the formula above, and the variance. Note that the estimates are based on the time between events.

Step 5: Determine the critical path.

The figures for each t_e are then entered on the PERT diagram network on the arrow between nodes. The lower section of Fig. 8.1 is extracted in order to illustrate (Fig. 8.2).

The next substep is to establish the times by which one might expect to accomplish each of the events as linked in the network. Expected time (T_E) is computed by simply adding the t_e's in the longest path to any event. Thus, the T_E of event 3 is 2. But the T_E of event 7 is 3, since event 7 is not only dependent on 1 → 7, but on 1 → 3 → 7 as well. Event 7 may not be completed until events 1 and 3 are completed.

The T_E's in Fig. 8.2 are as follows.

(T_E) 3 = 2	[1 →3]
(T_E) 7 = 3	[1 →3 →7]
(T_E) 15 = 5.83	[1 →3 →7 →15]
(T_E) 4 = 10.16	[1 →3 →7 →15 →4]

Table 8.2 Time calculations

Between Events		a	m	b	t_e	σ^2
1 & 8	Appointing the information coordinator	1	2	3	2	.11
1 & 3	Appointing the registrar-hostess	1	2	3	2	.11
1 & 7	Appointing group discussion leaders	1	2	3	2	.11
3 & 7	Appointment of registrar-hostess and group discussion leaders	.5	1	1.5	1	.03
7 & 15	Selecting group discussion rooms	1	3	4	2.83	.25
15 & 9	Group discussion room information to program	.5	1	1.5	1	.03
8 & 9	Designing of programs	3	5	7	5	.44
9 & 11	Typing of program materials and copy	2	3	4	3	.11
9 & 10	Preparation of news releases	3	5	8	5.16	.69
3 & 4	Planning building preparations	5	7	9	7	.44
15 & 4	Selection of group discussion rooms and final planning	3	4	7	4.33	.44
4 & 5	Ordering luncheon menu	3	5	7	5	.44
4 & 2	Ordering of registration supplies	1	2	3	2	.11
11 & 12	Transmitting materials to printer	1	1	2	1.16	.03
12 & 13	Printing of materials	4	10	10	9	1.00
10 & 6	Mailing of news releases	1	2	4	2.16	.25
6 & 17	The news release mailing and completed event (leaving time for publication)	4	6	8	6	.44
5 & 17	Luncheon menu preparation	6	8	10	8	.44
2 & 16	Delivery of registration supplies	3	7	12	7.16	2.25
14 & 17	Delivery of printed materials and readiness thereof	1	1	2	1.16	.03
16 & 17	Setting up registration materials	1	1	1	1	0

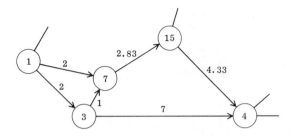

Fig. 8.2 Placement of t_e on PERT diagram.

One other time estimate necessary in PERTing is that of the latest completion time. This is circumscribed by Mr. Brown's deadline of one month for completing the in-service planning. The example noted that Mr. Brown had four weeks, or 20 working days, to finish his planning. This obligation date (20 days) is symbolized in PERT as T_S. The latest permissible completion time (T_L) for PERTing will equal the obligation deadline time or date.

To compute T_L, start with the final event (number 17 in our example) and work backward (from *right* to *left*), subtracting the t_e from the value of T_L for each succeeding event in a cumulative fashion. When more than one T_L is obtained, such as when an event precedes two or more events, use the smallest value.

Frequently, the value of T_E is placed above the event node; the T_L is placed beneath the node. By subtracting T_E from T_L, one will obtain the slack time, or the negative or positive difference between allowable time and necessary time.

A positive slack time indicates the degree of efficiency in the production; and such slack time indicates a point in the project where energy might be diverted to other events which have a negative slack time.

Figure 8.3 shows the completed network of the planning, including T_E and T_L computations.

The track with the least amount of slack time is called the *critical path*. In our example, the critical path is [1 →8 →9 →11 →12 →13 →14 →17]. The slack time for this path is -3.48 days. This means quite clearly that to follow the proposed planning scheme may well result in incomplete preparations for the in-service day. There are only 20 working days time left to complete the task, while the projected PERT planning would seem to require 23.48 days.

Step 6: Estimating probability.

In completing the calculations, one would typically determine the statistical probability of accomplishing the task within the given time. The formula for this calculation is:

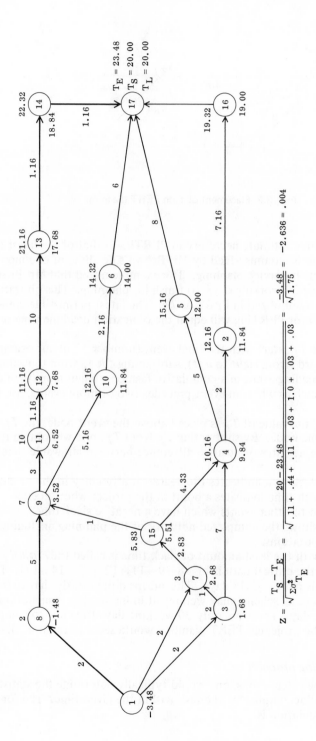

$$Z = \frac{T_S - T_E}{\sqrt{\Sigma \sigma^2_{T_E}}} = \frac{20 - 23.48}{\sqrt{.11 + .44 + .11 + .03 + 1.0 + .03 + .03}} = \frac{-3.48}{\sqrt{1.75}} = -2.636 = .004$$

Fig. 8.3 Completed PERT network and probability calculation.

$$Z = \frac{T_S - T_E}{\sqrt{\Sigma \sigma^2_{T_E}}}$$

Using this formula with Mr. Brown's projections, we find that there is only a .4 percent probability of success when the score from the above formula is associated with a probability table.

At this point it becomes obvious that Brown *must* use his PERT diagram effectively if he is to succeed in his in-service workshop planning. Further, examination of the critical path shows that Brown must do something to shorten it. He may wish to use more than one typist in order to minimize typing time, or he may try to secure a better production and delivery time from the printer. He may also allow less time for the appointment of his information coordinator, registrar-hostess, and group discussion leader. But, in any event, it is obvious that the T_E's in the PERT diagram's critical path must be tightened considerably for the planning to be successful.[4]

SUMMARY

The PERT technique is a viable means for intelligently scheduling the time necessary for accomplishing a task.[5] In itself PERT solves no problems. From it, however, an analysis of the subsystematic functioning is readily available with easily recognizable clues for the redistribution of energies when necessary in order to ensure a desired outcome.

For small work groups, or for a project with a reasonable number of events, a pen-and-paper PERTing is well within the realm of possibility. For extremely intricate computations, the computer is more feasible.

PERT is a means for identifying subsystem activities and for coordinating efficient subsystem relationships. One can readily see when too many demands are being made on one work group, or, for that matter, when too little is being asked of other groups. Thus, PERT is a valuable tool in achieving a truly synergistic interrelationship between action processing subsystems involved in complex system work.

NOTES

1. See, for example, F. K. Levy, G. L. Thompson, and J. D. Wiest, "The ABC's of the Critical Path Method," *Harv. Bus. Rev., 4,* No. 5 (September-October 1963), pp. 98-108.

2. Relative to educational applications, see D. L. Cook, *PERT: Applications in Education,* Cooperative Research Monograph No. 17, OE-12024, 1966, U. S. Government Printing Office, F55. 212:12024; and J. H. Justus, "PERT," *Sch. Mgt., 80,* No. 6 (December 1967), pp. 24-29.

3. For examples of PERTing in education, see A. E. Kent, "How Skokie Created a Program Budget," *Nations Schools, 82,* No. 5 (November 1968), pp. 56-59; and R. E. Meckley, I. E. Valentine, and Z. McCoy, "A Guide to Systematic Planning for Vocational and Technical Schools," Research Document 22, Center for Vocational and Technical Education, The Ohio State University, December, 1968.

4. For more detailed instructions on using PERT see J. D. Wiest and F. K. Levy, *A Management Guide to PERT/CPM.* Englewood Cliffs, N. J.: Prentice Hall, 1969; Federal Electric Corporation, *A Programmed Introduction to PERT.* New York: John Wiley & Sons, 1963.

5. D. L. Cook, "Better Project Planning and Control through the Use of System Analysis and Management Techniques," Educational Research Management Center, School of Education, The Ohio State University, November, 1967, 16 pp.

Chapter 9 / PPBS

Just as it is difficult to conceive of a discussion systems applications without a treatment of PERT (Chapter 8), it is likewise impossible to omit PPBS (the Planning Programming-Budgeting System) from any such consideration. This approach is variously referred to as PPBS, PPB System, PB System (Program Budgeting System), or just as the Program Budget. Regardless of its label, the planning-programming-budgeting system (PPBS, as we will call it) is the short- and long-range systematic budgeting scheme which was developed by the Rand Corporation and popularized by the Federal Government.[1] Often termed "McNamara's brain-child" in the press, because of former Secretary of Defense Robert McNamara's extensive use of this budgeting approach, PPBS to date has had its most extensive applications in the military arena.

Although advanced by some as "new" and "revolutionary," PPBS is more accurately a rather logical outgrowth in budgeting evolution and reform in the public sphere. The *planning* portion of PPBS can be traced to Keynesian economics and the *programming-budgeting* aspect to the performance budgeting of the Hoover Commission on Government Reorganization (1949), or to the "budgeting by programs" concept of Professor C. DeYoung in the field of educational administration of about the same time. The *system* aspect of PPBS originated in the futuristic, integrative mode of thought spawned by the systems movement. Also contributing were planning and budgeting procedures used by British military authorities during World War II. In any event, PPBS is not something unique or drastically different, nor is it a product of the past decade. Rather, it has numerous antecedents in the development and refinement of economics and budgeting, and, as Schick has observed, PPBS is a natural product in the evolution of public budgeting procedures from the early stages of, first, central control, then scientific management, to the present long-range planning, cost-benefit analysis approaches toward fiscal planning.[2]

In essence, PPBS is rational planning, optimization of scarcity, and systematic allocation of limited resources. It involves, simply, long range projections of goals (planning into the future) for organizational units or activities in terms of precise objectives (programming) with systematic cost-benefit analyses of alternative strategies and a resulting multi-staged financial plan (multiple year budgeting) in order to ensure maximum organizational goal realization through optimum use of resources. It represents analysis before the fact, as opposed to after-the-fact analysis, and implies continual evaluation and review of both organizational goals and financial strategy for realizing those goals. As Hitch has pointed out, PPBS links the *fiscal* (budgeting) and *substantive* (goals and objectives) aspects of planning.[3] In sum, PPBS has economical, political, theoretical (systems), and practical roots; however, its ethos, according to Hartley, is economic rationality.[4]

It is quite natural, then, that this approach is currently, gaining popularity in public and governmental fiscal planning and budgeting (whether for the military or for other governmental services including education) at the federal, state, and local levels. At the Federal government level, President Johnson stimulated the implementation of PPBS by using the approach throughout all departments and agencies in the preparation of the 1968 Federal budget. States such as Wisconsin and New York have been testing and experimenting with PPBS along with municipalities such as New York City. In education, institutions such as the Ohio State University and the University of California at Irvine, or school districts such as the Skokie, Illinois, School District 68, the Dade County Public Schools, and the Sacramento Public Schools have begun implementing PPBS procedures in full or in part.[5] Further, PPBS is viewed by some as a viable strategy for use by state departments of education, as attested by emerging applications in both California and New York State.

In fact, in any area where economic and political impingements are critical, PPBS is ultimately useful. To some adherents of the approach it is only a matter of time until educational organizations — school districts of all kinds, universities, and state departments of education — move in increasing numbers toward the implementation of PPBS. For any high priority function such as education, this approach to planning and allocating resources, with its economic, political, and practical rationality, has a number of significant advantages.

It should be clearly stated that PPBS serves primarily to facilitate organizational decision-making in public or governmental units by administrators, boards, or the electorate at large. Readily apparent in this approach are goals (long range targets) and objectives (specific outcomes desired), the display of programs or activities projected to realize goals and objectives, and the costs of each program or activity. Purposes are explicit and stated; programs or activities are spelled out in terms of their components; and costs are clearly linked to benefits or outcomes. This can be contrasted to the traditional year-by-year, line budget-planning process prevalent today, where goals and objectives are rarely (if ever) in evidence, programs or activities are obscured by line budget categories (such as salaries or supplies), and organizational costs are not displayed with any reference to benefits derived — and where, we may add, analysis takes place at the *end* of the budget year instead of *prior* to implementation, as is the case with PPBS. Also it should be underscored that planning is a crucial element in PPBS, and that this fact, along with the detailed but comprehensive nature of PPBS, contributes to the complexity of the approach. Indeed, moving to PPBS is quite a different matter than moving from an object to a function type of budget format. However, utilization of PPBS—a systematic framework for planning involving the examination of all possible relevant inputs, thereby entertaining more alternate strategies or solutions—ensures a more reasoned or rational, as opposed to "conditioned," response in decision situations concerned with the allocation of organizational resources.

These are not, however, the only purposes served by PPBS. Recently, Piele listed the following purposes served by the planning-programming-budgeting system approach with regard to education:

1. To make available to decision-makers more concrete and specific data relevant to broad decisions.
2. To spell out more concretely the objectives of school programs.
3. To analyze systematically and present for school board review possible alternative programs to meet these objectives.
4. To evaluate throughly and compare the benefits and costs of programs.
5. To produce total rather than partial cost estimates of programs.
6. To present on a multi-year basis the prospective costs and accomplishments of programs.
7. To review objectives and conduct program analysis on a continuing year-round basis.[6]

Put another way, the major purposes which may be realized through PPBS, in addition to the most obvious facilitation of decision-making purposes noted above, are the following:

1. Through PPBS, organizations and all key personnel must consciously and continually set and review goals and objectives; PPBS involves target setting and the concommitant planning necessary to reach the targets.
2. Also through this process, since all activities are costed and assessed in terms of benefits to be derived or outcomes to be realized, goals and objectives must be both realistic and operational.
3. PPBS causes organizations to exhaustively generate and analyze all categories of input and all reasonable alternative approaches to goals and objectives.
4. PPBS requires that all activities, or programs, must be related to goals or objectives. (In Novick's words it involves the "rational odering of inputs and outputs."[7]) Facilitated here is not only decision making.but also program implementation and review.
5. By the precise cost analysis evaluation of existing and projected activities and programs, the PPBS approach is helpful in the establishment of priorities which inevitably confront decision-makers dealing with an

abundance of need, but a scarcity of resources.

6. In the course of the comparing, evaluating, and unifying aspects of the planning and budgeting approach of PPBS, diverse elements of the organization are potentially related and integrated through precise specification of objectives and activities. Duplicative efforts are better avoided and less, or nonrelevant, activities or programs can likewise be more easily eliminated.

7. Decision-making by individuals or groups at all levels of the organization, and at all times, is facilitated by the explicit and exacting formulations and documentations of a PPB System, and all subunits gain a clearer perception of their role in the total organization as well as their relationship to all other subunits.

8. Organizational planning and development is greatly aided in that all subunits project goals and fiscal needs into the future and demonstrate the costs of projected outcomes beyond simply the next year or the most immediate future.

9. Organizational efforts and activities (programs) are consciously evaluated and assessed prior to implementation, thereby ensuring greater relevance and functionality as well as being subjected to continual review as these efforts or activities are in operation. At the present time innovative activities are seldom evaluated until after the fact, when little can be done to improve the impact of potentially good programs or to cut unworthy or marginal programs before excessive resources are wasted.

10. So crucial for educational organizations, PPBS results in both quantitative and qualitative information regarding "what the organization's outcomes or benefits are." Such information can be used with members of the organization as well as with clients (students) and constituents (the public at large) of educational organizations.

11. This kind of information should, further, be of great value in developing support (moral and financial) for school programs and personnel, and for use by the electorate and their representatives (school board members) in exercising their voice constructively toward budgetary matters, fiscal priorities, program priorities, and directions for their schools.

12. Finally, implementation of PPBS means involvement of personnel in the totality of organizational planning and budgeting. Since an ultimate Program Budget is a hierarchy of goals and programs, and is a collation of projections from organizational subunits, extensive participation of all organizational members is realized through this process. The advantages of participation—involvement, communication, and commitment—all accrue to those taking part in the process.

PPBS is, then, a rational process for both planning and budgeting that links the fiscal and substantive aspects of organizational programs in a systematic way with full attention to the benefits or outcomes of such programs. It is more than an accounting plan, and more than "armchairing" into the future. *Instead it is an integrative, systematic, and comprehensive approach to bridging from the present to the future.* The process further serves many other purposes, as we have noted, and thus has a potential for facilitating a wide range of organizational activities as well as such basic concerns as growth and development.

With this general introduction to PPBS we can now turn to the process itself and to the matter of implementation. Since PPBS is more encompassing and embracing than some systems techniques (in sum, more complex), the treatment of this planning-budgeting process here cannot be in terms of an illustrative problem as was the case in dealing with PERT. Rather, we will sketch in a more general fashion the logical steps through which an administrator would move in introducing PPBS into an educational organization, whether this is a school building, a school district, a university, or an intermediate or state educational agency. Illustrations will be made along the way and the interested reader is encouraged to consult the growing literature on PPBS[8] and to explore information on concrete or operational models from educational organizations using PPBS[9]. Because of the intricate nature of PPBS and its relatively embryonic state of development in educational organizations to date, a detailed discussion of the application of PPBS is not possible in this chapter. However, the basic process involved in the approach can be outlined in broad strokes, its strengths and weaknesses can be examined, and some guidelines can then be suggested for administrators interested in drawing on the planning-programming-budgeting system approach or its elements for organizational, fiscal, and program planning.

IMPLEMENTING PPBS

The potential of PPBS is attested somewhat by the variety of ways it can be (and is being) operationalized by governmental organizations. In the development of the Federal Budget of 1968 it was introduced totally into the entire Federal governmental structure and throughout the budgetary process. On the other hand, its initial use in the New York City schools revealed a concentration of effort on cost analysis rather than toward the development and implementation of a full-scale program planning structure and fiscal accounting system. Here the complexity of the New York City schools' budget apparatus and other problems of total implementation suggested use of the analysis phase of PPBS as *a step toward* more precise costing and more effective long-range planning. In addition, PPBS efforts in the New York City schools were initially directed primarily toward areas with prospects of generally high payoff. Or if, as Corbally suggests,[10] the greatest value of PPBS can be realized in terms of the crucial "ten percent" of the budget (that dealing with new and improved programs as opposed to the continuation portion of the budget), then organizations may wish to apply the approach initially only to new programs, or to proposals for modifying or changing existing programs. Or—as will be seen as the overall PPBS process is outlined—many elements, aspects, or techniques of the PPBS strategy might be tested or advantageously employed by practicing administrators using more traditional planning and budgeting approaches. To realize the ultimate potential of PPBS, however, implementation in the full totality and complexity of the concept is, of course, necessary.

At the outset it must be observed that there is no "royal road" to implementing PPBS. In other words, *there is no magical, standard, already-worked-out process (like PERT) that an administrator can study and then apply to his organizational work.* First of all, the comprehensiveness of the PPBS concept defies its reduction to a simple step-by-step procedure. Second, the nature of the concept is such that PPBS must be adapted to the organization using it, since the basic object of PPBS is to facilitate and link the major aspects of an organization's basic management functions. As Hartley has so cogently observed in working with educational administrators, PPBS is what you make it. There is, however, a generic or general process conception that can be set forth, but which must ultimately be tailored, fitted, and modified to the situation or organization at hand.

Before presenting this concept, however, it must in all honesty be noted that PPBS applications have met with varied success. Hitch has pointed out that even in the military PPBS works better for some branches of the service than others.[11] And in education, though the number of organizations trying or experimenting with PPBS, or elements of it, is growing, "exploration" is the characteristic of activity at present. Contributing to the reasons why a simple model or standard process cannot be devised is the fact that different kinds of organizations, such as the military and the schools, have different kinds of goals, objectives, inputs, operations, and outputs. Further, even schools themselves differ in this regard. And, since all organizations are staffed by people (and PPBS requires extensive involvement of people) this contributes greatly to the need to design unique PPB Systems for each organization wishing to capitalize on this refined approach for improving planning, budgeting, and in the end, decision-making.

Following is a discussion of the generic planning-programming-budgeting system process. It is a cyclic process that takes place continously throughout the year. Emphasis here is placed on the basic steps in the process in terms of an initial implementation of PPBS by an organization such as a school district.

STEPS IN PPBS

Step 1: The development of a unique PPBS scheme

At the beginning, an organization must first decide to what extent PPBS or its elements will be used—total implementation, PPBS for new or improved programs (proposals), PPBS for one or two selected programs (e.g., reading or science), cost analysis for budget requests, or whatever. Since the prospects for school districts, due to growing Federal and state governmental activity in this area argue for a view toward full implementation (more immediately by logic and possibly eventually by mandate), we will hereafter in our illustrations assume an essentially total implementation of the PPBS approach. Nevertheless, the first question for any organization in introducing PPBS is one of scope and extent.

The most crucial task in developing PPBS in an organization, once the extent of its employment is determined, is that of establishing a viable program structure. *A program can be defined simply as a set of goals, objectives, and activities (an input-output subsystem, if you will) under the aegis of an organization or a subunit of an organization.* Due to the nature of educational goals, objectives, and products, "programs" in education are often more difficult to define and operationalize than are those for other organizations such as hospitals or military groups. Nonetheless, there are several ways programs can be defined for educational organizations.

It is important to note that program structure is ultimately hierarchical in the same fashion that organizational goals and objectives are. For example, just as one of the school's objectives, "to teach children to read," has a subobjective of "reading for meaning" (which in turn has a subobjective of "developing word-concepts for specific words"), so the *reading program* for a school has a *primary level reading subprogram* which in turn has a *first grade reading subprogram* which likewise can typically be further subdivided into *readiness, primer, and first reader subprograms.* Program structure is at the heart of the entire PPBS process and the success of a PPB System is linked directly to the viability and functionality of the devised program structure for it is around this structure that all planning and budgeting occurs.

For public schools, program structure may take the form of various, learning "levels" such as (1) preschool programs, (2) primary programs, (3) intermediate programs, (4) junior high school programs, (5) high school programs, and (6) post-high school programs. In operation these may be further subdivided, such as the high school program into the (1) technical program, (2) comprehensive program, (3) college preparatory program, and (4) evening or adult school program.

Another approach to program structure would be to view the school's programs in terms of subject or content areas such as (1) language arts, (2) science, (3) mathematics, (4) social studies, (5) fine arts, (6) practical arts, (7) physical education, (8) special education, and so forth.

Still another approach to program structure would be in terms of goals (of education) statements such as programs for developing (1) saleable skills, (2) health and physical fitness, (3) citizenship, (4) family membership, (5) methods of science, (6) ethical values, (7) rational thinking, and so on.[1][2] Or some combination of these approaches may be used, as in the following outline:

1. Preschool education
   a) Social skills

   b) School routines
   c) Readiness (etc.)

2. Elementary education
   a) Kindergarten
   b) Grade one
   c) Grade two (etc.)

3. High school education
   a) Language arts
   b) Science
   c) Mathematics (etc.)

4. Post high school education
   a) Vocations and trades
   b) Arts and crafts
   c) Occupational retraining (etc.)

The above example is not suggested in any sense as an "ideal" but rather only to show the possibility of combining the level, subject matter, and broad goal approaches to developing a program structure. In fact, at the present stage of experience with PPBS in education, some type of combination approach offers real advantages in that it allows for flexibility within a large school organization, does not force or impose a drastically different way of thinking on staff, and can easily be tailored to existing program conceptions and many organizational procedures. At the outset, granted all of the uniqueness of PPBS for an organization, it seems advantageous to begin with program conceptions as already conceived and to modify these as needed when goals, objectives, and/or the organization itself changes.

In a like manner, programs in universities may take a variety of forms. Here programs may be in terms of levels (e.g., undergraduate, graduate, or post-graduate studies), in terms of disciplines (e.g., sociology, psychology, medicine, engineering, etc.), in terms of elements (e.g., faculty, support, plant, research, libraries, etc.), or again in terms of some combination of the foregoing. In this regard we should note that the implementation of PPBS at Ohio State University used that educational organization's basic administrative structure (and, hence, operating structure) as the PPBS program structure.[13] Programs were developed at the department level in terms of departmental objectives. These were then passed on to the college level for review, evaluation, and collation, and then in turn to the central university administration level. No attempt was made to determine program structure or goals for the university; rather the organizational structure itself served as the "program structure." Programs, therefore, were defined and conceived at the operational level by the most competent "specialists." Review and decisions at the college and finally university levels were used to bring together the total organizational planning and budgeting. This approach to program structure appears most beneficial in large complex organizations, where personnel are highly specialized, and where goals and objectives are diverse and outcomes often subjective. Also, the approach utilizes existing and known operational, decision-making, and communications systems which can, in and of themselves, facilitate and be facilitated by, the PPBS process.

The most crucial aspect of the initial step in implementing PPBS is, then, the development of a viable program structure. *This program structure serves as the framework for developing operational programs (activi-*

*ties), for setting operational objectives, for short- and long-range planning,
and for budgeting.* There are, as suggested above, numerous ways to create
a program structure, but ultimately this structure must be devised in terms
of the particular organization at hand.

The next step in the initial phase of implementing PPBS is to make decisions about procedures, time-scheduling, responsibilities, decision and review techniques, program revision mechanisms, and other specifics of the
overall system process design. Particularly the planning, goal and objective
setting, cost analysis, program reporting, and program revision procedures
need to be determined in the light of the program structure to be utilized.
These in turn need to be placed in chronological sequence so that operations
at the program development level can be accomplished and processed
through the program structure hierarchy in order for the total program plan
and budget to be developed in time for funding and implementation. Specific responsibilities of all employees (e.g., for goal and objective setting,
program planning, cost analysis, coordination, review, and subunit or unit
budget-making) must be spelled out along with decision and review responsibility at each higher level of the organization. Relatedly, procedures for
handling differences of opinion about program needs and priorities (revisions) should be determined along with communication and feedback procedures among and between all levels. Other specifics such as reporting
format and style, appropriate cost-analysis techniques, criteria for determining needs and priorities, and the length of time to be used in long-range
projections need to be determined. Obviously the short-range aspect of
PPBS is the annum or biennium, and the long-range aspect may extend 4,
5, 6, or even more years into the future. These matters, of course, must be
worked out in advance and are a part of the rules of the game for any planning, programming, budgeting system.

Other details such as the keying of the PPBS planning and budgeting
structure to (1) existing board of education reporting formats (e.g., for
board meetings, annual meetings, or reports to the public), (2) mandated
fiscal accounting or reporting formats at the state level, or (3) special project accounting and monitoring systems (e.g., from fund-granting agencies),
also should be devised to ensure smooth operation and greatest relevancy of
the PPBS process.

Finally, a communication network should be established to facilitate
the flow of reports and information in the process of reviewing component
programs, and in the review of the total planning and budgeting package.
Attention should be given here to feedback down the program-structure
hierarchy relative to needed program revisions, as well as to horizontal information and feedback between related or proximate (interfacing) subunits. This will ensure continual understanding and knowledge of the PPBS
process and will contribute to the relating and meshing of all operations as
well as to minimizing duplicative or wasteful efforts at all organizational
levels.

Step 2: Orientation of members of the organization

Once the particular PPBS scheme has been developed for an organization, staff must be oriented to it and to their roles in PPBS. All staff participating in the planning-programming-budgeting system will need some general introduction to PPBS and its strengths and weaknesses, as well as detailed instructions regarding the particular scheme to be introduced or used. Technical documents and guides should be developed, circulated, and discussed so that all staff are aware of their responsibilities and the operation of the PPB System. Illustrative materials should be used and various techniques such as goal setting, objective writing, program planning. long-range projecting, cost analyzing, plan reporting, and budget reporting should be focused upon. Report forms, memoranda forms, and feedback procedures should be discussed and their use illustrated. Workshops and training sessions are necessary for all staff at this point, and key staff—administrators, coordinators, chairmen, and planners—will need intensive instruction. *It is important that all staff be aware of their task, the overall scheme, and the benefits that will accrue.*

Step 3: Sub-unit planning, programming, budgeting

Following orientation, program planning and budgeting is initiated throughout the organization at the operational level of the organization or PPBS structure. Whether this be the individual teacher, a grade-level group, a subject-matter department, or a teaching team, goals (targets without a time referent) and objectives (specific operational outcomes desired at a specified time) are determined—first in terms of the coming budget annum or biennium (short-range planning) and then for 4 or more years in advance (the long-range period). Programs (or activities) to achieve these goals are then formulated and projected in terms of staff needs, space needs, materials and equipment needs, and all other program requirements. Alternative program specifications are generated, and costed in detail. The various alternatives are compared by cost-benefit analysis techniques, and memoranda (documents setting forth program policy, recommendations, justifications, and the results of analyses made) are prepared for each program or major portion of a program. Such information is helpful in communicating (or in relating) to other subunits and in reporting to higher administrative levels. The memoranda are used as the basis for developing the subunit's multi-year program plan, and its multi-year financial plan (budget).[14] These plans, the multi-year program and financial plans, are then submitted to the next administrative level in the organization for review, analysis, and decision relative to program and financial plan development at that level.

Step 4: Review of subunit program and financial plans

Priorities in terms of goals and objectives are established at each level in an organization's PPB System. Subunit or operational level plans are reviewed at the next higher level. When reviewed, some aspects of the subunit's projections will be altered, modified, postponed, or even rejected. Feedback to the subunit in this regard permits the subunit to know continually what the status of its projections are. If revisions are called for, subunits may be requested to revise their work (that done in step three). To the extent projections or projects are modified or postponed, the subunits' multi-year plans will need revision. Once all subunit plans are in order, the administrative unit collates the selected program plans and financial projections along with its own administrative plans and budget (each administrative unit in an organization has its own "programs" or requirements *qua* administration, including administrative support programs), and then passes its total plan (program and financial) on to the next higher administrative unit. This process continues until the highest administrative level in the organization's PPB System structure is reached.

Step 5: Collation of the organizational program budget

At the top administrative level the various unit program and financial plans are reviewed, and along with these, the program and financial plans for top level administration are collated into the complete organizational program budget. Here they are keyed to other budget impingements (funds or grants) or accounting formats. The preparation of the total organization budget and its supporting documents (program plans, long-range projections, and crucial memoranda) are worked out by appropriate specialists in central administration for submission in the form of proposals for funding purposes. The budget is then passed on to the board, the state, the electorate, and/or other agencies according to appropriate procedures for the funding decision(s).

Step 6: Budget decision

The funding source or sources review the organization's program plan and budget and pass judgment on the total fiscal-program plan. If revisions or adjustments are needed, these are realized in the same way the program budget was developed (e.g., as in steps one through five above). Hopefully, the PPBS process will result in less need for revision at this (decision) stage and will result in fewer negative decisions on program and budget plans.

Step 7: Implementation

Once funded, or to the extent funded, the organization is free to implement its program and financial plan for the specified time period. Once in operation the PPBS plan and budget serve ultimately as an improved means for organizational control, operations, and as a basis for evaluation of work done by the organization.

Step 8: Review and recycling of the process

Simultaneously with step seven, or shortly after, the organization should evaluate the efficacy and effectiveness of its planning-programming-budgeting system and should make any changes or modifications deemed desirable. As soon as such adaptations are made the process should be recycled—that is, begun again for the next budget period and respective long-

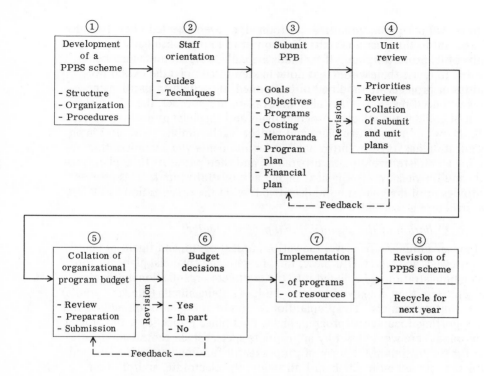

Fig. 9.1 A flow chart of PPBS.

range periods (4 or more years). Also, as programs are implemented, program evaluation procedures are set in motion. Evaluations of all program activities then become input data (in terms of effectiveness and efficiency) for subsequent planning and budgeting. It should be apparent that much subsequent PPBS activity becomes an updating or an expansion of the previous year's work. But the continual program budget and planning process, constantly looking into the future and modifying goals and directions accordingly, should greatly facilitate organizational decision-making, growth and development, and the organization's contribution to those it serves.

The generic process indicatively described above can be set forth and summarized in a flow chart. Figure 9.1 illustrates the major dimensions of the process. With this background on the PPBS approach and process, the major strengths and weaknesses of PPBS can now be explored.

STRENGTHS AND WEAKNESSES OF PPBS

As noted in Chapter 1, all systems approaches have problems as well as prospects, and PPBS, like PERT (in Chapter 8), is no exception. Thus, although the writers have thus far "glorified" the planning-programming-budgeting system approach, they should also note its weaknesses and problems. It is no cure-all, no panacea; in fact, in addition to being subject to numerous problems in implementation, PPBS as an approach has some imposing drawbacks not the least of which are its inherent complexity and current embryonic stage of development. Some of the more prominent weaknesses are the following:

1. PPBS as a rational process is no better than the people working with it.

2. PPBS is a complex, time-consuming process demanding time and effort by all involved in it. To the degree that organizations are already overburdened with inadequate staff and insufficient resources for doing organizational work, PPBS will only add to such problems (until such time as its outcomes or effects are felt).

3. PPBS requires rather elaborate and sophisticated analyses, and if such analyses are based on poor or inadequate data, little can be expected from the process. It is imperative that management information and data for use in PPBS be sufficient and adequate for the task at hand.

4. PPBS requires explicit and operational objectives. This has always been difficult in education because of the nature of the teaching-learning task.

5. PPBS requires, further, the specification of objectives in terms of outcomes or outputs that can be measured against criterion standards. In order to realize the full benefits of PPBS, the results of education will need to be determined in greater specificity, and ways will need to be found to measure the degree to which such outcomes are achieved, as well as to assess the utility of alternate routes to such outcomes.

6. PPBS will require better administrative review techniques and the establishment of sound criteria that can be used in both program and financial plan review. Choice must be exercised when dealing with scarcity, and careful choice is needed for avoiding arbitrary or capricious decisions relative to needs and priorities.

7. PPBS tends to foster and promulgate a centralizing bias in program and financial planning which limits operational freedom and restricts the possible positive effects of specialization in organizational sub-units.

8. PPBS requires certain specially trained competencies which are in short supply (and, thus, are at present costly) and which are not available in most personnel trained for school or educational positions.

9. In its strategy, PPBS, through its short-range (one- or two-year) and long-range (multiple year) formats, does not in fact account effectively for emergencies, immediate action situations, or "hot," innovative ideas unless such provisions are built into the process. PPBS schemes must be flexible and viable enough to accommodate crises and to enable staff to seek funding at appropriate times when need dictates—such as from granting agencies when such funds are made available "on the spot."

Ways should be provided to incorporate valuable new activities and programs outside of the existing long-range format.

10. PPBS requires a comprehensive and effective communication system throughout an organization with maximal speed, feedback, and capacity for information transmission. A PPB System breaks down quickly when communications are impeded.

11. Although PPBS provides a logical and pragmatic political strategy (that is, costs are related to systematic planning to achieve specified outcomes), the political arena surrounding public organizations such as schools has irrational and expressive elements which may conflict with or hamper the logic of strategic rationality.

12. PPBS is in its infancy relative to applications in educational organizations. Time and the experience of experimentation and practice (PPBS applications) will begin to reveal its true potential for schools.

These limitations or problematic features are, however, in no way intended to dampen enthusiasm for the PPBS approach. Rather they are identified to keep PPBS in perspective and to suggest that administrators need to weigh the pros and cons of PPBS before blindly adopting or using it. Certainly advantages such as those which follow counterbalance and even outweigh the potential drawbacks, or at least indicate that with some attendant problems, PPBS can facilitate the administration of educational organizations. For PPBS does cause organizations to:

1. plan,
2. formulate goals and objectives,
3. develop programs and activities to meet organizational goals and objectives,
4. formulate alternate routes to realizing desired outcomes,
5. cost-analyze in detail varying approaches to goal achievement,
6. set priorities,
7. review constantly the efficacy of programmed activities,
8. look continually to the future in terms of growth and development,
9. relate financial planning and objectives,
10. link related subunits and activities (thereby avoiding duplication and waste while increasing effect),
11. focus on the total organization and all of its elements,
12. involve staff at all levels in organizational planning,
13. monitor programs and activities continually,
14. allocate resources for maximal effect,
15. assess new and improved activities systematically before they are implemented, and
16. accumulate and organize hard data that can be used to keep constituents informed, or to spell out areas of need.

All in all, PPBS has both prospects and problems. Insightful educational administrators, through careful implementation, will determine the real utility of the process for educational organizations. Practice in the field of educational administration to date at best suggests some guidelines for implementing PPBS in educational organizations to which we can now turn.

SOME GUIDELINES, IN SUMMARY

In a capsule, PPBS is one of the most promising, though involved, systems approaches presently on the horizon. Its potential value for a field of practice such as educational administration is underscored by its growing implementations in governmental circles and by its increasing use by forward-looking administrators in a number of educational organizations.[15] Based on the emerging planning-programming-budgeting system utilization in education, the following guidelines for implementation are suggested to administrators.

Tailor the PPB System to your organization. Do not adopt a PPBS scheme or format from another organization, but instead assess the value of the overall approach and its components for your organization and develop a PPB System designed to best meet your particular needs.

Seek expertise in designing and implementing a PPB System. In developing a PPB System, seek help from systems experts, planning experts, cost-analysis experts, and others with competence in using this approach or its component techniques and procedures. Also visit and consult with other educational administrators who are using PPBS, in order to gain advice based on experience and to avoid problems they have encountered.

Involve staff. Since broad staff involvement is necessary in PPBS, it is essential to involve staff early in the design and development of a PPB System. At the same time it is necessary to look at the competencies of existing staff relative to some of the kinds of competencies needed in the PPBS approach. Then staff can be utilized or trained as necessary for program and financial planning of the type desired.

Pay careful attention to PPB System Program Structure. Possibly the most crucial aspect of PPBS is the program structure. Priority and time should be given to the development of this structure, both its form and its function.

Develop an organizational structure for PPBS. Most administrative organizations in education are formulated along classic or pragmatic lines. PPBS inevitably places extreme demands on such structures and requires explicit attention to planning, communication, analysis, review and feedback functions not often provided for in these structures. This requires that PPBS implementors restructure their organization's administration with appropriate attention to the roles, functions, and relationships dictated by their PPB System.

Orient staff for PPBS. Even with staff involvement in designing a PPB System it is still essential to train and orient staff once a PPB System has been developed. And, as implemented PPB Systems are modified and improved, staff retraining will be called for.

Begin PPBS activities as close to operation as possible. The planning of programs, cost benefit analysis, and financial projections should begin at the operational level and work upward through an organizational structure in order to maximally realize the benefits of PPBS. Program planning can be achieved at top levels, but this, in and of itself, restricts the range of benefits that can be realized. Full staff involvement in analyzing programs and in planning for the future, including the identification of resource requirements, will certainly enhance the effects of the organization's activities.

Devise a flexible PPB System. A too-rigid PPB System will not enable the organization to capitalize on new and innovative ideas or to adjust to changing or emergency situations. Some flexibility in the process and its procedures is necessary if the organization is to remain viable.

And, if you see merit in the PPBS concept, try it! Whether for full-scale implementation or for a new program idea, if PPBS (or any PPBS elements) is appealing, try it out. Many promising administrative procedures (support systems) are never tested because of reluctance to try something new or the comfort of existing approaches. PPBS has potential on both a small and grand scale. Just as it might be ultimately helpful in selling the budget for next year to the school board or the taxpayers, so might it help in introducing a new remedial reading program or an innovative program for school dropouts to the school staff.

The linkage of substantive and fiscal planning through PPBS has a double effect: goal realization is enhanced, and wise use of resources is ensured. PPBS, as a recent evolution in public budgeting, can contribute to educational administration and decision-making in education through rational planning and optimal allocation and use of scarce resources.

NOTES

1. H. J. Hartley, "PPBS: The Emergence of a Systematic Concept for Public Governance," *Gen. Syst., 13* (1968), p. 149.

2. A. Schick, "The Road to PPB: The Stages of Budget Reform," *Publ. Adm. Rev., 26,* No. 4 (December 1966), pp. 243-258.

3. C. J. Hitch, "What are the Programs in Planning, Programming, Budgeting?" Address at the U. S. O. E. Symposium on Operations Analysis of Education, Washington, D. C., November 21, 1967.

4. H. J. Hartley, *Educational Planning-Programming-Budgeting.* Englewood Cliffs, N. J.: Prentice Hall, 1968, p. 94.

5. See *ibid.* for a comprehensive enumeration and some description of such applications of PPBS in education.

6. P. Piele, "Planning Systems in Education," *CASEA-ERIC/CEA News*

Bulletin, University of Oregon, (Winter 1969), p. 4. Paraphrased from *U.S. Bureau of the Budget Bulletin* 66-3, October 12, 1965, p. 3.

7. D. Novick (ed.), *Program Budgeting,* Supt. of Documents, U. S. Government Printing Office, Washington, D. C., 1964, p. xii.

8. H. J. Hartley, *op. cit.;* D. Novick, *op. cit.;* S. J. Mushkin and J. R. Cleaveland, *Planning for Educational Development in a Planning, Programming, Budgeting System.* CEF: NEA Committee on Educational Finance, National Education Association, 1968.

9. Dade County Board of Public Instruction, "A Program Budget Research Proposal," Miami: the Board of Public Instruction, 1966, 75pp.; New York City Board of Education, " PPB: An Introduction," New York: prepared for the Office of PPB and the Stanford Research Institute, June 1967, 15 pp. (OPPB Bulletin, No. 1); State of California, *Programming and Budgeting System.* Sacramento: State Department of Finance, May 1967, 210 pp.; University of Pennsylvania, Government Studies Center, Fels Institute of Local and State Government, *Planning-Programming-Budgeting System Procedures Manual for School Districts.* Philadelphia: The Government Studies Center, 1969; The Western New York School Development Council. *An Operational Model for the Application of Planning-Programming-Budgeting Systems in Local School Districts,* Pre-Pilot Test Version. Williamsville, N. Y.: The Council, 1970; or the articles on PPBS and the Skokie, Illinois public schools appearing in various issues of *Nations Schools* in 1968 and 1969.

10. J. E. Corbally, Jr., "Planning, Programming, Budgeting in the University Setting." Presentation to the eighteenth UCEA Career Development Seminar, held at Syracuse University, April 1968.

11. Hitch, *op. cit.*

12. After the classic "Ten Imperative Needs of Youth," taken from: Educational Policies Commission. *Education for all American Youth: A Further Look,* Washington, D. C.: National Education Association, 1951.

13. Corbally, *op. cit.*

14. Muskin and Cleaveland, *op. cit.,* p. 12.

15. See Hartley, *op. cit.,* for a listing and discussion of applications in schools, universities, and state departments of education.

Chapter 10 / Systems study: problems and their solution

Traditionally and increasingly, schools have been subjected to formal evaluations and assessments. Some evaluations have been internal, that is, they have been made by school personnel — teachers and administrators. Other evaluations or assessments have been external, that is, they have been made by people outside of the school organization. The "Citizens' survey of Their Schools," the state department of education evaluations, the accreditation visits of various accrediting agencies, or the university bureau of school services' survey of schools are all examples of external analysis. And some approaches to school evaluation have been cooperative in the sense that several groups, internal and external, have taken part in the evaluative procedure. For example, the school surveys of the Kellog-supported Cooperative Program in Educational Administration (CPEA) in the 1950's typically involved university personnel (external experts), citizens, and school staffs in a comprehensive study of schools and their community settings.[1]

In fact, few schools or school people have not had at least some experience with the study of the educational enterprise — its structure and function. Critical evaluation of schools or educational organizations is not new. Rather, it is a continuing, ongoing process that involves a growing number of educators each year. School studies, surveys, and analyses of the past have served a vital function in illuminating problems, pointing up weaknesses, showing the shortcomings, and focusing attention on needed modifications or changes in the schools. To the degree that local school district personnel used (or were able to use) the efforts of these evaluations, schools were improved.

However, the typical school study or school survey has several limitations, despite its widespread use and the attempts made over the years to refine this process. In the first place, most such evaluations are "comprehensive" studies of the schools. They are, therefore, global, and in attempting to examine the full picture, they often fail to come to grips with the real problems or dynamics of the situation. The charge is voiced that such surveys seldom get beyond "symptoms" to "real" dysfunctions. Even a brief perusal of the recommendations of many of these studies indicates a high level of generality.

Secondly, these studies characteristically use relatively unsophisticated data gathering procedures, tapping only after-the-fact data in a reputational manner (e.g., questions of what happened in the past relying heavily on the perception and memory of the respondents). Relatedly, the data used in such studies are general or summated (e.g., group achievement scores or percentages of students going on to higher education) and imprecise (e.g., "I think the schools are doing a good job," or "We try to do the best we can in teaching mathematics"). It has been cogently observed that even the most sophisticated and rigorous handling of poor data yields but poor results; approximations with adequate data are, in fact, far better.

Finally, these studies tend to be "in-house" studies. That is, the supposedly "external" agents in school surveys are citizens (in-house, in that they are members of the school-community along with a school's staff) and professionals from universities, state departments, or accrediting agencies (in-house, in that they, like the school staff, are educators). Thus the chance for the mutual-admiration-society approach to school study is ever present.

The systems movement, in addition to numerous facilitators for administrative practice, also has a potential for contributing to the study or evaluation of schools. Inherent in the movement and in numerous systems devices—some of which have been identified and discussed in previous chapters —are techniques and approaches which can facilitate and improve the study of the schools. Operations research, systems analysis, linear programming, cost-benefit analysis, and many other systems procedures can add greatly to the quality and ultimate payoff of school study.

First of all, the use of systems approaches involves a look at problems. As pointed out in Chapter 1, to the systems specialists, problems are simply the dysfunctional aspects of systems. There are no psychological or sociological problems, or financial or personnel problems per se. Rather, there are problems of motivating underpaid teachers, of funding a new program for remedial reading in the high school, or of obtaining qualified, responsible school bus drivers. The disciplines or professional skill areas offer only ways of looking at such problems. In any event, systems approaches are specific; to be successful the systems specialist must get at what *is* wrong and not merely verbalize about the easily identified symptoms or characteristics obvious at a given time.

Secondly, systems approaches are based on maximizing the quantification of variables relative to a system and, of course, using the best data available. Here one's feelings about the schools are not of as great value as are data, for example, from accurate measurement of attitudes and opinions about the school regarding precise events or activities. Rather than working with a notion that "taxes are too high" the systems specialist must know what the taxes are, what incomes are, and what all categories of personal expenditures are in determining the ability of citizens to pay (based on wants and capacity) for schools. Thus systems approaches seek hard, accurate data and use these data in drawing conclusions.

Thirdly, systems approaches in the tradidion of Operations Research or Systems Analysis are interdisciplinary. Since exhaustive exploration of relevant data and alternatives is a goal, systems study of problems draws on personnel from as many disciplines as possible. The more perspectives utilized in examining a problem and generating solutions, the better the chance of reaching the "best" or optimal solution. Possibly if schools would use sociologists, political scientists, economists, and others in examining why, for example, tax levies or bond issues fail, greater insight would be gained that in turn could be used to formulate better strategies and approaches for the future.

Additionally, systems study is typically rigorous, before-the-fact analysis, as opposed to the prevalent after-the-fact evaluations of schools. Certainly the better the data and the better the analysis of alternatives, the greater the chance of making the best decision or taking the most appropriate action. Systems approaches also do not leave the situation with just study and conclusions; in assessing alternatives and modeling or designing solutions, they actually provide the "solutions" for problems and typically indicate guidelines for implementation. Instead of being hypercritical or "tearing down," the systems approach to problem solution constructively builds and naturally bridges to "what will be."

THE GOALS OF SYSTEMS STUDY

Numerous goals can be ascribed to systems approaches to the study of organizational problems. However, at the heart of all systems activity is the goal of locating problems or dysfunctions in order to correct them. Ultimately the systems approach is directed toward "system" (or school organizational) improvement and the highest level of system or organizational development possible. *Systems study seeks most directly to make better systems.*

We could also say that systems study or analysis seeks to uncover critical malfunctions or nonfunctions; to explore alternate routes to solving these problems; to analyze in terms of costs and benefits all such alternatives; to model the optimal problem solution; and to provide guides and controls for eventual practical implementation. The process is premised on asking the right questions, using quantifiable data, specifying precisely desired outcomes or objectives, and analyzing the full range of system and solution effects. Further, the process is pragmatic and either heuristic or algorithmic; it is less qualitatively judgmental, or "questionative," or "hunchy." At the end of systems study one knows what one has and how it will work. The generalities and suggestive nature of other approaches pale in comparison.

There are, of course, other goals of systems study such as:

1. improving the productivity, or "effect," of a system,
2. making a system maximally efficient (that is realizing greatest results from costs),
3. facilitating system operations,
4. ensuring system relevancy,
5. guiding system growth and development,
6. improving system processes, procedures, and personnel,

7. fostering improved data for decision-making,
8. providing a basis for system accountability,
9. exercising quality control,
10. maximizing resource allocation and utilization, and
11. unearthing other system problems or dysfunctions.

Such goals can be generated indefinitely, and when dealing with specific organizations at particular times the list can be even further magnified. In sum, system study is multipurposed, though its basic goal as noted above is most fundamental.

And there are, of course, many kinds of systems studies, or numerous different focuses or approaches for systems study. For example, systems study may be concerned with organizational structure of function (or both). That is, it may be directed toward the dysfunctionality of the administrative organizational *structure* of a school district in order to find out why crucial decisions are abrogated, or are not made. Or it might be directed to the *functionality* of the administrative communication system.

Likewise, system study may be directed toward organizational design or performance. In the former vein, system study might be directed toward the *design* of a grievance, or salary negotiation, mechanism for the schools. In the other case, system study, in seeking to improve *performance* or productivity, may be directed toward finding the best way to convey current events content in the junior high school social studies program.

Systems study also may be more or less objective. Although quantification is the goal of all systems approaches, the various extant systems strategies or techniques can be globally categorized as more or less objective or subjective. To illustrate, Operations Research and Systems Analysis are often equated, but they can, in fact, be differentiated in this way. Wildavsky and Hartley are of help here. The former has noted that Systems Analysis tends to be used in situations in which crucial variables cannot be reduced to quantification. He notes that "the less that is known about objectives, the more they conflict, the larger the number of elements to be considered, the more uncertain the environment, the more likely (the approach) will be called systems analysis."[2] He adds that in systems analysis more "judgment" and "intuition" are relied on, and correspondingly less reliance is placed on quantitative methodology. Operations research, on the other hand, through its total utilization of mathematical procedures in both analysis and modeling, is maximally quantitative in nature. Systems Analysis is, therefore, a "subjective" approach to systems study while Operations Research is an "objective" strategy. Put another way, Hartley observes that Systems Analysis tends to be heuristic while Operations Research is algorithmic (or based on calculation).[3]

In this chapter it is not feasible to indicate or illustrate all of the possibilities for systems study in schools or in education. We will, however, indicate briefly several directions for the "objective" approaches and then will turn to two descriptive illustrations of "subjective" (or Systems Analysis) approaches for study of the school setting. We choose indicative treatment of the "objective" approaches, and deal more with the "subjective," and we do so for the following reasons: First, and most importantly, the present nature of data and the state of educational science lends itself best to the subjective approaches to systems analysis. That is, the inability to quantify many aspects of the educational realm rules out purely quantitative approaches in many instances. Secondly, for the interested reader, detailed descriptions of the "objective" approaches are increasingly readily available. It seems best that the concentration here be on the area of greatest applicability and need. We will, then, identify several of the possible applications of objective systems study in education. Following this we will illustrate two more subjective approaches to the systems study of schools or school problems.

OBJECTIVE APPROACHES:
OPERATIONS RESEARCH AND MATHEMATICAL PROGRAMMING

Of all the "objective" or quantitative approaches in the systems movement, Operations Research (OR) is best known. OR (sometimes also called operations analysis) relies on computational and mathematical procedures as techniques within the interdisciplinary application of the scientific method to the goal of improving the operations of man-machine systems. Through OR it is hoped that better data and the systematic solution of problems will provide the basis for improved operations and decision-making.

The model of OR views effectiveness E or organizational performance P as a function f of controllable C_i and noncontrollable V_j variables.[4]

$$E = f(C_i, V_j) \quad \text{or} \quad P = f(C_i, V_j).$$

Although in actual practice this equation becomes more complicated and other more extensive and elaborate formulae are often required, the above equation presents the underlying structure of OR solutions to organizational problems. In OR, the equation constitutes a model of the system and the problem or dysfunction to be solved.

Solutions in OR may be either analytical (that is, mathematical deduction) or numerical (trial and error iteration).[5] Sometimes the solution of the problem in the OR equation(s) can be determined deductively from the structure of the mathematical model employed. If this is not the case, one can use the inductive approach of conducting experiments (actually simulations) on the model. Since the value of the solution is contingent on the equation or the model's being a true representation of reality, both the model itself and the solution require testing and evaluation. Such testing and evaluation are, however, of the model and solution in abstract form prior to implementation in the organization context. Thus extensive before-the-fact assessment and refinement contribute to the eventual value of the solution for the real world setting.

Ackoff has noted that "since the objective of OR is not merely to produce reports but to improve the performance of systems, the results of the research must be implemented if they are accepted by the decision-maker."[6] It is here that the ultimate test of the operations research (systems study) occurs and is also the point at which the systems scientist contributes to improved practice.

The stages of the OR process are as follows:

1. Formulating the problem
2. Constructing the model
3. Deriving a solution
4. Testing the model and evaluating the solution
5. Controlling the solution
6. Implementing the solution.[7]

Operations Research in Education

To date there has not been very extensive use of Operations Research (OR) in educational organizations. In part, the inability to quantify goals and outcomes of education mitigates against its application in schools. It is also true, however, that educators resist quantification and reject such approaches in solving problems; this, coupled with the scarcity of OR talent (which is co-opted quickly by industry and priority military projects), contributes to the lack of OR's use in this field.

The United States Office of Education has initiated activity in this area through a symposium on "operations analysis in education," held in late 1967.[8] As a result of such activity in the USOE, the use of resource allocation, model building, and quantitative solutions to educational problems through OR, economic or econometric models, and mathematical approaches have all received greater impetus. Through the symposium mentioned and other activities of the USOE Division of Operations Analysis (which is what USOE calls OR), the potential usefulness of OR for education has begun to be established and pilot projects and applications are under way. As Mood and Stoller have indicated, some of the highest priority topics for development before the USOE are those that follow:

1. Pupil flow model: analyzes the flows of pupils on the basis of grade levels, private-public schools, advanced rates, trade schools, higher education, region, race, and socioeconomic status.
2. Teacher flow model: traces flows of college graduates into teaching, migration rates, salaries, experience, age, and other characteristics.
3. Operational cost accounting: traces flows of funds.
4. Manpower and employment: uses 1970 census data.
5. Benefit-cost analysis: provides a basis for national policies regarding resource allocations for education.[9]

Such priorities by the USOE and the activities of personnel from the Division of Operations Analysis, along with the projects their efforts have stimulated, indicate a growing desire in the profession to utilize quantitative systems approaches such as OR, econometrics, and other mathematical approaches to improve educational organizations through better data and analysis for decision-making.

Mathematical Programming in Education

Also revealing the growing interest in systems approaches to educational administrative problems was a recent UCEA-Syracuse University Seminar on management support systems in education.[10]   At this seminar several mathematical approaches to educational problems were introduced which can be identified here. The interested reader can explore these kinds of applications further, if he so desires, in the publications of the Educational Systems and Planning Center directed by Frank Banghart at Florida State University.[11] Admittedly, a very thin line separates OR, mathematical programming, and linear programming. And rather than dwell on such distinctions, which might be of interest only to the mathematically inclined, we might best devote our attention to a brief indication of the particular applications. Suffice it to say that OR is a general methodology, while mathematical and linear programming are particular mathematical techniques used in OR for solving problems.

In one presentation to the UCEA-Syracuse Seminar, Richard O'Brien of USOE described the use of linear programming to solve an urban school location problem.[12]   A simulation was developed, data about alternatives collected, alternatives modeled, and a "solution" derived by linear programming techniques. O'Brien's work in this area illustrates the potential for "quantifying" a decision problem in education which heretofore had usually been approached in a highly subjective way. Although his work has not resulted in a sure-fire procedure for use by urban administrators, it does suggest the viability of this approach, an approach which, with refinement and testing, may be of help in the future.

In another presentation at the Syracuse Seminar, Frank W. Banghart described his development of a mathematical programming model for planning school lunch menus and a linear programming algorithm for a school transportation problem.[13] Banghart's work in this respect has been maximally productive and his planning program for school lunch menus is currently in operation in at least one school district and can be readily modified for use in other districts. His school transportation program has completed the final stages of testing and has a real potential for application in school districts.

In working on the school lunch menu planning problem, Banghart observed that "the school lunch program is the largest nonprofit feeding system in the world." As such, management problems here are great. Since these deal with both allocation and mixture problems, mathematical programming techniques offer a procedure for dealing effectively with the management problems of this particular school program. Approached by a large city school system with a school lunch program annually in need of subsidizing, Banghart sought to design a computerized procedure through which the most economical school lunch menu could be selected from a stockpile of preplanned Type A menus, taking into account nutritional requirements, student taste, aesthetic qualities of menu items, and the full range of costs and preparation variables. Mathematical programming procedures were used to generate menus, and a complete systems study of the school lunch program was undertaken in terms of costing out recipe items, labor, equipment, overhead, and other related factors in order to provide an economical school lunch program operation. Although still in its early years of implementation (the *true* test of systems or any other kind of study), the model and procedures have well demonstrated the promise of their ultimate utility.

School transportation represents a significant aspect of school operations nationally in terms of both cost and management. Typically, school busses are routed by school administrators in what is, at best, a pseudo-scientific fashion, with little attention paid to much other than the best way for a bus to travel in order to get a full load and be at school on time. Administrators usually give little attention to costing or to maximum system efficiency. In this regard, Banghart has sought "to design and test a linear programming model which would optimize transportation costs." In doing so, he has used linear programming procedures to model a school transportation situation. He has applied linear programming to the vehicle routing problem and used cost analysis procedures with all other aspects of the transportation system. Resulting from his work is a computer program that can be used to maximize the economy of a school transportation system and to optimize its operation.

Summary

In sum, objective or quantitative systems approaches such as OR and mathematical programming have a potential for solving educational problems. *Wherever allocation of scarce or limited resources is concerned and quantification can take place, OR provides a valuable systems approach to problem study and solution.* The utility of mathematical programming has already been indicated for solving problems of urban school site selection, school lunch menu planning, and transportation scheduling and operation. We can now look to the less "objective" approaches of systems study and how they can be applied to the problems of the educational administrator.

SYSTEMS ANALYSIS APPROACHES: COST-BENEFIT ANALYSIS AND COMPREHENSIVE SYSTEMS STUDY

It has already been noted that systems analysis is often equated to, or confused with, Operations Research. Systems analysis, like OR, is the interdisciplinary scientific approach to problem solving and is also a refined "systems" process for business and industrial problem solving. However, *in contrast to OR, systems analysis tends to be less objective and correspondingly more subjective. Thus, when goals are vague, not quantifiable, or in conflict, when a large number of factors must be considered, and when there is a high level of situational uncertainty, systems analysis approaches (or heuristic, as opposed to algorithmic, approaches) should be used.* OR further basically works on problems in the context of an organization as a given entity. In systems analysis the approach is, however, less restrictive. Here wholes are broken into parts and ultimately reassembled into some kind of a whole (that is, the same whole, an entirely new whole, or a somewhat different one). Analysis in this approach involves reduction of complex entities or problems into their component parts so that each part can be scrutinized and functionally realigned. Systems analysis involves (1) *systems decomposition* (analysis), or the dissection of a system, and (2) resulting *system synthesis* (design) into a revitalized whole. Components, functions, activities, and relationships, whether or not they can be quantified or which elude quantification, are used to restructure a system for improved operation.

Systems analysis approaches have had a wide range of applications, from airplane design in industry to tank and submarine development in the military, from traffic flow analysis in urban centers to work flow analysis in hospitals. Wherever complexity and lack of quantifiability exists, this approach, whether applied in a procedure such as cost-benefit analysis or to organizational study of a more comprehensive type, has utility. In this light two applications of subjective systems study or systems analysis can be set forth. First, we will show how cost-benefit analysis, without full quantification, might be used to help an overburdened principal solve the problem of being overworked. Then we will illustrate how a systems analysis approach to the comprehensive study of an educational organization might be structured.

Cost-Benefit Analysis

Hartley has succinctly defined cost-benefit analysis as "the enumeration and evaluation of all relevant costs and benefits over a period of time."[14] He further points out in clear terms the goal of cost analysis: the outcomes of an activity (that is, benefits) should ideally exceed the costs. Or, $B/C > 1$. Although cost-benefit analysis in the OR sense is fully computational, the technique in PPBS or the systems analysis framework may contain both quantitative and qualitative variables. In the latter cases quantification of costs and benefits goes as far as is possible, so that decision makers are not forced to deal solely with vague qualitative judgments or hunches. The basic process of cost-benefit analysis contributes, further, to the sophistication of these procedures in that in dealing with a problem, all elements, quantitative and qualitative, are enumerated, related, and assessed.

Since educational administrators are usually confronted with limited resources — financial, human, and material — systematic analysis of all possible solutions to a problem is most relevant, particularly since problems do not arise in isolation. Through cost-benefit analysis the administrator is able to assess individually and collectively the costs, benefits, and consequences of all alternatives at a given time. As the full picture of costs and gains is revealed, questions of priority and greatest positive effect can be objectively answered.

Mushkin and Cleaveland cogently define and describe cost-effectiveness analysis as:

> . . . a process of systematically asking relevant questions about full cost implications and benefits of program alternatives to satisfy objectives and assembling information that bears on those questions. The questioning starts by defining program purposes or objectives and by asking what alternative courses may be followed in meeting those objectives. Analysis calls for estimating costs and gains in meeting those purposes by alternative programs. It calls for inquiring about the uncertanity of those estimates. It calls for documentation of the information that is brought together to give greater precision to the "pros and cons" (gains and costs) of alternatives for meeting stated objectives by quantified description where possible and to qualitative statements where quantification is not possible.[15]

The four major steps in cost-benefit analysis are then:

1. Asking the right question(s) (in terms of one's objectives).
2. Projecting alternative ways to meet the objectives.
3. Documenting all problem data, assumptions, and reasoning in a written statement.
4. Analyzing the costs and gains (two sets of information) of each alternative.

To illustrate how cost-benefit analysis can be used to solve a typical problem in the field of educational administration we might use the rather common problem of the "overburdened" administrator. Let us assume that Principal Smith is the head of a growing suburban high school. Pupil enrollment has grown persistently over the last six years, though not dramatically, and now that the enrollment has reached 900, Principal Smith and his two secretaries seem constantly harassed and unable to get the work done. In a nutshell, they are living from crisis to crisis. Historically, some seven years ago, when Smith was appointed principal, the school had 600 pupils. He and his one secretary were able to handle the job well. When the school enrollment reached 700, he was able to add another secretary and things continued, at least for a short time, to go along smoothly. The last couple of years, however, have not. Enrollments creep up, and due to mounting teacher demands for higher salaries and the taxpayers' reluctance to provide additional funds for school operations, personnel additions in administrative or classified (nonprofessional) areas have been restricted. At this point Principal Smith, like many other exhausted principals, feels at a visceral level that he just *must* have an assistant principal!

Utilizing cost-benefit analysis to solve this problem, Principal Smith would move through the following steps:

1. *Asking the right question.* In analysis it is incumbent on Smith to ask the right question. A gut-level reaction would be to ask "Why should I not have an assistant principal?" But since the problem is one of principal and secretarial (total school office) overload, the objective is to provide relief for both Smith and his secretaries. The more appropriate question might be "How can we best staff the school office in order to get the work done?"

Smith would need to get specific about objectives for relieving the situation. He might determine that he needs help with a snowballing number of discipline cases and a mounting number of observations of teachers to fulfill his role in staff evaluation. Also, he may need relief from the filling out of endless statistical reports and the handling of daily correspondence. In regard to these latter problems he may find that the endless statistical reports wind up on his desk because his secretaries are not good with numbers and tabulations. Pressure from his correspondence may result from the fact that neither secretary can take shorthand and no dictaphone equipment is available, thus imposing a persistent, burdensome longhand approach to this problem. Likewise, his secretaries may find their load resulting from size (that is, more teacher *and* office work to handle), more telephone calls and office procedures confronting them, and the need to handle minor disciplinary or administrative problems due to the principal's load. As such problems are identified by Smith, the objectives to guide overall problem solution will become explicit and the right question or questions will evolve. Here it seems to be that of "how to staff the school office." Principal Smith can then turn to step two of cost-benefit analysis.

2. *Projecting alternative ways to meet the objectives.* Although an initial response might be to add an assistant principal and/or secretary, there may well be some other alternatives. The questions of "How can we divide the labor in the office?" and "What can we do?" will facilitate the search for alternatives. And, instead of an either/or solution (which may be unfeasible or unpalatable to the superintendent or school board) there may be gradations of solutions. For example, some alternatives may be:

a) Hire an assistant principal and another secretary and appropriately portion out the duties.

b) Hire an assistant principal to handle discipline, office reporting, and office management, and utilize student help (free) to alleviate secretarial routing (e.g., hall passes, deliveries to teachers, telephone calls, and duplicating).

c) Hire an executive secretary to manage the office, handle reports, take care of the principal's correspondence (one who could take

shorthand or use a dictaphone, in which case this should be pur-
chased) and assign greator disciplinary responsibility to guidance
personnel and greater teacher evaluation responsibility to department
heads.

d) Appoint two part-time assistant principals, one to manage the office,
the other to handle discipline, and employ an office worker or assistant for the secretaries to do routine work such as serving as recep-
tionist, duplicating, running errands, and so forth.

e) Appoint one part-time assistant principal and another full-time secretary and divide the duties appropriately.

f) Etc.

There are obviously many solutions to this problem. As the reader can
see, we have just mentioned five possibilities, and the elements of these
could be combined in numerous ways to provide other solutions. But once
the alternatives are identified, Smith can turn to step three in cost-benefit
analysis.

3. *Documenting all problem data, assumptions, and reasoning in writing.*
Principal Smith would then take each alternative identified and develop a
written statement about it. For example, he would set forth data about the
situation as it was discovered in step one (Asking the right question) and
would firm up situational objectives. He could next document the assumptions and reasons for each problem alternative. In regard to the first alternative identified in step two, some assumptions might be:

a) Since teacher evaluation is a basic function of the principal, a full-
time assistant is needed to relieve the principal for this important
work.

b) Since office secretaries are overburdened, additional competent secretarial help is needed.

c) Full-time, qualified employees are preferable to part-time or less
qualified personnel, and so forth.

His reasoning behind the alternative may be spelled out in similar fashion:

a) Since the enrollment growth will continue and additions to the
school plant will be made, additional full-time personnel will be
needed (in this case these are not in any sense temporary employees).

b) Although improving teachers' salaries contributes to teacher motivation, failure to provide administrative and office support to
teachers will mitigate against any such gains.

c) Full-time qualified personnel additions tend to be more permanent
and are more easily assimilated into an organization than are part-
timers, and so forth.

The function of this documentation of all alternatives is to set forth

Table 10.1 Costs of Principal Smith's five alternative solutions.

A	B	C	D	E
Assistant principal $12,500	Assistant principal $12,500	Discipline and teacher evaluation help -0-	Two part-time assistant principals + $2,000 + $2,000	One part-time assistant principal + $2,000
Secretary $4,200	Student office help -0-	Executive secretary $6,200	Additional teacher $6,500	Half-time additional teacher + $3,100
			Office worker $3,200	Secretary $4,200
Total A $16,700	Total B $12,500	Total C $6,200	Total D $13,700	Total E $11,300

Table 10.2 Gains of Principal Smith's five alternative solutions.

	A	B	C	D	E
Handling of discipline	++	++		+	+
Teacher evaluation	++	++		++	
Office reports	++	++	++	+	
Correspondence	++	+	++		++
Office load	++	+	+	+	++
Office procedures	++	+	+	+	++
Etc.	Etc.	Etc.	Etc.	Etc.	Etc.

systematically the full parameters and complexity of the problem and to enable others to review and assess (understand) what is being projected. Principal Smith can then move to the fourth step in cost-benefit analysis.

4. *Analyzing costs and gains.* Two sets of data are needed here, one to enumerate the costs of each alternative and the other to set forth the gains. Tables 10.1 and 10.2 illustrate this kind of information in quite global terms.

After the problem objectives have been determined and all aspects of alternative solutions have been quantitatively and qualitatively assessed through the preceding four steps of cost-benefit analysis, Principal Smith and his superiors, the superintendent and board, can select the optimal solution to the problem confronting the effective operation of the high school office.[16]   In addition, such rigorous before-the-fact analysis also provides the basis for evaluating the effectiveness of the implemented problem solution.

Comprehensive Systems Study[17]

Systems analysis approaches can also be applied to the comprehensive evaluation or study of schools in the extant school survey tradition. Such approaches are, however, interdisciplinary in nature and seek different goals from those normally pursued in a school survey. The systems approach would focus more on the identification of problems, the solution of each problem, and the overall synthesis of these solutions into a total design for organizational improvement, adaptation, or restructuring. The goals, procedures, and outcomes of a systems study of a school administrative organization can be suggested, and how one theoretical vehicle can be used to facilitate this type of study can be illustrated. For obvious reasons, space forces this discussion to be indicative and illustrative at best.

1. *Goals to be realized through systems study.* The following outcomes would be relevant to a systems analysis study of a school district's administrative organization or administrative performance system (APS):

a) The analysis of existing administrative structure, function, and procedures in order to design new and more appropriate elements for the administrative support aspect of the educational organization.

b) The improvement of organizational decision-making through the systematization of viable choice (decision) procedures and through the development of operational administrative support and information systems.

c) The general development of the administrative sector (APS) of the organization to a more vital, dynamic state as a result of critical assessment (evaluation) and subsequent organizational modification or redesign.

d) The testing and application of a heuristic process for organizational change and evolution (through "experiencing" and undergoing systems study).

e) An in-service experience for all organizational administrators and allied specialists through cooperative participation in the systems study and the interdisciplinary, pragmatic, problem-seeking approach to organizational problems.

2. *Procedures in systems study.* The application of systems analysis to the administrative performance system requires the use of both intraorganizational personnel and a study team representing certain disciplines external to the organization. Those individuals within the organization who

function as management decision-makers and those who represent operational units within the major subsystems of the organization would comprise the *intraorganizational* group. The *external* team members would have interdisciplinary backgrounds and would be drawn from disciplines such as education, sociology, psychology, business management, and engineering. Study team leadership would be provided by specialists in either administration or educational administration and organization. Additionally, team members would be selected for their competence in special areas, such as cost-benefit analysis, quantitative methods, information processing, man-machine systems design, and organizational design.

Critical to the success of this kind of venture is a true team approach. No group which is external to the system under study can accomplish its objectives without a close partnership work relationship with those in administrative and allied positions within the school organization.

The major categories of activity in such a systems study might take the form of those outlined below:

a) *Identification* of components (their structure, function, and procedures) of the existing APS.

b) *Classification* of support system components and relationships through the use of a model, such as decision-taxonomy framework.

c) Analysis of existing administrative performance system *elements, functions,* and *operations.*

d) *Delineation* of desired administrative support system performance specifications.

e) *Synthesis* of a model APS support system with appropriate testing and evaluation.

f) *Development* of a viable management information system component (using categories (a) through (e) above to determine the information requirements within the model or organizational decision-making framework used).

g) *Design* of operational APS support systems, associated APS information system, and implementation controls and strategies in terms of an organizational decision-making model.

3. *An analysis vehicle.* To focus and guide a systems study of an educational organization, some model or analytic framework is necessary. Such an analytic vehicle enables the study of the APS to be focused on relevant variables and to avoid any tendency to digress or pursue less relevant (tangential) concerns. Any model or framework also provides a research construct and an overall scheme for projecting and designing APS modifications and improvements as a result of the study. Further, assuming a generic model or framework, a general concern for the totality of relevant activity will be ensured.

One appropriate model for the systems study of the administrative sector of an educational organization would be a framework derived from the science of organizational decision processing. This can be illustrated here both through the derivation of such a model and its application to systems study.

Since administration exists to support, maintain, and develop an organization (or, put another way, to direct and control organizational activity), it is constantly confronted with choosing between alternative courses of action. Choice of courses of action, or decision-making, is the *central task* of those administering an organization. Thus, for any APS the quality and utility of its decision-making processes are central to its fulfillment of its basic organizational function.

The APS and the various definable APS support systems function essentially to direct and control organizational activities. Some of this direction and control is achieved through the application of laws, rules and regulations, and organizational policy. Choices or decisions of this kind are, in a sense, "rule following," and are characteristically prescribed or made within well-defined boundaries or limits. Administrative choices not so easily handled are channeled into formal or informal organizational decision processes.

These may be dealt with by either fixed or programmed procedures or nonprogrammed (unfixed) procedures. In the former instance, the decision variables are known and are susceptible to a predetermined set of operations for their solution (e.g., mathematical formula, or a computer program). The latter, nonprogrammed decisions, involve a number of unknowns, and their solutions rest on the heuristics of man and man-machine resolution.

As an analysis framework for systems study of an APS we may consider the taxonomy of organizational decision-making which appears in Fig. 10.1. The taxonomy provides a ready classification device for use in the analysis of existing organizational decision-making and can easily be applied to APS support systems in an educational organization. The taxonomy also provides a framework for designing improved decision strategies and configurations for the organization. Finally, the taxonomy can be used in determining the dimensions, nature, and scope of an allied APS information system.

A few observations about this taxonomy might be appropriate. Typically, decisions in educational organizations are of the 2.11, 2.12, 2.211, or 2.221 types. Or, characteristically, decisions in educational organizations are either the applications of rules or policy to situations, or individual or routine choices. A range of other choice or decision procedures is often ignored or used to a negligible extent. These are certain of the programmed procedures (2.212, 2.213 and 2.214), nonprogrammed simulation, and group-decision processes. Inherent in the logic of this taxonomy is the notion that all branches (procedures) in the taxonomy need to be employed by an organization in order to cope effectively with that which the organization wishes to control. If individuals or groups make decisions that could be made through mathematical formulas or computer programs, it is obvious that they will not have maximal time for making decisions that are

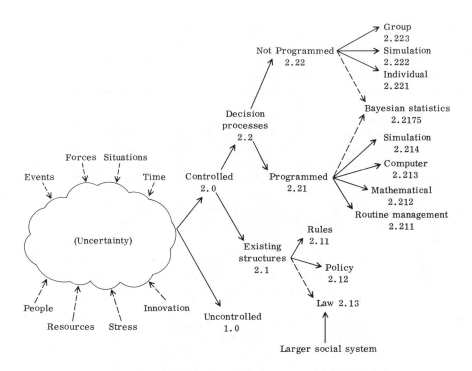

Fig. 10.1 A logical taxonomy of organizational decision-making.

basically nonprogrammatic. Put another way, *the many human relations and interpersonal decisions confronting those administering educational organizations can only hope to receive proper attention and adequate resolution as certain routine, reoccurring decisions are made by programmed procedures.*

It has already been noted that the decision taxonomy has implications for the APS information system that underlies all administrative choice. To meet the requirements for information system components and procedures is essential. This means that we need an adequate data base (information), and procedures for obtaining, storing, and retrieving such data when necessary. Just as organizational decision strategy can be projected through the decision taxonomy, so can decision information requirements be determined and an APS information system be designed.

Organizations need to decide how best to decide by organizing their decision-making and information base in terms of the full range of decision procedures available. This is central to the concept of administrative support in an organization; a systems study is one way to analyze and design such support for the educational organization.

4. *Applying the analysis vehicle.* The use of the above "logical" taxonomy of organizational decision-making in a systems study can be briefly illustrated relative to a school system. In this way we can, further, convey both the general analysis and design aspects of a subjective systems study. In order to make our illustration as meaningful as possible we will apply the taxonomy to a precisely delimited administrative support system — that dealing with the deployment of personnel — which is only one small part of a total comprehensive systems study of an APS. This system is actually a subsystem of the larger personnel system and represents a well-defined and very specific realm of APS activity. This is to say, the personnel deployment support system is concerned only with the utilization of organizational members.

The analysis phase of a systems study by an internal-external systems study team using the decision taxonomy may produce the following kinds of findings:

a) Decisions regarding the deployment of personnel are essentially rule-following or policy-guided choices made by individuals (e.g., primarily the superintendent, the assistant superintendent, and the principals). (2.1)

b) There are conflicting policies regarding the deployment of personnel (e.g., one position holds that teachers are to be used only in their primary area of certification; another position is that teachers with multiple certification may be assigned according to existing needs, with seniority as the basic criterion). (2.12)

c) Some rules regarding personnel deployment are difficult to enforce (e.g., teachers are not to be given extra duties for pay if they accept any form of outside employment). (2.11)

d) Group decision procedures are vague and individuals involved in decision situations often have conflicting desires and expectations (e.g., in the assignment of a teacher, no procedure is specified for resolving a conflict between the assistant superintendent and the principal in a case where the principal feels the teacher will do better in grade two and the assistant superintendent feels the teacher should teach first grade). (2.223)

e) Decisions about personnel deployment can be capricious and without due regard for the organization or the organizational member under consideration (e.g., a principal can assign an excellent kindergarten teacher to the second grade for one year to avoid losing her to another principal). (2.221)

f) Many matters regarding personnel deployment are not covered by existing policy or rules (e.g., little thought has been given to the utilization of special-subject teachers). (2.1)

g) Information regarding organizational members is not consciously collected or stored in such a way that it can be retrieved and used efficiently in organizational decision-making (e.g., only limited information is stored centrally in employee folders and thus much information, or what information there is, is idiosyncratic in nature and filed in various administrative offices). (2.21)

h) Etc.

On the basis of such data and findings as the above, the design phase of the systems study would project such modifications in the decision-making activities of the personnel deployment subsystem as the following:

a) The development of appropriate rules and policies covering the assignment of special-subject teachers. (2.1)

b) The rectification of all vague or conflicting aspects of school district rules and policy. (2.1)

c) Operationalization of all rules, including ways they can be enforced. (2.11)

d) Development of a precise scope of decision authority and resolution procedures for all decisions involving more than one person. (2.223)

e) The development of district-wide personnel utilization policy and procedures to maximize the use of the talents of all staff members. (2.12 and 2.21)

f) Design of relevant components for a management information system such as centralized, IBM data packets on all employees with up-to-date information of biographical, special interest, job performance, anecdotal, and similar nature. (2.21)

g) The development of programmed decision procedures such as: (2.21)

-A linear program to deploy the maintenance force on a district-wide basis during vacation periods. (2.212)

-A computer inventory system to scan teacher data packets (an aspect of the management information system) to identify competencies and interests relative to emerging developmental or innovative projects. (2.213)

-A program for evaluating objective data (obtained, stored, and available through the management information system) regarding teachers near the tenure decision. (2.211 and 2.213)

-A simulation designed to identify prospective leadership talent among employees. (2.214)

-Etc.

h) The development of appropriate group decision-making procedures for complex decisions involving large groups of organizational members. (2.223)

i) An inservice seminar on modern organizational decision-making for all administrative employees. (2.2)

j) Etc.

Although this illustration is hypothetical and somewhat brief, it can be seen that a model, such as the decision taxonomy, can serve as an analytic framework for facilitating a systems study of a school administrative organization. It is particularly relevant for any survey focusing on the organizational administrative performance system and APS support systems. The taxonomy provides a perspective for both analysis and design, the dual dimensions of systems study.

5. *A flow chart of a systems study.* The general activities of a comprehensive systems study and their relationships can be set forth in a flow chart to graphically show the possible evolution of such a study. Thus, a chronology of events illustrates in a time-sequence perspective the major aspects of systems study and further helps operationalize the systems study approach relative to an educational organization. Beginning with an initial introduction to systems study, Fig. 10.2 illustrates the dimensions and aspects of the systems approach to organizational analysis in education.

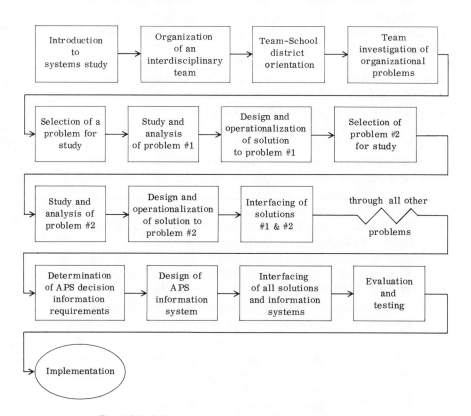

Fig. 10.2 A flow chart of a comprehensive systems study.

Summary

In conclusion, less objective or "subjective" systems analysis approaches are most relevant at the present time for the evaluation of problems in educational administration. Cost-benefit analysis can be used both quantitatively and qualitatively with problems, and the comprehensive, interdisciplinary systems study approach briefly sketched above can contribute greatly in the general tradition of the school survey movement.

THE POTENTIAL OF SYSTEMS STUDY

Through the systems study of schools, a number of advantages can be realized. First: the approach is *problem-oriented* and gets at dysfunctions. Second: it not only deals with problem analysis but also *the design and implementation of problem solutions;* Third: quantification and the systematic and explicit use of qualitative information *objectifies* problem variables and ensures a maximally relevant data base for decisions. Fourth: through systems approaches, *objectives are clarified,* and thereby the liklihood of asking the *right* question (s) is enhanced. Fifth: systems approaches draw knowledge from many disciplines and optimize *before-the-fact evaluation and assessment* of actions. And, finally: systems study forces the analyst to look at *all relevant elements of a system and the system in totality.*

NOTES

1. See for example, M. Z. Pond and H. Wakefield, *Citizens Survey Their School Needs.* Columbus, University Press, The Ohio State University, 1954.

2. A. Wildavsky, "The Political Economy of Efficiency: Cost-Benefit Analysis, Systems Analysis, and Program Budgeting," *Publ. Adm. Rev. 26,* No. 4 (December 1966), p. 229.

3. H. J. Hartley, *Educational Planning-Programming-Budgeting,* Englewood Cliffs, N. J.: Prentice Hall, 1968, pp. 36 and 37.

4. R. L. Ackoff, "The Development and Nature of Operations Research and Its Relevance to Educational-Media Research." Paper presented to a Conference of the Center for Instructional Communications of Syracuse University, April 2-4, 1964, p. 11.

5. C. W. Churchman, R. L. Ackoff, and E. L. Arnoff, *Introduction to Operations Research.* New York: John Wiley & Sons, 1957, p. 13.

6. Ackoff, *op. cit.,* p. 12.

7. *Ibid.*

8. A Symposium, "Operations Analysis in Education," sponsored by the U. S. Department of Health, Education, and Welfare, Office of Education, National Center for Educational Statistics, Division of Operations Analysis, Washington, D. C., November, 19-22, 1967.

9. A. M. Mood and D. S. Stoller, "USOE is Knee-Deep in Operations Analysis," *Nats. Sch. 80,* No. 4 (October 1967), p. 74. By permission of McGraw-Hill, Inc. All rights reserved.

10. The Eighteenth UCEA Career Development Seminar on "Management Systems and Educational Organizations," held at Syracuse University, April 1968. Also see J. Alan Thomas. *The Productive School: A Systems Analysis Approach to Educational Administration.* New York: John Wiley & Sons, 1971; and the available publications from Florida State University's Educational Systems and Planning Center (directed by Prof. Frank Banghart).

11. See any of a number of technical reports from the Educational Systems and Planning Center, *ibid.*

12. R. O'Brien, "Management Support Systems and Operations Analysis," Presentation to the Eighteenth UCEA Career Seminar, at Syracuse University, April, 1968.

13. F. W. Banghart, "A Management Support Systems Approach to Food Service and Transportation." Presentation to the Eighteenth UCEA Career Seminar, at Syracuse University, April, 1968. See also Frank W. Banghart. *Educational Systems Analysis.* New York: MacMillan, 1969.

14. Hartley, *op. cit.,* p. 253.

15. S. J. Mushkin and J. R. Cleaveland, *Planning for Educational Development in a Planning, Programming, Budgeting System.* Committee on Educational Finance, National Education Association, Washington, D. C., 1968, pp. 25 and 26.

16. See *ibid.* for an even more detailed illustration of cost-benefit analysis to an administrative problem in education.

17. The authors are indebted to Prof. James Manwaring of Syracuse University's Bureau of School Services who helped in the formulation of many of the ideas contained in this section.

Epilogue

Obviously, the systems movement has meaning for theory and research in educational administration in addition to the practice of administration. Those areas, however, are beyond the scope of this document, as is a truly comprehensive, detailed treatment of all the practical relevancies of the systems movement. Our intent has been to be indicative, to point to the kinds of applications systems thought and procedures can have for educational administration. No attempt has been made to exhaust the potential. We hope only that we have whetted the reader's appetite in opening up the prospects *vis-a-vis* the systems movement.

It should be stressed finally that, really, systems concepts and approaches are not a panacea; in fact, they do not offer anything startlingly revolutionary. The systems movement has, however, attempted to compile the laws and findings of many sciences and disciplines, natural and social alike, into a complex, multifaceted, one-conceptual mode of thought which facilitates the analysis of a wide variety of pheonomena. For the object under scrutiny, be it a learning unit, a school, a flowering plant, a nation, or a universe, has a set of properties which can be assessed in terms of notions from many disciplines, and which when "collated" into a relevant judgment, leads to increased understanding. Too, this movement has spawned many procedures and devices which enable one to cope more adequately with the objects and problems confronting him.

The field of systems is both challenging and rewarding.

The references cited throughout provide a source list for additional readings, more specific, more rigorous, and, perhaps, even more cogent.

Index

Index

ABCDEFGH79876543